Safe AI Systems

Sponsored by:

Socrates – Assurance Case™ Editor is a collaborative platform that helps your team build better assurances cases. Socrates is designed by engineers for engineers to help tackle the challenge of assuring today's complex systems.

Socrates users benefit from a range of innovative features for creating and maintaining "live" cases that evolve alongside your system including support for multiple notations (GSN, CAE, and EA), modular arguments, safety case patterns, performance indicators, traceability to technical standards, terminology management, and rule-based static analysis. Socrates can be deployed on your organization's IT infrastructure, so that you can keep your data secure.

Learn more at https://criticalsystemslabs.com/socrates

Related Titles

Engineering Systems for Safety
Proceedings of the Twenty-third Safety-critical Systems Symposium, Bristol, UK, 2015
Parsons and Anderson (Eds)
978-1505689082

Developing Safe Systems
Proceedings of the Twenty-fourth Safety-critical Systems Symposium, Brighton, UK, 2016
Parsons and Anderson (Eds)
978-1519420077

Developments in System Safety Engineering
Proceedings of the Twenty-fifth Safety-critical Systems Symposium, Bristol, UK, 2017
Parsons and Kelly (Eds)
978-1540796288

Evolution of System Safety
Proceedings of the Twenty-sixth Safety-critical Systems Symposium, York, UK, 2018
Parsons and Kelly (Eds)
978-1979733618

Engineering Safe Autonomy
Proceedings of the twenty-seventh Safety-Critical Systems Symposium, Bristol, UK, 2019, SCSC-150
Parsons and Kelly (Eds)
978-1729361764

Assuring Safe Autonomy
Proceedings of the twenty-eighth Safety-Critical Systems Symposium, York, UK, 2020
SCSC-154
Parsons and Nicholson (Eds)
978-1713305668

Systems and Covid-19
Proceedings of the twenty-ninth Safety-Critical Systems Symposium, Online, 2021
SCSC-161
Parsons and Nicholson (Eds)
979-8588665049

Safer Systems: The Next 30 Years
Proceedings of the thirtieth Safety-Critical Systems Symposium, Bristol, UK, 2022, SCSC-170
Parsons and Nicholson (Eds)
9798778289932

The Future of Safe Systems
Proceedings of the 31st Safety-Critical Systems Symposium, York, UK, 2023, SCSC-179
Mike Parsons (Ed)
9798363385520

Mike Parsons
Editor

Safe AI Systems

Proceedings of the 32nd
Safety-Critical Systems Symposium
(SSS'24)
13-15 February 2024

SCSC-188

thescsc.org   SCSC SSS'24   scsc.uk

Editor

Mike Parsons
SCSC
mike.parsons@scsc.uk

While the authors and the publishers have used reasonable endeavours to ensure that the information and guidance given in this work is correct, all parties must rely on their own skill and judgement when making use of this work and obtain professional or specialist advice before taking, or refraining from, any action on the basis of the content of this work. Neither the authors nor the publishers make any representations or warranties of any kind, express or implied, about the completeness, accuracy, reliability, suitability or availability with respect to such information and guidance for any purpose, and they will not be liable for any loss or damage including without limitation, indirect or consequential loss or damage, or any loss or damage whatsoever (including as a result of negligence) arising out of, or in connection with, the use of this work. The views and opinions expressed in this publication are those of the authors and do not necessarily reflect those of their employers, the SCSC or other organisations.

ISBN: 9798868463440

Published by the Safety-Critical Systems Club 2024.

Individual chapters © as shown on respective first pages in footnote.

All other text © Safety-Critical Systems Club C.I.C.

Cover design by Alex King

Download (free to SCSC members): scsc.uk/scsc-188

Hardcopy available on Amazon

Preface

The rapid evolution of AI has shocked the world and further step-changes are likely. Not only does this change the picture regarding safety-critical applications utilizing AI: self-driving vehicles, drones and medical image recognition systems, but it has the potential to revolutionize the way we produce critical systems, everything from AI-generated designs to AI-authored safety cases.

System safety practices and approaches must adapt to deal with and make best use of, these new AI applications and uses, and ways must be found to assure systems utilizing AI which are meaningful, understandable and trustworthy.

Systems are also getting ever more complex and connected, and in some cases, more fragile. We do not have established tools and techniques to analyse and manage such systems: they are too opaque, have too many parts, interfaces and interactions for the old techniques to work. Two new SCSC Working Groups, the Safe AI Working Group (SAIWG) and Safer Complex Systems WG (SCSWG) have been set up to look at the issues and produce new guidance in these areas.

The existing SCSC Working Groups have evolved and expanded to cover new areas such as Safety of the Environment. The groups have all continued throughout the year and their work was presented again in the form of posters.

As always, this forward-looking symposium addressed some of these new challenges and presented work towards practical and industrially-relevant solutions.

The Safety-Critical Systems Club has operated in support of the safety community since 1991. This volume is the proceedings for the 32nd Club Symposium in February 2024 held at the Bristol Royal Marriot Hotel, Bristol, UK.

The symposium was for both experienced members of the safety community and those at earlier stages of their careers. It was a great opportunity to learn, develop experience and also build up useful connections and create technical and social networks.

SSS'24 extended across three days of presentations, grouped into key themes. There was a special session on Safety of AI on the Wednesday. Key features were: Seven keynote presentations, Primary themes of: Future Aviation, Assurance Cases, Future Rail, Safety of AI, New Thinking and Automotive and Autonomy, 'Safe AI' session and panel, Poster sessions including updates from the SCSC Working Groups, Entertainment on the Tuesday afternoon, Symposium Banquet on the Wednesday evening with after-dinner speech, Working Group meet-up on the Wednesday morning and Bristol social activities.

The SCSC is very grateful to all those who helped organise and contribute to the event.

Mike Parsons

SCSC Mission and Aims

Mission

To promote practical systems approaches to safety for technological solutions in the real world.
> Where *"systems approaches"* is the application of analysis tools, models and methods which consider the whole system and its components; *"system"* means the whole socio-technical system in which the solution operates, including organisational culture, structure and governance, and *"technological solutions"* includes products, systems and services and combinations thereof.

Aims

1. **To build and foster an active and inclusive community of safety stakeholders:**
   a. "safety stakeholders" include practitioners (in safety specialisms and other disciplines involved in the whole lifecycle of safety related systems), managers, researchers, and those involved in governance (including policy makers, law makers, regulators and auditors)
   b. from across industry sectors, including new and non-traditional areas
   c. recognising the importance of including and nurturing early career practitioners
   d. working to remove barriers to inclusion in the community
2. **To support sharing of systems approaches to safety:**
   a. enabling wider application
   b. supporting continuing professional development
   c. encouraging interaction between early career and experienced practitioners
   d. using a variety of communication media and techniques to maximise coverage
   e. highlighting the lessons which can be learned from past experience
3. **To produce consistent guidance for safety stakeholders where not already available.**
   a. "consistent" meaning the guidance is consistent within itself, and with other guidance provided by SCSC; although SCSC will also aim to co-ordinate with external guidance this is more difficult to achieve
4. **To influence relevant standards, guidance and other publications.**
5. **To work with relevant organisations to provide a coordinated approach to system safety.**
6. **To minimise our environmental impact wherever possible.**

The Safety-Critical Systems Club

organiser of the

Safety-Critical Systems Symposium

Avoiding Systems-Related Harm

This is a very exciting time for the discipline of system safety. There are new technologies and approaches using AI which are likely to revolutionise the way safety systems are designed and assured. New applications are near operational, including self-driving vehicles and delivery drones, which will rely on complex autonomous functions. The SCSC runs working groups looking at such systems, and also the environment in which they operate, with a mission to produce practical guidance. This is the mission of the SCSC: using systems approaches to prevent harm.

We should not forget that many safety-critical systems in everyday life work as expected day-in day-out. Safety of these systems is accepted as routine: airbags in vehicles, air-traffic control and infusion pumps are some of the critical systems in use, on which life and property depend.

That safety-critical systems and services do work is because of the expertise and diligence of professional engineers, regulators, auditors and other practitioners. Their efforts prevent untold deaths and injuries every year. The Safety-Critical Systems Club (SCSC) has been actively engaged for over 30 years to help to ensure that this is the case, and to provide a "home" for safety professionals.

What does the SCSC do?

The SCSC maintains a website (thescsc.org, scsc.uk), which includes a diary of events, working group areas and club publications. It produces a regular newsletter, *Safety Systems*, three times a year and also a peer-reviewed journal published twice a year. It organises seminars, workshops and training on general safety matters or specific subjects of current concern.

Since 1993 it has organised the annual Safety-Critical Systems Symposium (SSS) where leaders in different aspects of safety from different industries, including consultants, regulators and academics, meet to exchange information and experience, with the content published in this proceedings volume.

The SCSC supports industry working groups. Currently there are active groups covering the areas of: Assurance Cases, Autonomous Systems, Data Safety, Multicore, Risk Ontology, Security Informed Safety, Service Assurance,

Safer Complex Systems, Systems Approach to Safety of the Environment and Safety Culture. A new working group, SAIWG (Safe AI Working Group) is starting up at SSS. These working groups provide a focus for discussions within industry and produce new guidance materials.

The SCSC carries out all these activities to support its mission:

> ... *To promote practical systems approaches to safety for technological solutions in the real world....*

Origins

The SCSC began its work in 1991, supported by the UK Department of Trade and Industry and the Engineering and Physical Sciences Research Council. The Club has been self-sufficient since 1994. In 2021 it became a separate legal entity.

Membership

Membership may be either corporate or individual. Membership gives full web site access, the hardcopy newsletter, other mailings, and discounted entry to seminars, workshops and the annual Symposium. Membership is often paid by employers.

Corporate membership is for organisations that would like several employees to take advantage of the benefits of the SCSC. Different arrangements and packages are available. Contact alex.king@scsc.uk for more details.

There is also a short-term Publications Pass which, at very low cost, gives a month's access to all SCSC publications for non-members.

More information can be obtained at: scsc.uk/membership

Club Positions

The current and previous holders of the club positions are as follows (past holders in *italics*):

Director
Mike Parsons   2019-
Tim Kelly   *2016-2019*
Tom Anderson   *1991-2016*

Newsletter Editor
Paul Hampton   2019-
Katrina Attwood   *2016-2019*
Felix Redmill   *1991-2016*

eJournal Editor
John Spriggs   2021-

Website Editor
Brian Jepson   2004-

Steering Group Chair
Roger Rivett   2019-
Jane Fenn (deputy)   2019-
Graham Jolliffe   *2014-2019*
Brian Jepson   *2007-2014*
Bob Malcolm   *1991-2007*

University of York Coordinator
Mark Nicholson   2019-

Coordinator/Events Coordinator/Programme Coordinator
Mike Parsons   2014-
Chris Dale   *2008-2014*
Felix Redmill   *1991-2008*

Safety Futures Initiative Lead
Zoe Garstang (joint)   2020-
Nikita Johnson (joint)   2023-
Nikita Johnson   *2020-2021*

Manager
Alex King   2019-

Diversity, Equity and Inclusion Lead
Wendy Owen	2023-

Administrator
Alex King	2016-
Joan Atkinson	*1991-2016*

Honorary Solicitor
Dai Davis	2023-

Working Group Leaders
Assurance Cases	Phil Williams
Autonomous Systems	Philippa Ryan
Data Safety Initiative	Mike Parsons
Multicore	Lee Jacques
Risk Ontology	Dave Banham
Safe AI	Alan Simpson
Safer Complex Systems	Mike Parsons
Safety Culture	Michael Wright
Security Informed Safety	Stephen Bull
Service Assurance	Kevin King
Systems Approach to Safety of the Environment	James Inge

SCSC Organisation

The SCSC is a "Community Interest Company" (CIC). A CIC is a special type of limited company which exists to benefit a community rather than private shareholders. The SCSC has:

- A 'community interest statement', explaining our plans;
- An 'asset lock'- a legal promise stating that our assets will only be used for our social objectives;
- A constitution, and
- Approval by the Regulator of Community Interest Companies.

Our community is that of Safety Practitioners. As a distinct legal entity the SCSC has more freedom and can legitimately do things such as make agreements with other bodies and own copyright on documents.

There is no change to the way we do things, or the membership we serve.

Our Company Number is 13084663.

Papers

In first named author order. See also **Abstracts for Presentations** at page xv and **Poster Abstracts** at xvii. The **Title Index** is at xix. See also full **Author Index** at page 297.

Sanity Checking Autonomous Vehicle Specifications using ZDRa.
Lavinia Burski.. 27

The 'Golden Thread' of Information: A Systems Approach to Construction Safety
Mikela Chatzimichailidou.. 37

Byzantine Generals Attack an Airbus A320
Dewi Daniels.. 53

Ensuring Safety and Effectiveness of Medical Devices in the Presence of Electromagnetic Disturbances through Unified EMC Assurance: A Compliance Pattern
Vikas Ghatge, Laure Buysse, Dries Vanoost, Johan Catrysse, Rob Kleihorst, Davy Pissoort.. 71

System-Theoretic Process Analysis Approach to Analyse EMI-related Hazards and Prioritise Loss Scenarios
Miriam Gonzalez-Atienza, Dries Vanoost, Rob Kleihorst and Davy Pissoort.. 95

Red Cars are Killing Left-handed People
Paul Hampton... 115

The Safety Case as a Process Driver
Chris Hobbs 143

Driving the Development Process from the Safety Case.
Christopher Hobbs, Simon Diemert, Jeff Joyce... 157

Safety and Certification Considerations of eVTOL Aircraft
Benita Lawrence, George Head 173

Implementing autonomy in nuclear robotics: an experience-informed review of applying SACE
Phillip Mulvana, Lacey-Jo Marsland, Tom Boden, Guy Burroughes, Richard Hawkins, Matt Osborne 203

How do we make the case for "Safe" software and AI systems? - the Horizon Example
David Slater 229

Seeing beyond the Post Office Horizon
Harold Thimbleby 243

Safety Monitoring for Large Language Models: A Case Study of Offshore Wind Maintenance
Connor Walker, Callum Rothon, Koorosh Aslansefat, Yiannis Papadopoulos, Nina Dethlefs 253

A Position Paper on Safety Culture Assessment and Improvement
Michael Wright 275

Abstracts for Presentations

In first named author order. See also **Papers** index at page xiii and **Poster Abstracts** at xvii. The **Title Index** is at xix. See also full **Author Index** at page 297.

Autonomous Systems Safety by Design
Adiac Aguilar 23

Measuring and Forecasting Safety of Autonomous Systems in the Automotive Sector
Carmen Carlan 35

Project Bluebird: AI for Air Traffic Control
Richard Everson, Edmond Awad, Ben Carvell, Richard Cannon, George De Ath, Tim Dodwell, Marc Thomas 67

Achieving railway resilience to climate change using dynamic system risk assessment
Vincent Ganthy 69

ISO-26262 - The unfriendly, the friendly and the friend-in-need
Islem Jouini, Sai Pavan Kumar Eswara, Mikhail Tchernikov 169

Breaking the Tyranny of Net Risk Metrics for Automated Vehicle Safety
Philip Koopman, William H. Widen 171

Towards Formal Verification and Robustification of Neural Systems in Safety-Critical Applications
Alessio Lomuscio 191

RAFIA - Using open-source software in an Automotive safety application - a case study
Gavin McCall 197

System Analysis on Driver Monitoring System for Mainline Railway
Niki Mok 199

How to Assure a Cloud
Mike Parsons 221

Assurance 2.0: experience and automation
Ben Philips 223

Lithium-ion Batteries: Safety in Second-Life Applications
Anne Seldon 227

Safety in unmanned aviation - how much have we got and how much do we need?
Steve Wright 293

System Safety for Complex Projects – The Crossrail Approach
Hayat Zerkani 295

Poster Abstracts

In first named author order. See also **Papers** index at page xiii; **Abstracts for Presentations** at page xv. The **Title Index** is at xix. See also full **Author Index** at page 297.

Dynamic Risk Assessment in Automated Vehicles: An elaborated Approach to HARA
Nikita Bhardwaj Haupt, Peter Liggesmeyer 141

Digitalisation of Rail
Stephen Bull, Kath Uthay 25

Ensuring SOTIF for Off-Highway Autonomous Vehicles
Paul Darnell, Pavan Kumar, Ross McMurran, Ravindra Sabbella 65

Towards Trustworthy AI: Legislation, Techniques and Challenges
George Mason, Greg Chance 193

Using Rust for Safety-Critical Systems
Jonathan Pallant 219

Adaptive Safety Measures: A Concept to Optimize Safety in Automated Driving Systems
Anil Ranjitbhai Patel, Peter Liggesmeyer 225

SafeLLM: A Novel Framework for Safety Evaluation of Large Language Models: A Case Study of Offshore Wind Maintenance Planning
Connor Walker, Callum Rothon, Koorosh Aslansefat, Yiannis Papadopoulos, Nina Dethlefs 273

Title Index

In alphabetical title order. See also **Papers** index at page xiii; **Abstracts for Presentations** at page xv and **Poster Abstracts** at xvii. Also see also full **Author Index** at page 297.

A Position Paper on Safety Culture Assessment and Improvement 275

Achieving railway resilience to climate change using dynamic system risk assessment 69

Adaptive Safety Measures: A Concept to Optimize Safety in Automated Driving Systems 225

Assurance 2.0: experience and automation 223

Autonomous Systems Safety by Design 23

Breaking the Tyranny of Net Risk Metrics for Automated Vehicle Safety 171

Byzantine Generals Attack an Airbus A320 53

Digitalisation of Rail 25

Driving the Development Process from the Safety Case 157

Dynamic Risk Assessment in Automated Vehicles: An elaborated Approach to HARA 141

Ensuring Safety and Effectiveness of Medical Devices in the Presence of Electromagnetic Disturbances through Unified EMC Assurance: A Compliance Pattern 71

Ensuring SOTIF for Off-Highway Autonomous Vehicles 65

How do we make the case for "Safe" software and AI systems? - the Horizon Example 229

How to Assure a Cloud 221

Implementing autonomy in nuclear robotics: an experience-informed review of applying SACE 203

ISO-26262 - The unfriendly, the friendly and the friend-in-need 169

Lithium-ion Batteries: Safety in Second-Life Applications 227

Measuring and Forecasting Safety of Autonomous Systems in the Automotive Sector 35

Project Bluebird: AI for Air Traffic Control 67

RAFIA - Using open-source software in an Automotive safety application - a case study 197

Red Cars are Killing Left-handed People 115

SafeLLM: A Novel Framework for Safety Evaluation of Large Language Models: A Case Study of Offshore Wind Maintenance Planning 273

Safety and Certification Considerations of eVTOL Aircraft 173

Safety in unmanned aviation - how much have we got and how much do we need? 293

Safety Monitoring for Large Language Models: A Case Study of Offshore Wind Maintenance 253

Sanity Checking Autonomous Vehicle Specifications using ZDRa 27

Seeing beyond the Post Office Horizon 243

System Analysis on Driver Monitoring System for Mainline Railway 199

System Safety for Complex Projects – The Crossrail Approach 295

System-Theoretic Process Analysis Approach to Analyse EMI-related Hazards and Prioritise Loss Scenarios 95

The 'Golden Thread' of Information: A Systems Approach to Construction Safety 37

The Safety Case as a Process Driver 143

Towards Formal Verification and Robustification of Neural Systems in Safety-Critical Applications 191

Towards Trustworthy AI: Legislation, Techniques and Challenges 193

Using Rust for Safety-Critical Systems 219

Autonomous Systems Safety by Design

Adiac Aguilar

Volvo Cars

Abstract *In the rapidly evolving landscape of autonomous systems, ensuring safety is paramount. As these systems become increasingly integrated into our daily lives, we must adopt a proactive approach to mitigate risks and prioritize safety from the very inception of design. This keynote presentation, titled "Autonomous Systems Safety by Design," delves into the critical intersection of technology and safety, emphasizing the imperative to embed safety principles into the DNA of autonomous systems design.*

The presenter, Adiac Aguilar, Autonomous Systems Safety expert, will explore the foundational principles and methodologies that underpin the concept of safety by design in autonomous systems. Adiac works on the System Safety Architecture within the Core System Platform at Volvo Cars, contributing to the design of system architecture and requirements for SPA2 Core System Platform, introduced in Polestar 3 & Volvo EX90, to ensure a safe and redundant computing architecture.

During the presentation, Adiac will navigate through the intricate web of challenges posed by the dynamic nature of autonomous technologies, such as artificial intelligence, robotics, and deep learning. Key themes will include the incorporation of fail-operational mechanisms, robust testing protocols, and end-to-end System Reliability.

Drawing on real-world case studies and the latest advancements in autonomous systems, he will shed light on industry best practices and emerging standards.

The keynote will not only emphasize the technological aspects of safety but will also delve into the ethical considerations surrounding autonomous systems. It challenges attendees to think beyond technical solutions and consider the broader societal implications, addressing questions of accountability, transparency, and public trust.

© Adiac Aguilar 2024.
Published by the Safety-Critical Systems Club. All Rights Reserved.

Poster: Digitalisation of Rail

Stephen Bull and Kath Uthay

Ebeni Ltd

Abstract *Software is embedded in all aspects of our life and, without it, our lives would be completely different. Can you imagine your typical day without a smartphone or a laptop? Even for our daily commute, whether we use cars, trains or electric bikes, software is essential for them to function and provide additional services such as train timetables or the name of the next station. So, what is software? How do we ensure it is fit for purpose? And, how do the standards help us achieve this? Ebeni tackle these questions and look to provide an overview of the key software standards in rail, and their evolution. We also discuss the latest developed software standard for railway applications, explaining the significant changes, additional guidance on lifecycles and the consideration of model-based design, as well as how some requirements have been rewritten to aid interpretation and understanding.*

Sanity Checking Autonomous Vehicle Specifications using ZDRa

Lavinia Burski

SCSC Safety of Autonomous Systems Working Group (SAWG)

Abstract *Safety-critical systems need a lot of work and expertise to determine they are safe before being deployed into the public domain. Therefore, the safety case of these systems must be robust and comprehensible. This paper presents a potential solution to verifying safety-critical systems at the requirements stage of the project lifecycle by checking for loops within system requirements in the reasoning and totalization of a system specification. By undertaking these checks at an earlier stage in the project lifecycle both time and money can be saved.*

Keywords: *Connect Automated Vehicles, Smart Cities, Human Autonomy Teaming, Autonomous Vehicles, System Safety, Verification and Validation.*

1 Introduction

Autonomous cars, autonomous trains, autonomous planes. They are all, if not already, becoming a reality. Most of the technology driving these systems is becoming more practical but the largest barrier to further testing and deployment, is the public acceptance of these systems. Original Equipment Manufacturers (OEMs) are presented with the challenging task of persuading the public of the safety of their systems, so testing in real-world environments can proceed. Running autonomy software in a simulated environment is not enough verification and validation to cover all possible scenarios, therefore, more needs to be done. This paper explores one approach to check the correctness of autonomous systems specifications to ensure a high level of rigour and thus create evidence for safety cases.

Over time, public acceptance or public trust should gradually increase the more reliable a system proves to be, therefore we can assume the following equation:

$$\uparrow trust = \uparrow reliability + \uparrow time$$

© Lavinia Burski, 2024. lavburski@gmail.com
Published by the Safety-Critical Systems Club. All Rights Reserved.

One approach to persuade the public that these systems are safe is to have a solid safety case which includes:

1. Sufficient verification and validation to check that the system meets the requirements and specifications and it fulfils its intended purpose.
2. Sufficient safeguards as a back-up for any unexpected behaviour by the system.
3. Sufficient testing to verify that all the systems and subsystems work together as they should.

Before deployment to open, public-accessible environments, autonomous vehicles (AV's) and their technology should be tested in simulated environments as well as using other verification methods. It's important to note that AV's should be considered as high integrity systems and therefore their development should be treated as such. The CertiCAV project (Catapult, 2021) describes an assurance framework to support approval to market which shows that this area of research is paramount to public acceptance. Verification and validation methods should be applied at all stages of the project life cycle and not just at the end of the system's development. This paper suggests one way in which a verification technique could be applied at the design stage of the project.

2 Background and Notation

Currently, autonomous vehicles are subject to simulation testing before being allowed to be tested on public environments. The code of practice written by the UK department for transport (Transport, Department for Transport, 2015) states that:

> "*All software and revisions have been subjected to extensive and well documented testing. This should typically start with bench testing and simulation, before moving to testing on a closed test track or private road. Only then should tests be conducted on public roads or other public places.*"

However, simulation frameworks for autonomous vehicle testing are limited and may not cover all scenarios with gaps, assumptions, and simplifications potentially leading to unpredictable behaviour and accidents. One must investigate multiple scenarios to help the autonomy make safe decisions. However, what is an unsafe decision? What one human may do in one scenario may be completely opposite to another human. So who is right? - The programmer? The designer? In decision making we don't want to make these comparisons so all you can do is compare against the Advanced Driver Assistance System reference system

(European Commission, 2016) or check conformance to a formal specification (Catapult, 2021), Recent publications have addressed this challenge such as Objective COM4.2 from (Alexander, 2020) which discusses the issue that software behaviour does not result in incorrect outputs from the algorithm. If we look at applicable standards such as ISO 26262 (ISO, 2018)- the standard itself doesn't specify what safety measures should be used but it does require evidence that the safety mechanisms you do provide are sufficient. One technique to check for errors early in the software lifecycle and thus assure safety to some degree, is to use formal methods or rigorous arguments for the software of the autonomous vehicles. This paper presents a framework to check for loops in the reasoning of an autonomous vehicle specification. For ease the specification can be written either formal or natural language.

3 Writing requirements and applying ZDRa

Currently, simulation environments are used to verify and validate autonomous vehicle systems. However, by the simulation stage significant work has been done on the autonomous vehicle system. Safety checks can be completed earlier in the project lifecycle, during the requirements phase. Writing requirements for any complex system, especially an autonomous system, is difficult.

One way to check for possible safety-related issues at the earlier stage of Connected Autonomous Vehicle (CAV) development is to check for circular reasoning in the list of requirements. This aspect is called the Z Document Rhetorical aspect (ZDRa), taken from (Burski, 2019). Initially, this check for loops in reasoning was devised for formally defined specifications, as such it can check for loops in reasoning in informal specifications as well.

For example, say we had the following list of requirements:

1. The autonomous vehicle shall follow instructions from the passenger
2. The autonomous vehicle shall stop at a red light.
3. The passenger of an autonomous vehicle shall follow instructions from vehicle manufacturers.
4. The autonomous vehicle shall not harm any pedestrian.
5. The vehicle manufacturers shall follow instructions from passengers.

Fig. 1. Example requirements for a CAV

We can then label the requirements in LaTeX with the following:

1. \draschema{req1}{The autonomous vehicle shall follow instructions from the passenger}

2. \draschema{req2}{The autonomous vehicle shall stop at a red light.}
3. \draschema{req3}{The passenger of an autonomous vehicle shall follow instructions from vehicle manufacturers.}
4. \draschema{req4}{The autonomous vehicle shall not harm any pedestrian.}
5. \draschema{req5}{The vehicle manufacturers shall follow instructions from passengers.}

\uses{req1}{req3}
\uses{req3}{req5}
\uses{req5}{req3}

Fig. 2. ZDRa labeled requirements.

The syntax from the ZDRa is highlighted in red. We use the notation draschema (a Z specification schema (Bowen, 2001) annotated in ZDRa notation (Burski, 2019)) to denote each requirement is a Document Rhetorical aspect schema-a schema or function in Z which has been annotated in ZDRa (Burski, 2019). We then use the notation to denote which requirements use another requirement. Moreover, which requirement is dependent on each requirement.

We use the ZMathLang (Burski, 2019) framework to compile Figure 2 as a LaTeX document and the following pdf is generated:

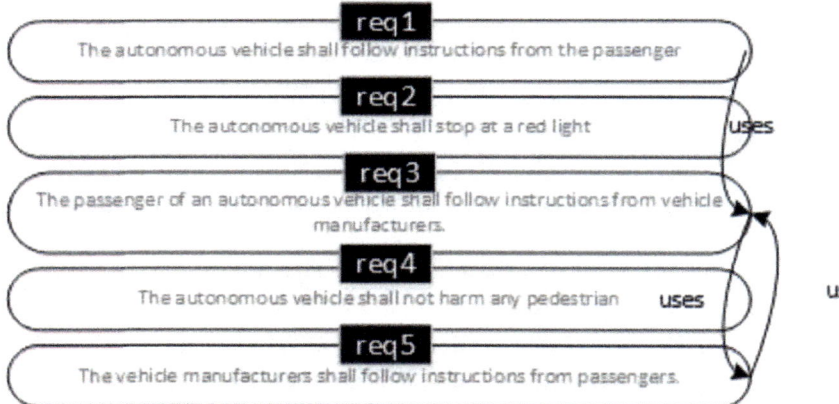

Fig. 3. Requirements labelled and compiled using ZDRa

The compiled document clearly demonstrates a loop between requirement 3 and requirement 5, where each requirement is dependent on each other. This is not a good idea for a high integrity system specification, as the program would find itself in a continuous loop if there is no exit condition (Charles Waite, 2006). The example uses the manually added relationship between the requirements using the ZDRa annotations. If a relationship is not annotated and missed by the user than a potential loop may not be picked up. This is not an ideal situation and is therefore a clear area of future work.

The ZMathlang tool also outputs the following dependency graph, which is a graph representation of Figure 3.

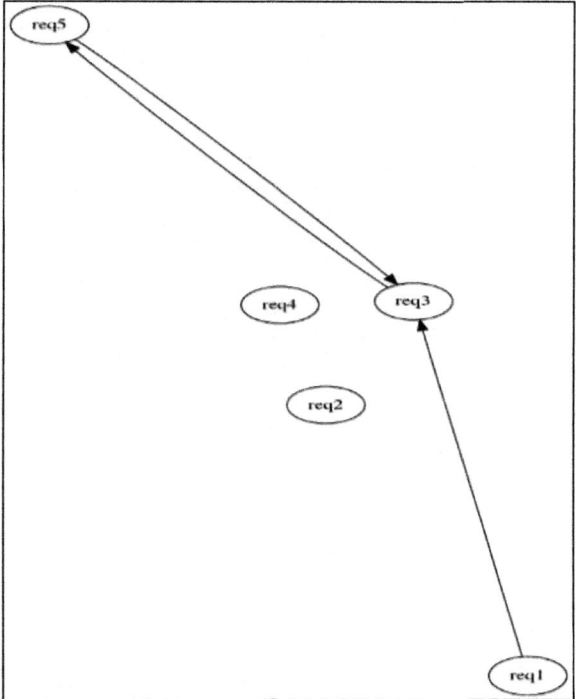

Fig. 4. Dependency graph for sample requirements

The dependency graph shown in Figure 4 is helpful to see which requirements are dependent on each other without the requirements themselves. This graph would be particularly useful with a large system specification with many requirements. The graph clearly shows that requirement 1 is dependent on requirement 3 which does not pose a problem. However, requirement 5 is dependent on requirement 3 and requirement 3 is dependent on requirement 5. This dependency could potentially pose a problem in a high integrity system such as an autonomous vehicle as the system could end up in loop. Safety-critical systems are usually programmed in languages such as SPARK Ada (Spark, 2023) where if a program doesn't terminate, it needs to enter the same state twice which can then be checked (Setzer, 2004). By using the ZDRa checker such elements of a program can be identified at the specification stage of the project lifecycle.

4 Sanity checking the specification using ZDRa check

The document rhetorical aspect can check for loops withing the reasoning of a specification. In a large software specification with many aspects and functionalities this is important to find out to ensure a safe system. Not only does the ZDRa tell the user if there are any loops it also shows where these loops are and therefore what parts of the specification need to be re-analysed. Inconsistencies and loops within a specification are quite common when there is more than one person working on a specification (which is often the case in software/system development for safety-critical systems).

The ZDRa model is intended to be used as evidence in the safety case of autonomous vehicle development. Failures in autonomous vehicle systems can be catastrophic and shouldn't be taken lightly. That is why we propose that a ZDRa system is used in addition to simulation testing to enhance safety. The ZDRa system gives a visually representative overview of the requirements and how they link to each other. One can then move onto to translate their specification into a theorem prover in order to complete further proofs. However moving to this stage usually requires an expert in the chosen theorem prover or to follow a translation path such as ZMathlang. The ZDRa can also check for totalization, that is for every precondition that isn't satisfied there must be an alternative solution. This is very important for high integrity systems such as autonomous vehicles because the vehicle must have a solution in every scenario.

5 Conclusion

Public acceptance is a large hurdle to overcome in deploying autonomous systems. Clients, stakeholders, regulators and governments want to know these systems are sufficiently safe before deploying them in real-world scenarios. One way for policy-makers to and to do this is via a convincing safety case. In this paper we have demonstrated how a specification written in natural language can be checked for loops in the reasoning. This allows anyone to be able to check for loops and totalization of specifications without needing to be an expert in formal methods or verification and validation. The ZDRa check can be used as evidence within the safety case of autonomous vehicles and be presented in a way in which everyone in the project team can understand. This allows stakeholders with an interest in the safety of autonomous vehicles to be satisfied that the system in question will always have some kind of outcome no matter what the situation. In addition, identifying problems this early in the process can prevent massive amounts of rework and expense.

References

Alexander, R. H. (2020). *Safety assurance objectives for autonomous systems.* Safety Critical Systems Club.
Bowen, J. P. (2001). https://link.springer.com/chapter/10.1007/978-1-4471-0701-9_1. *Formal Approaches to Computing and Information Technology FACIT*, 3-19.
Burski, L. (2019). *From Formal Specification to full proof: A stepwise method.* Edinburgh: Doctoral dis-sertation, Heriot-Watt University.
Catapult, C. P. (2021). *CertiCAV Assurance Paper.* U.K: Connected Places Catapult.
Charles M. Waite, R. D. (2006). The Rhetoric of "Software Complexity" - Beyond the Smoke and Mirrors,. *SAE 2006 World Congress & Exhibition* (p. 10). ProDesCon, Process Design Consultants, Inc.
European Commission. (2016). *Advanced driver assistance systems.* European Road Safety Observatory.
ISO. (2018). *ISO 26262-1:2018, Road vehicles, Functional safety.*
Setzer, A. (2004). *Critical Systems course slides.* Retrieved from Swansea University: http://www.cs.swan.ac.uk/~csetzer/lectures/critsys/03/critsysdraft.pdf
Spark. (2023, 11 23). Retrieved from Adacore: https://www.adacore.com/about-spark
Transport, D. f. (2015). *The Pathway to Driverless Cars, Summary report and action plan.* DfT Publications.

Measuring and Forecasting Safety of Autonomous Systems in the Automotive Sector

Carmen Carlan

Edge Case Research

Extended Abstract

Based on the media reports, interviews, and survey reports, such as the reports conducted by the RAND Corporation, the public expects that autonomous vehicles (AVs) are at least as safe as conventional vehicles. Consequently, as required by various stakeholders such as the European Union Commission, the German Ethics Commission, and the ISO TR 4804, the risk assessment framework of choice for AVs is Positive Risk Balance (PRB). PRB requires that a newly developed system is as good as a similar existing system. In the context of PRB, AVs are compared with human driver performance in exemplary situations, according to published crash statistics and analysis of human behaviour. While applying PRB, the risk associated with different types of harm (e.g., injuries of people in the car, injuries of vulnerable road users (VRUs), fatalities of people in the car, fatalities of VRUs), and the distribution of risk (e.g., the system shall not discriminate because of age, religion, skin colour) are taken into consideration. Also, when comparing risks associated with different systems (i.e., human driver versus computer driver), the compared risks shall have been measured given comparable operating conditions.

PRB is challenging to demonstrate, especially before deployment, because of a lack of historical data about the behaviour of AVs in the entire operational design domain. To compensate for this, Positive Trust Balance (PTB) was proposed. The safety argument behind PTB is that 1) the AV developer has a solid safety culture, and feedback related to system safety is gathered from different stakeholders and addressed; 2) the system has been developed following an engineering process, including an extensive V&V process, aligned with the relevant safety standards and best practices; 3) all operational controls and system maintenance are correctly in place after deployment and the behaviour of the system after deployment is monitored, and the monitored information is analyzed to improve the system performance continuously and to ensure that the assurance properties hold.

A solid safety culture may be established by using a Safety Management System (SMS). An SMS is an approach from the aerospace domain that supports

© Carmen Carlan 2024.
Published by the Safety-Critical Systems Club. All Rights Reserved.

organizational safety in a systematic and integrated way. It guides the establishment of the safety practices within a company, together with the safety roles, and sets up organizational safety objectives. An SMS also guides safety risk assessment and management, handles the monitoring, analysis, and measurement of overall safety performance, and specifies the activities to be executed within an organization to promote safety.

To demonstrate that the risk of the known hazardous scenarios is "as low as reasonably possible", safety standards, such as ISO 26262 and ISO 21448, engineering processes, and best practices are followed. Also, conformance with applicable regulations shall be demonstrated. To document identified hazards, a Quantitative Fault Tree (QFT) may be used. To build up the QFT, first, a preliminary hazard analysis defines what loss events can occur and lists what hazards can lead to these loss events. Second, a functional hazard analysis allocates the occurrence of hazards to functions in the autonomy stack and builds the fault tree. Third, a system/subsystem hazard analysis process allocates functions to components in the architecture and can employ techniques such as failure modes and effects criticality analysis to further define what causal factors need to be tracked, including hardware failures and software defects.

Risk targets can then be allocated to each node in the QFT. For each identified hazard, a causal chain leading to the occurrence of harm can be evaluated based on processes described in standards like ISO 21448 and ISO 26262. Initially, this can be used to define a risk budget for the autonomy stack and operations. However, the complexity of AVs and their operational domain make it impossible to identify before deployment all unsafe scenarios. Consequently, before deployment the risk budget can only be estimated and then refined – with feedback from simulation, on-road testing, and operation.

Safety performance metrics measured in operation reinforce or update the estimated rates of causal factors in the QFT. Violations of the estimated risk and statistical deviations between simulation results and real-world operation can be used to identify new trigger conditions (i.e., unknown safe scenarios) for the already identified hazard. The newly identified triggering conditions will be fed to the SMS to address them.

The 'Golden Thread' of Information: A Systems Approach to Construction Safety

Mikela Chatzimichailidou[1]

Department of Civil, Environmental and Geomatic Engineering, UCL[2]

London, UK

Abstract *To improve efficiency and productivity in the construction industry, governments around the world encourage the development of modular buildings. Meanwhile, worker safety is an important aspect that the construction industry has been concerned with, as there is still much room for improvement. Furthermore, accidents like London's Grenfell Tower fire in 2017 demonstrate the imperative need to consider construction safety systemically. However, as pointed out in the academic literature and experienced in practice, there is an apparent disconnect between worker safety and building safety. For this reason, this paper sets the ground for a holistic approach to safety by bringing together worker and building safety under the 'golden thread of information' as introduced by the British government. The golden thread calls for more integrated safety information management, which could be achieved with the use of Building Information Modelling (BIM) throughout the entire construction and building lifecycle. BIM is regarded as a holistic process of creating and managing information for built assets. Its simulation and visualisation functions can improve safety in all types of construction; this paper concentrates on modular construction.*

Keywords: *BIM; building safety; golden thread; modular construction; system safety; worker safety.*

---

[1] mikela.chatzi@ucl.ac.uk

[2] Professor Mikela Chatzimichailidou, Department of Civil, Environmental and Geomatic Engineering, UCL, London, UK

© Mikela Chatzimichailidou 2024.
Published by the Safety-Critical Systems Club. All Rights Reserved

1 Background and motivation

1.1 Safety considerations in construction

The construction industry is one of the most dynamic and hazardous industries (James et al. 2012). According to the 2020 Construction statistics in Great Britain report (Health and Safety Executive 2020), there was an estimated 81,000 construction work-related ill health cases (new or long-standing). Figure 1 presents a comparison between heath incidents in general construction and other industries with similar work activities. It therefore becomes apparent why workplace health and safety – also known as occupational health – is the main priority for the construction industry (James et al. 2012).

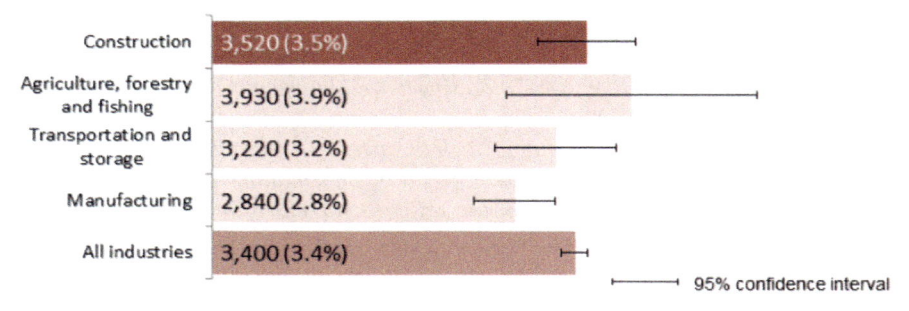

Fig. 1. Work-related ill health cases in construction (Health and Safety Executive, 2020)

Compared to traditional stick-built construction methods, modular construction has environmental, economic, and social advantages (Mao et al. 2015; Liu et al. 2020). A simple overview of the main stages of the modular construction process is provided in Figure 2. However, the safety risks pertaining to innovative methods of construction like modular are less known or different from those of conventional construction methods. Thus, the safety risk management of modular construction plays a key role in unlocking its full breadth of benefits and, in turn, its wider employment (HM Government 2020).

Here, the term modular construction is adopted as the most frequently used in contemporary literature. Modular construction refers to a process of factory-built building units (i.e., the modules) being fabricated and/or partly assembled in a manufacturing plant away from the construction site, then transported to and assembled on-site (Lu and Korman 2010; Li, Shen, and Xue 2014). Figure 2 shows the main stages of the modular construction lifecycle. In this paper, attention is prominently drawn on modular construction due to the fact that its process is quite different than conventional on-site construction, as depicted in Figure 2.

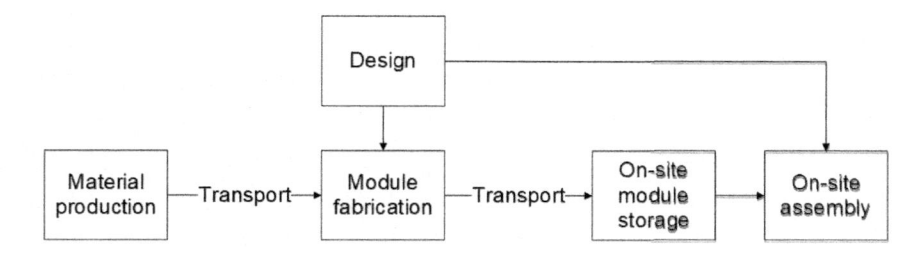

Fig. 2. Main stages of modular construction lifecycle
(adapted from Kamali, Hewage, and Sadiq 2019, Figure 1)

The work done offsite (Figure 2, "Module fabrication") can reach 70%-80%, which greatly reduces the amount of vertical work at height (Jeong et al. 2021). However, a report released by the United States Bureau of Labor Statistics in 2017 argues that the accident rate of the modular construction industry was much higher than the average level of the general construction and manufacturing industries mainly because the construction of modular buildings involves offsite production as well as on-site installation (James et al. 2012; Jeong et al. 2021). Seemingly, although the physical footprint on-site is reduced, some safety risks have been altered or transferred to the manufacturing and transportation processes of modules (Ahn et al. 2020). For instance, according to Kim, Nussbaum, and Jia (2012) the modules produced in a factory are usually larger and heavier than the components used in conventional buildings and usually require partial assembly offsite. Additionally, offsite assembly requires the use of tools, such as ladders and mobile scaffolding, so falls may also occur in the manufacturing phase (Jeong et al. 2021). Furthermore, multiple workers need to perform installation tasks on-site (e.g., lifting, carrying, erecting), which put them at a risk of ergonomic exposure and injury (Kim, Nussbaum, and Jia 2012).

In 2019 in the United Kingdom, specialists from the Department for Levelling Up, Housing and Communities (formerly Ministry of Housing, Communities and Local Government) (HM Government 2019) developed a framework to regularise and refine the term Modern Methods of Construction (MMC) – as an alternative and more inclusive term for modular construction – by defining a broad spectrum of seven innovative construction techniques. With the corresponding document, one of the main priorities of the UK government is for the construction industry to demonstrate the highest standards of building safety and quality, without sacrificing innovation in the built environment (HM Government 2021b). It has become apparent that the new safety challenges brought by innovations in the built environment, such as modular construction, cannot be ignored (El-Abidi and Ghazali 2015).

1.2 Added value of paper

This work builds on previous research published by Chatzimichailidou and Ma (2022) in the Safety Science[1] journal. Chatzimichailidou and Ma (2022) summarised the existing literature on the application of Building Information Modelling (BIM) in the safety management of the construction industry in general, as well as the main safety hazards of modular construction. The authors analysed the application of BIM in the safety risk management of modular construction as a joint topic. This was the main contribution of the previous paper, as there was very little research being done to link all three subjects together. The findings showed that BIM technology has a great application potential in modular construction, and specifically in the training of staff, safety inspection, and crane management. By adopting BIM-based solutions it is likely to improve worker safety awareness, detect hazardous factors and scenarios, and optimise site layout.

As a continuation of the previous work (Chatzimichailidou and Ma 2022), in this paper modular construction is seen as the process of fabricating building modules offsite and assembling them on-site (Figure 2). Nonetheless, the perception of the building as the final product of the modular production process should not be disregarded. This process-product relationship is illustrated in a simple manner in Figure 3. It is also worth to mention that the building is not a static final product but has a lifecycle itself and evolves with time (e.g., retrofitting, repair, maintenance etc.), hence the loop around "Building" in Figure 3.

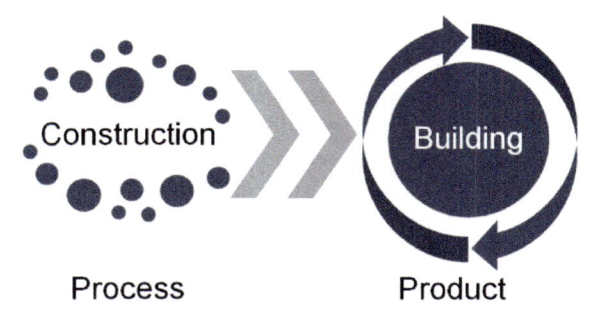

Fig. 3. The relationship between construction and building

Although the safety of personnel during the construction process is of paramount importance, the safety of the building – and in turn of its occupants – is also very crucial. This notion has been strongly emphasised recently after major fatal accidents like the Grenfell Tower fire in London in 2017 and the Surfside condominium collapse in Florida in 2021.

---

[1] https://www.sciencedirect.com/journal/safety-science

In the literature, it is recognised that worker safety and building safety are disconnected and that further research is needed in the area (Harvey, Waterson, and Dainty 2019). To address this gap, this work emphasises the need to cater both for worker safety as well as for building safety and for this reason it initiates a discussion around system safety, which encompasses both the construction process (i.e., construction) and the product (i.e., building) (Jones et al. 2021). This paper makes high-level recommendations about how to bring together occupational safety and building safety under the 'golden thread of information' (Hackitt 2018; HM Government 2021a). It is also argued that Building Information Modelling (BIM) solutions can bring great value in the safety risk management of modular construction by facilitating the creation and maintenance of the golden thread of information. Especially in the case of modular construction, BIM solutions can bring significant advantages due to the standardisation of design and processes (e.g., Yeoh, Wong and Peng, 2016; Abanda, Tah and Cheung, 2017; Tak et al., 2021).

2 A holistic view of construction safety

Occupational safety is mainly concerned with preventing injuries to personnel that can result from incidents associated with the job they perform during the construction process (Aloqaily 2018). This section, however, initiates a discussion around system safety, which encompasses the entire lifecycle from manufacturing to construction to building operation. It concludes by making high-level recommendations about how to bring together worker safety and building safety under the golden thread of digital information.

2.1 System Safety

Referring to its theoretical underpinnings, system safety emerges from the application of systems theory. Systems theory offers a more holistic perspective, emphasising that safety in a complex system is more than the sum of its parts (Leveson 2011). Recent studies in the area of high-rise (also known as high-risk) buildings (Hackitt 2018; Cidik and Phillips 2021) recognise the technological, organisational, and social underpinnings of safety and also the need to manage buildings as complex systems where the actions of many different people (e.g., designers, engineers, workers, occupants, maintainers) can compromise the integrity of the building throughout its entire lifecycle covering design, construction, and maintenance.

In practice, accidents like London's Grenfell Tower fire demonstrate the imperative need to consider construction and building safety as a system (Hackitt 2018), as opposed to a series of competing or isolated objectives. Moreover, building safety is not limited to the building itself, but incorporates all the people in or in the vicinity of the structure. In view of this, the UK government committed itself to instigate an upgraded Building Safety Programme that will also study modular construction as per the Construction Playbook (HM Government 2020). The post-Grenfell reformed regulatory system further established the importance of a holistic, lifecycle approach to drive a more responsible building industry (HM Government 2021a). To maintain building safety, especially for higher risk residential buildings, Dame Hackitt (2018) identified the need for the golden thread of information, so that the original design intent is preserved, and changes can be managed through a formal review process. To address the golden thread of information will require organisations to have a mature understanding of the design process, the associated requirements and capability in handling digital data to provide the surety that they can deliver and operate the final product (i.e., the building) in accordance with the Building Safety Bill.

2.2 The 'golden thread of information'

Following the Grenfell tower fire accident, the UK government appointed Dame Judith Hackitt to lead an independent review of building regulations and fire safety; similar considerations were put forward earlier by Park et al. (2014). In her report, 'Building a safer future', Dame Hackitt (2018) recommended the introduction of a golden thread as a tool to manage buildings as systems and allow people to use digital records to safely and effectively design, construct, and operate their buildings. The government set out that the golden thread will apply to all buildings within scope of the new more stringent building safety regime in the UK, being introduced through the Building Safety Bill (HM Government 2021a). The Department for Levelling Up, Housing and Communities specified that the golden thread will (HM Government 2021a):

- use digital tools and systems to enable key information to be stored and used effectively to ensure safer buildings
- support duty holders and accountable persons throughout the lifecycle of a building (during the gateways process, building registration process, the safety case approach and throughout occupation) by recording the original design intent and ensuring subsequent changes to buildings are captured and preserved

- incorporate all the information needed to understand a building and how it should be managed so that the building and above all the people in and around a building are safe, both now and in the future
- make information easily available to the right people at the right time
- put in place a new higher standard of information-keeping which will support the building safety regulator in being assured buildings are being managed safely

In summary, the golden thread covers the information, documents, management processes and platforms used to support building safety. The new UK Building Safety Bill will require the golden thread to be maintained through the series of three gateways; that is, planning, construction, and operation (HM Government 2021a). Therefore, given its wide span and nature, it can be argued that the golden thread of information can support and improve both worker safety and building safety as well. This relationship between the two forms of safety is shown in Figure 7 and can refer to general construction, modular construction as well as the corresponding operable buildings produced through the construction process, whether conventional or not.

2.3 Safety benefits of BIM

BIM is a computer-aided modelling and simulation technology based on objects and their development process. It can simulate the actual information of construction projects through 3D geographic figures and non-geographical figures including materials for building components, weight, price, size, program, and scale (Migilinskas et al. 2013; Xu, Ma, and Ding 2014). In terms of project and system lifecycle, BIM is designed to facilitate collaboration and visualisation during the design and construction phases, and can also serve as a digital database when the project is completed. A digital twin, on the other hand, is intended for the building's operations and maintenance. The two technologies complement each other, with BIM being the stepping stone to digital twins[2].

The significant advantages of BIM technology in facilitating the coordination and management of complex projects have attracted widespread attention in the construction industry (e.g., High Speed Two railway, HS2) and academia (Fargnoli and Lombardi 2020). A new research trend has emerged, that is, using BIM technology and tools to help early risk identification, accident prevention, and risk communication (Zou, Kiviniemi, and Jones 2017). With BIM model simulation, unsafe factors can be identified and based on the results of the visual identification, construction personnel can take appropriate protective measures in

---

[2] https://www.mottmac.com/views/bim-before-you-digital-twin

time to eliminate (or minimise) the safety risks at the construction site (Wang et al. 2015).

To summarise some literature findings: the main safety-related challenges that modular construction is faced with are shortage of skilled workers (Fard et al. 2017), demanding planning phase (Lu and Korman 2010), large demand and complicated dispatching of large-scale machinery and equipment (Getuli, Capone, and Bruttini 2020), which leads to the most frequent accidents such as workers falling from heights and being hit by falling objects (Fard et al. 2017; Jeong et al. 2021). This is practically where BIM technology has proved to be helpful (Abanda, Tah, and Cheung 2017; Tan, Li, and Wang 2020). BIM technology can improve workers' safety awareness (Ahn et al. 2020) by providing them with a visual experience of the workspace and early warnings of potential safety hazards (Tan, Li, and Wang 2020). BIM technology not only helps designers check possible conflicts in the planning stage, but also safety managers to monitor site dynamics and check safety issues real-time during the construction process (Tak et al. 2021). This supports the optimisation of construction plans and strengthens protection measures (Yingbo, Yanyao, and Yan 2019). In terms of crane management, the models and animations offered by BIM provide help for crane selection, layout, and scheduling (Yeoh, Wong, and Peng 2016). By utilising BIM-based solutions and other related technologies (e.g., augmented reality) it is possible to achieve a safer working environment in both the offsite manufacturing stage and the on-site assembly and installation stage of modular construction.

All in all, BIM technology can make a big contribution in providing visual and interactive innovative methods for worker training (Figure 4), optimising site layout and construction plans (Figure 5), and automatically detecting safety issues, such as collisions and lack of protection facilities (Figure 6) during the construction process to improve the safety management efficiency (Chatzimichailidou and Ma 2022).

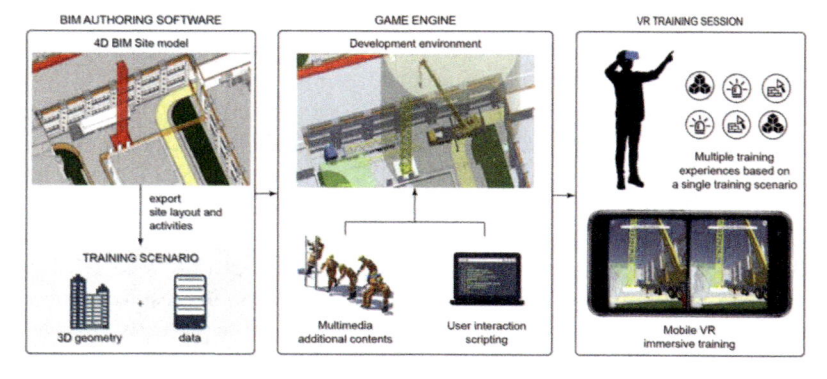

Fig. 4. BIM-enabled virtual reality training experience (Chatzimichailidou and Ma 2022)

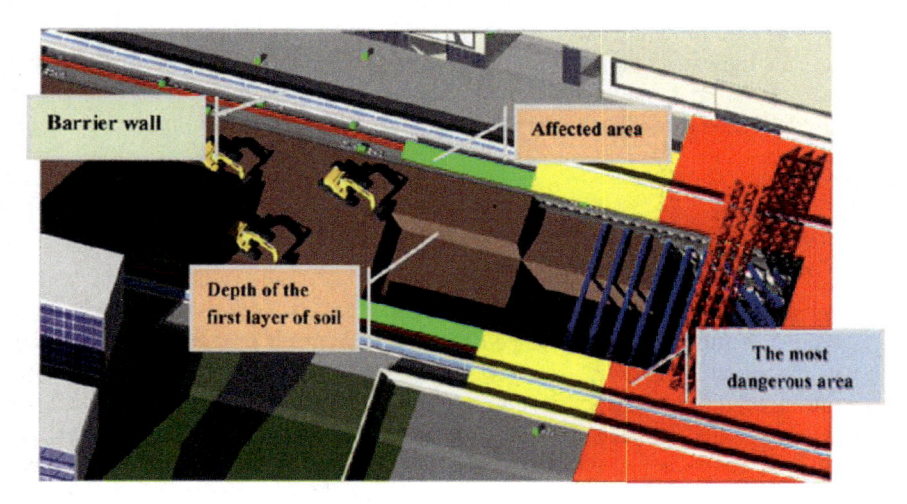

Fig. 5. Determination of risk level in impacted working area (Chatzimichailidou and Ma 2022)

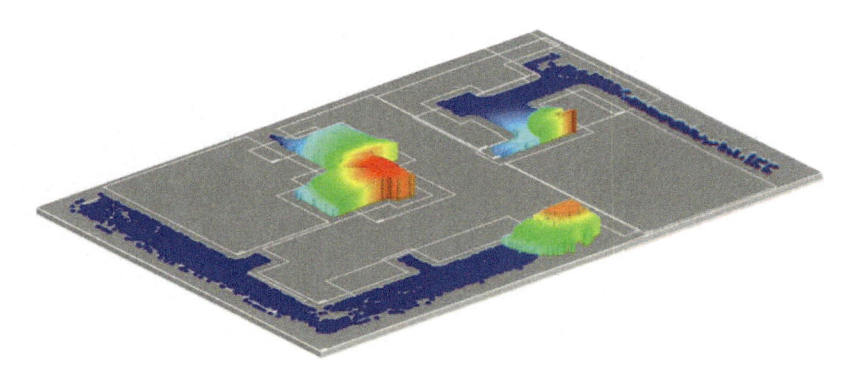

Fig. 6. Crane occupancy (Chatzimichailidou and Ma 2022)

Looking beyond worker safety, BIM can serve the need for through-life safety. It can enable building safety information to be stored in an organised way and used effectively by the right people at the right time. By capturing information from the planning stage and recording the original design intent it can ensure that subsequent changes to buildings are captured and preserved. BIM can help incorporate all the information needed to understand a building throughout its lifecycle and how it should be managed so that the building and above all the people (i.e., construction professionals, buildings occupants and the wider public) in and around a building are safe.

This indicates that BIM has a great application potential in promoting a holistic safety risk management for construction projects and buildings either those are delivered through conventional methods or through modular construction.

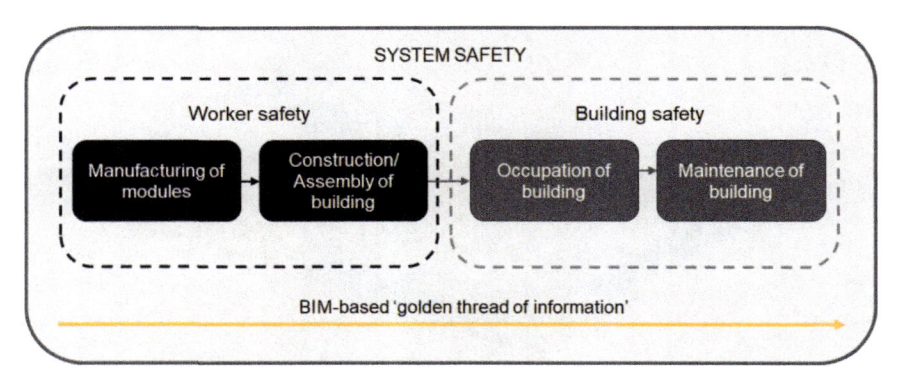

2.4 A system safety framework for modular construction

As shown in Figure 7, building safety (grey dotted frame on the right) refers to the occupation and maintenance of the building itself (i.e., when the building is in place), whereas worker safety (black dotted frame on the left) is of concern during manufacturing and assembly. It is worth to mention that worker safety can be also considered during the maintenance of the actual building, but for clarity reasons and to avoid confusion this is not depicted in Figure 7. System safety, on the other hand, should cover the entire building lifecycle spanning from planning to maintenance (Hackitt 2018; Cidik and Phillips 2021). In the case of modular construction, system safety will also incorporate the manufacturing of modules, which of course is not applicable in general construction.

Fig. 7. System safety framework for modular construction

Here it is recommended that the golden thread requirement can be satisfied through the use of BIM-based solutions. In the literature (e.g., Yeoh, Wong, and Peng 2016; Fard et al. 2017; Abanda, Tah, and Cheung 2017; Yingbo, Yanyao, and Yan 2019; Hossain, and Ahmed 2019; Ahn et al. 2020; Getuli, Capone, and Bruttini 2020; Tan, Li, and Wang 2020; Jeong et al. 2021; Tak et al. 2021), there are several examples of how BIM can cater for the occupational safety of workers in modular construction (Figure 7, black dotted frame on the left). Referring to building safety (Figure 7, grey dotted frame on the left), as the other component of system safety,

> *"a BIM system can enable the duty holders to ensure accuracy and quality of design and construction, which are crucial for building-in safety up front. Having BIM-enabled data sets during occupation means that duty holders will have a suitable evidence base through which to deliver their responsibilities and maintain safety and integrity throughout the lifecycle of a building. Information can be updated as and when changes are made during the building lifecycle"* (Hackitt 2018).

So, it is suggested that the golden thread can be realised through BIM. By using BIM systems from planning to maintenance we can create a complete digital twin where the risks of workers and occupants can be securely stored, visually depicted, shared and updated by different duty holders. Another benefit of using BIM for holistic safety management is that interfaces between building subsystems, such as façade, gas, mechanical, electrical, fire installations, tolerances and forces become visible and interrelating safety risks can be also identified. By knowing the specific building subsystem – and the humans involved – where safety risk is seen as high, targeted and hence more effective mitigation strategies can be applied depending on the stage of the construction process or the building lifecycle.

Fundamentally, the golden thread is a systems approach to storing, sharing, and monitoring safety-related information across the construction and building lifecycles and can be practically achieved by adopting BIM as a process. The preliminary model introduced with Figure 7 is an important prerequisite for paving the way for a new safety culture in the construction sector that embraces a holistic view of potential risks impacting the safety of modular construction and general construction as well.

3 Concluding remarks and future directions

Accidents like the Grenfell Tower fire have shifted the way construction professionals see construction and building safety, at least in the UK. Although the safety of personnel during the construction (and maintenance) process is admittedly of paramount importance, the safety of the building – and in turn of its occupants – is also crucial.

So far, the literature has not devoted much attention to incorporating worker and building safety into system safety. To start bridging the gap, this paper initiated a discussion around system safety, which encompasses both process (i.e., construction) and product (i.e., building) (Jones et al. 2021) based on the conception that a building is the final product of the construction process (Figure 3). It is now recognised that there is an imperative need to consider construction, irrespective of the method (i.e., stick-built or modular), as a system (Hackitt 2018), as opposed to a series of competing or isolated objectives.

The UK is one of the first countries to embark on a process of reforming their regulatory framework through the upcoming Building Safety Bill, the ongoing Building Safety Programme and the already published Construction Playbook (HM Government 2020). The Construction Playbook encourages the application of modular construction and the use of BIM solutions for a more efficient and sustainable construction sector. To achieve better information and safety management, Dame Hackitt (2018) proposed the creation and maintenance of the golden thread of information that could run through the entire lifecycle of the construction process and the building operation as well.

To address the golden thread of information in practice, this paper argues that digital technologies can support and improve risk management. With the use of BIM already from the early stages of construction planning, the golden thread of information can be created and further maintained throughout the phase of module production, assembly and construction, building occupation and maintenance. In this way, BIM will capture information pertaining both to occupational health as well as building safety, including design and operational safety of the building, safety of occupants and also the safety of the society that leaves around and interfaces with the building. The notion of system safety and the function of BIM as the foundation for the golden thread of digital information were shown in Figure 7.

As depicted in Figure 8, BIM is a synthesis of aspects integrated in a single model. The model is populated with data that describes the geometry, materials, systems, and components of the built asset. Input data for BIM may consist of, but are not limited to, schedules, requirements, standards, emails, spreadsheets, contracts, documents, designs. The BIM software (e.g., Autodesk Revit, Navisworks) works by creating three-dimensional (3D) objects that construct a virtual model that can be viewed from multiple angles and perspectives by using devices, such as tablets, smart phones, laptops and desktops etc. Mobile devices are particularly useful for those on site.

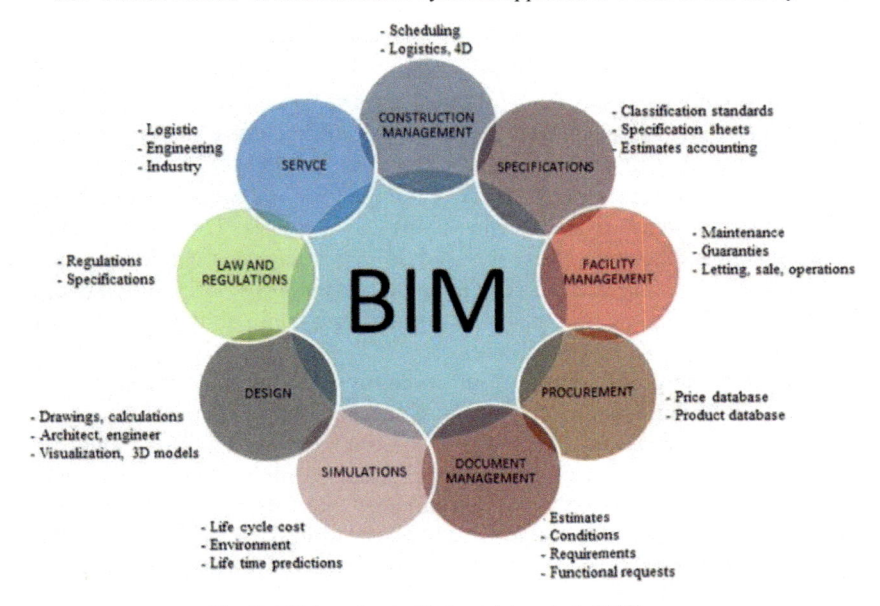

Fig. 8. BIM synthesis (Reizgevicius et al. 2018)

The golden thread of information calls for better information management, which can be achieved through BIM. BIM appears to address the principles of the golden thread as these are described by HM Government (2019):

- Accurate, trusted, understandable, simple to access and secure information from the golden thread as the single source of truth
- Culture change within the industry with new competencies and updated processes that focus on information management and control
- Clear accountabilities to those designing, building or maintaining a building; information being formatted in a way that can be easily handed over and maintained over the entire lifetime of a building to achieve longevity and shareability of information
- Relevant and proportionate information - the objective of the golden thread is system safety and therefore if information is no longer relevant to worker or building safety it does not need to be kept

In this paper, it has become apparent that the golden thread of information – through the functions of BIM – can improve the overall safety management. The initial framework on Figure 7 proposes a way to create the golden thread of information during the early stages of a construction project and maintain it until the late stages of the building lifecycle. Further conceptual work and applications will validate this proposed framework and the initial recommendations made herein. Additionally, future studies around how the golden thread can be maintained throughout the building lifetime can strengthen the argument that the golden thread, and in turn BIM, create a new safety culture in the construction industry according to which worker safety and building safety are part of the same mission, i.e., system safety. Developing a new safety culture will require overcoming resistance to new technologies and practices. Therefore, to support future practice, research endeavours should aim at tackling challenges such as accuracy of modelling, acceptance and use of digital tools, information overload and situational awareness, intellectual property and commercial interests, cost of new technologies, shortage of new skills.

Of course, the golden thread of information was originally introduced in the UK and will become mandatory in this region only, however the author appreciates that this concept and the proposed solutions can benefit other countries as well, depending on the local regulatory regime. As global trends favouring urbanisation bring more people to cities and more high-rises (e.g., Grenfell Tower in London, Torre dei Moro apartment block in Milan) are constructed to house those people, the need for a systems approach to construction safety will only increase in the coming years.

This paper recognises the opportunity for the construction sector to develop a capability that enables us to foresee, monitor, and track how earlier safety-critical decisions can impact later stages of the building lifecycle, therefore laying the foundation for the introduction of more proactive and better-informed risk mitigation plans.

Acknowledgments I would like to thank my MSc student Yue Ma for working tirelessly to complete her MSc thesis, which laid the foundation for our journal paper ("Using BIM in the safety risk management of modular construction.") published in Safety Science, and led to this paper as well. I would also like to thank Mike Parsons for providing constructive feedback that improved the quality of this paper.

Disclaimers This is a working paper, and hence it represents research in progress. This paper represents the opinions of the author, and is the product of empirical research. This work has not received any funding.

References

Abanda, F. H., J. H. M. Tah, and F. K. T. Cheung. "BIM in off-site manufacturing for buildings." Journal of Building Engineering 14 (2017): 89-102.

Ahn, Seungjun, Luke Crouch, Tae Wan Kim, and Raufdeen Rameezdeen. "Comparison of worker safety risks between onsite and offsite construction methods: A site management perspective." Journal of Construction Engineering and Management 146, no. 9 (2020): 05020010.

Aloqaily, Arafat. Cross Country Pipeline Risk Assessments and Mitigation Strategies. Gulf Professional Publishing, 2018.

Çıdık, Mustafa Selçuk, and Stephen Phillips. "Buildings as complex systems: the impact of organisational culture on building safety." Construction Management and Economics (2021): 1-16.

Chatzimichailidou, Mikela, and Yue Ma. "Using BIM in the safety risk management of modular construction." Safety science 154 (2022): 105852.

El-Abidi, Khaled M. Amtered, and Farid Ezanee Mohamed Ghazali. "Motivations and limitations of prefabricated building: an overview." In Applied Mechanics and Materials, vol. 802, pp. 668-675. Trans Tech Publications Ltd, 2015.

Fard, Maryam Mirhadi, Seyyed Amin Terouhid, Charles J. Kibert, and Hamed Hakim. "Safety concerns related to modular/prefabricated building construction." International journal of injury control and safety promotion 24, no. 1 (2017): 10-23.

Fargnoli, Mario, and Mara Lombardi. "Building information modelling (BIM) to enhance occupational safety in construction activities: Research trends emerging from one decade of studies." Buildings 10, no. 6 (2020): 98.

Getuli, Vito, Pietro Capone, and Alessandro Bruttini. "Planning, management and administration of HS contents with BIM and VR in construction: an implementation protocol." Engineering, Construction and Architectural Management (2020).

Hackitt, Judith. "Building a Safer Future." Independent Review of Building Regulations and Fire Safety: Interim Report (2018).

Harvey, Eleanor J., Patrick Waterson, and Andrew RJ Dainty. "Applying HRO and resilience engineering to construction: Barriers and opportunities." Safety science 117 (2019): 523-533.

Health and Safety Executive, 2020. [online]. Available from: https://www.hse.gov.uk/statistics/industry/construction.pdf

HM Government. 2019. "Modern Methods of Construction: Introducing the MMC Definition Framework." Department for Levelling Up, Housing and Communities. https://www.gov.uk/government/publications/modern-methods-of-construction-working-group-developing-a-definition-framework

HM Government. 2020. "The Construction Playbook. " Cabinet Office. https://www.gov.uk/government/publications/the-construction-playbook

HM Government. 2021a. "Building Safety Bill: draft regulations. " Department for Levelling Up, Housing and Communities. https://www.gov.uk/government/publications/building-safety-bill-draft-regulations

HM Government. 2021b. "Transforming Infrastructure Performance: Roadmap to 2030." Infrastructure and Projects Authority. https://www.gov.uk/government/publications/transforming-infrastructure-performance-roadmap-to-2030

Hossain, Md Mehrab, and Shakil Ahmed. "Developing an automated safety checking system using BIM: a case study in the Bangladeshi construction industry." International Journal of Construction Management (2019): 1-19.

James, Joel, Laura H. Ikuma, Isabelina Nahmens, and Fereydoun Aghazadeh. "Influence of lean on safety risk exposure in modular homebuilding." In IIE Annual Conference. Proceedings, p. 1. Institute of Industrial and Systems Engineers (IISE), 2012.

Jeong, Gilsu, Hyunsoo Kim, Hyun-Soo Lee, Moonseo Park, and Hosang Hyun. "Analysis of safety risk factors of modular construction to identify accident trends." Journal of Asian Architecture and Building Engineering (2021): 1-13.

Jones, Kell, Luigi Mosca, Jennifer Whyte, Andrew Davies, and Jacqueline Glass. "Addressing specialization and fragmentation: product platform development in construction consultancy firms." Construction Management and Economics (2021): 1-16.

Kamali, Mohammad, Kasun Hewage, and Rehan Sadiq. "Conventional versus modular construction methods: A comparative cradle-to-gate LCA for residential buildings." Energy and Buildings 204 (2019): 109479.

Kim, Sunwook, Maury A. Nussbaum, and Bochen Jia. "The benefits of an additional worker are task-dependent: Assessing low-back injury risks during prefabricated (panelized) wall construction." Applied Ergonomics 43, no. 5 (2012): 843-849.

Leveson, Nancy G. Engineering a safer world: Systems thinking applied to safety. The MIT Press, 2011.

Li, Zhengdao, Geoffrey Qiping Shen, and Xiaolong Xue. "Critical review of the research on the management of prefabricated construction." Habitat international 43 (2014): 240-249.

Liu, Huazan, Yukang He, Qichao Hu, Jianfei Guo, and Lan Luo. "Risk management system and intelligent decision-making for prefabricated building project under deep learning modified teaching-learning-based optimization." Plos one 15, no. 7 (2020): e0235980.

Lu, Na, and Thomas Korman. "Implementation of building information modeling (BIM) in modular construction: Benefits and challenges." In Construction Research Congress 2010: Innovation for Reshaping Construction Practice, pp. 1136-1145. 2010.

Mao, Chao, Qiping Shen, Wei Pan, and Kunhui Ye. "Major barriers to off-site construction: the developer's perspective in China." Journal of Management in Engineering 31, no. 3 (2015): 04014043.

Migilinskas, Darius, Vladimir Popov, Virgaudas Juocevicius, and Leonas Ustinovichius. "The benefits, obstacles and problems of practical BIM implementation." Procedia Engineering 57 (2013): 767-774.

Park, Haejun, Brian J. Meacham, Nicholas A. Dembsey, and Mark Goulthorpe. "Integration of fire safety and building design." Building Research & Information 42, no. 6 (2014): 696-709.

Reizgevičius, Marius, Leonas Ustinovičius, Diana Cibulskienė, Vladislavas Kutut, and Lukasz Nazarko. "Promoting sustainability through investment in Building Information Modeling (BIM) technologies: A design company perspective." Sustainability 10, no. 3 (2018): 600.

Tak, Ala Nekouvaght, Hosein Taghaddos, Ali Mousaei, Anahita Bolourani, and Ulrich Hermann. "BIM-based 4D mobile crane simulation and onsite operation management." Automation in Construction 128 (2021): 103766.

Tan, Yi, Silin Li, and Qian Wang. "Automated Geometric Quality Inspection of Prefabricated Housing Units Using BIM and LiDAR." Remote Sensing 12, no. 15 (2020): 2492.

Wang, Jun, Xuedong Zhang, Wenchi Shou, Xiangyu Wang, Bo Xu, Mi Jeong Kim, and Peng Wu. "A BIM-based approach for automated tower crane layout planning." Automation in Construction 59 (2015): 168-178.

Xu, Xun, Ling Ma, and Lieyun Ding. "A framework for BIM-enabled life-cycle information management of construction project." International Journal of Advanced Robotic Systems 11, no. 8 (2014): 126.

Yeoh, Justin KW, J. H. Wong, and L. Peng. "Integrating crane information models in BIM for checking the compliance of lifting plan requirements." In ISARC. Proceedings of the International Symposium on Automation and Robotics in Construction, vol. 33, p. 1. IAARC Publications, 2016.

Yingbo, Ji, Li Yanyao, and Liu Yan. "Prefabricated building hoisting safety risk identification and control." In IOP Conference Series: Earth and Environmental Science, vol. 371, no. 3, p. 032004. IOP Publishing, 2019.

Zou, Yang, Arto Kiviniemi, and Stephen W. Jones. "A review of risk management through BIM and BIM-related technologies." Safety science 97 (2017): 88-98.

Byzantine Generals Attack an Airbus A320

Dewi Daniels

Software Safety Limited

Trowbridge, UK

Abstract *Airbus recently published an article in their safety magazine describing a serious incident where the thrust reverser remained deployed on one engine during a go-around. The aircraft veered to the left but became airborne just before reaching the edge of the runway. The flight crew were able to land the aircraft with one engine inoperative. Airbus is to be commended for publishing such a clear and honest account of the incident. This appears to be a variant of Leslie Lamport's Byzantine Generals Problem, which I described in my SSS'22 paper, but not one that I have seen described before. In this case, an implementation of the Byzantine Generals solution would have allowed the two engines to agree whether to stow and lock the thrust reversers. Byzantine failures are rare events, but they seem to keep happening. I'm reminded of the Terry Pratchett quote, "million-to-one chances crop up nine times out of ten". I wonder whether Leslie Lamport's 1982 paper on the Byzantine Generals Problem is now so old that it has begun to fade from memory?*

1 Introduction

Two years ago, at SSS'22, I described an instance of the Byzantine Generals Problem that resulted in all three primary flight control computers being shut down on an Airbus A330 (Daniels 2022).

The Byzantine Generals Problem is a very well-known problem in computer science, with a solution that has been mathematically proven to be correct (Lamport et al 1982). The Byzantine Generals solution would have prevented this serious incident. However, the final report on this serious incident (TTSB 2020) did not mention the Byzantine Generals Problem.

Airbus claimed that no other such incident had been reported since the A330/A340 family entered service. They implemented a software update that would reduce the probability of the incident recuring but did not implement the Byzantine Generals solution.

© Dewi Daniels 2024.
Published by the Safety-Critical Systems Club. All Rights Reserved.

In this paper, I describe another serious incident, this time involving an Airbus A320. I aim to show this is another instance of the Byzantine Generals Problem, which the Byzantine Generals solution would also have prevented.

Neither the Airbus article (Airbus 2023) nor the press release and updates from Accident Investigation Board (AIB) Denmark (AIB 2022a, AIB 2022b, AIB2023) mention the Byzantine Generals Problem. Again, Airbus claimed this is a rare event and that only Airbus A320 and A340 aircraft fitted with this specific type of engine are affected.

It is surprising that an apparently well-known problem in computer science does not appear to be known to the airframe manufacturer, certification authorities or accident investigators. I conclude by discussing how we can improve awareness of the Byzantine Generals Problem and its solution.

2 The Byzantine Generals Problem

The Byzantine Generals Problem is a very well-known problem in computer science. It was first formulated by Leslie Lamport in 1982. Leslie Lamport is an eminent American computer scientist and mathematician who was the winner of the 2013 Turing Award. He is best known for his work in distributed systems but is also well-known for having developed the LaTeX document preparation system. In the early 1980s, Leslie Lamport was working on one of the earliest fly-by-wire systems, which used majority voting. He realised that majority voting could fail when the redundant processors failed to agree on the input values to be used.

Fig. 1. Leslie Lamport © Leslie Lamport

Leslie Lamport chose to describe the problem as a story involving Byzantine[1] generals. A story such as this makes the problem and its solution much more memorable, as Catherine Menon and Austen Rainer described in their presentation at SSS'22 (Menon and Rainer 2022). The disadvantage is that it can be difficult to see how the story relates to computer systems.

In Leslie Lamport's story, the Byzantine army are camped outside an enemy city. There is a commanding general in overall charge and several lieutenant generals, each in command of a single division. The generals can communicate with each other only by messenger. They must implement a common plan of action. They could all attack or they could all retreat. If only some of them attack, they will be defeated.

However, some of the generals are traitors. The commanding general could be a traitor, in which case he will command some lieutenant generals to attack and others to retreat. Some of the lieutenant generals could also be traitors, trying to spread misinformation about the orders issued by the commanding general.

The Byzantine Generals Problem seems deceptively simple. Consider the case where there is a commanding general and two lieutenant generals. If the commanding general is a traitor, he could command one lieutenant general to attack and the other to retreat. One would suppose this could easily be detected by having the two lieutenant generals compare their orders. They will realise that the commanding general has given them conflicting orders and that he is therefore a traitor.

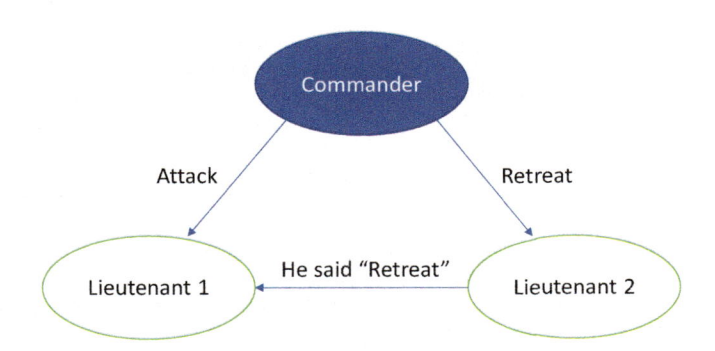

Fig. 2. The commander is a traitor

However, if one of the lieutenant generals is a traitor, he could tell the loyal lieutenant general that he was ordered to retreat when he was told to attack. The loyal

---

[1] The Byzantine Empire was the continuation of the Roman Empire in the East following the fall of the Western Roman Empire in 476. The Byzantine Empire continued until the fall of Constantinople to the Ottoman Empire in 1453

lieutenant would wrongly conclude that the loyal commanding general was a traitor and would fail to carry out his orders.

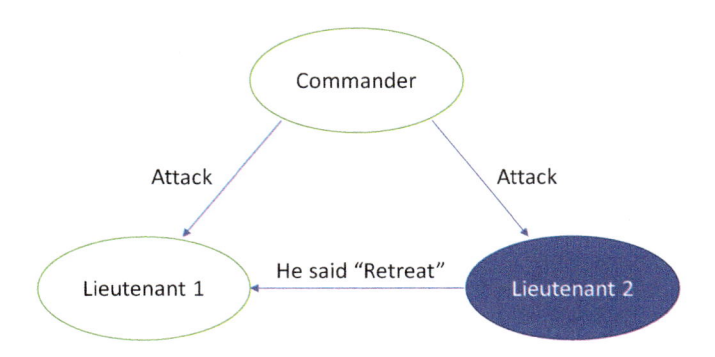

Fig. 3. Lieutenant 2 is a traitor

Leslie Lamport presented a solution to the Byzantine Generals Problem, together with a mathematical proof of the correctness of that solution. He inductively defined the Oral Message algorithms OM(m), for all nonnegative integers m, which a commander sends an order to $n - 1$ lieutenants. He showed that OM(m) solves the Byzantine Generals Problem for $3m + 1$ or more generals in the presence of at most m traitors.

Algorithm OM(0).
The commander sends his value to every lieutenant.
Each lieutenant uses the value he receives from the commander or uses the value RETREAT if he receives no value.

Algorithm OM(m), $m > 0$.
The commander sends his value to every lieutenant.
For each i, let v_i be the value Lieutenant i receives from the commander, or else be RETREAT if he receives no value. Lieutenant i acts as the commander in Algorithm OM($m - 1$) to send the value v_i to each of the $n - 2$ other lieutenants.
For each i, and each $j \neq i$, let v_j be the value Lieutenant i received from Lieutenant j in step (2) (using Algorithm($m - 1$)), or else RETREAT if he received no such value.
Lieutenant i uses the value *majority*($v_1, \ldots, v_{n-1}$).

Consider the following scenario where the commander is the traitor. This time, the loyal lieutenants can figure out that the traitorous commander ordered most of the lieutenants to attack, so that is what they all agree to do.

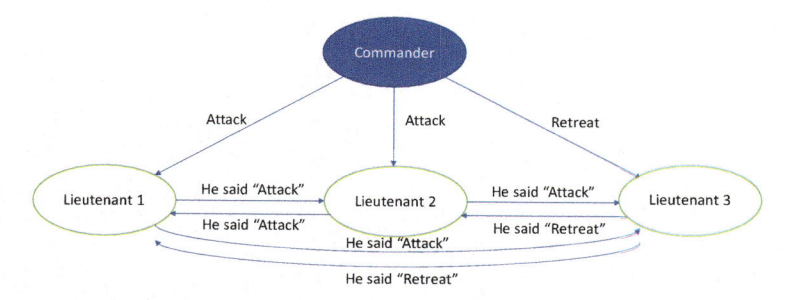

Fig. 4. Commander is a traitor (Byzantine Generals solution)

Consider the following scenario where one of the lieutenants is the traitor. This time, the loyal lieutenants can figure out that the traitorous lieutenant is lying. The loyal lieutenants both agree to attack, as ordered by the loyal commander.

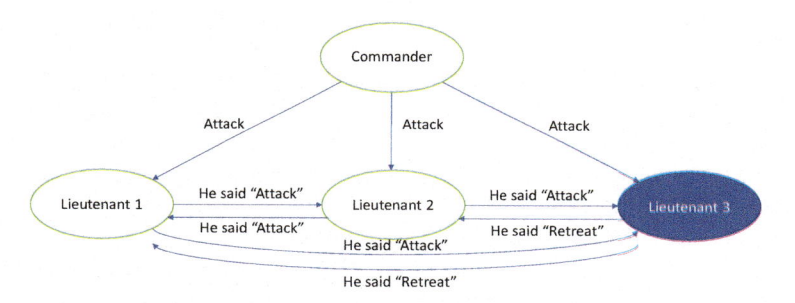

Fig. 5. Lieutenant 3 is a traitor (Byzantine Generals solution)

How does this apply to computer systems? Leslie Lamport explained that other than using intrinsically reliable circuit components, the only way we know to implement a reliable computer system is to use several different processors to computer the same result, and then to perform a majority vote on their outputs to obtain a single value. This means that a faulty processor will be ignored. With sufficient redundancy, multiple faulty processors will be ignored.

However, the use of majority voting to achieve reliability assumes that all the nonfaulty processors produce the same output. A malfunctioning input unit can give different values to different processors. Ensuring that all processors read the input from the same wire does not avoid this problem. A faulty unit could send a marginal signal along the wire that is interpreted by some processors as a zero and by others as a one. Furthermore, nonfaulty processors can get different values from a nonfaulty input unit if they read the value at different times. Implementation of the Byzantine Generals solution ensures that every nonfaulty processor uses the same input value and therefore produces the same output.

3 The Previous Incident

Fig. 6. The aircraft stopped at the end of the runway (from the TTSB final report)

At SSS'22, I described a serious incident involving an Airbus A330 (Daniels 2022). All three primary flight control computers shut down while an A330 was landing at Taipei in 2020. The aircraft stopped only 10 metres from the end of the runway. I showed how this was an instance of the Byzantine Generals Problem.

The Taiwan Transportation Safety Board (TTSB) final report did not mention the Byzantine Generals Problem. Airbus claimed that no other such incident had been reported since the A330/A340 family entered service. The A330/A340 fleet had accumulated 44.3 million flying hours. They also claimed their investigations had found no other issues that could result in a similar incident.

Airbus implemented a software update that will reduce the likelihood of the incident recurring. This software update did not implement Leslie Lamport's Byzantine General solution.

4 The Latest Incident

Fig. 7. The aircraft involved in the incident at Copenhagen.
© Anna Zvereva CC BY-SA 2.0 Deed | Attribution-ShareAlike 2.0 Generic | Creative Commons

Only two months after I presented my SSS'22 paper, TAP Air Portugal flight TP754, an Airbus A320, was landing in Copenhagen. Immediately after touchdown, the flight crew decided to abort the landing and the Pilot Flying (PF) initiated a go-around. The aircraft started veering to the left and did not climb as expected by the flight crew, which made it difficult for the flight crew to maintain control of the aircraft. The flight crew regained control of the aircraft and established a single engine climb.

The flight crew declared an emergency. The aircraft landed on runway 22L without any further issues.

So, what happened? The PF initiated the flare at 30 ft Radar Altitude (RA), set the thrust levers to idle at 11 ft RA and set the thrust levers to maximum reverse at touchdown. The thrust reversers were applied once both left and right Main Landing Gear (MLG) were compressed.

The thrust reversers were not fully deployed by the time the PF applied Takeoff/Go-Around (TO/GA) thrust. The Thrust Reverser Stowage Logic (on CFM56 Engines) is as follows:

- If the computed status is "ground", the Engine Control Unit (ECU) will send a stow command until the thrust reversers are stowed.

- If the computed status is "flight", the ECU does not send a stow command[2].

Engine 1 computed status to be "flight" using information from Landing Gear Control and Interface Unit (LGCIU) 1. ECU 1 did not send a stow command. Engine 2 computed status to be "ground" using information from LGCIU 2. ECU 2 sent the stow command.

Fig. 8. Photos of left and right sides of engine no. 1 (from the AIB Denmark press release)

According to Airbus, a short asynchronism between the computation of the ground/flight status by both ECUs, combined with a bounce of the left landing gear, explains the different behaviours of the ECUs.

Airbus determined that only A320 and A340 aircraft equipped with CFM56 engines can be affected by this potential for the thrust reversers to not retract if the crew decides to perform a go-around after the thrust reversers are selected.

An update of the ECU software for CFM56 engines is under development. It includes an enhanced stow logic in the case of a rejected landing with reversers already selected.

At first glance, this seems a very different incident to the one I reported at SSS'22. However, I believe this to be another instance of the Byzantine Generals Problem.

The Byzantine Generals Problem relates to implementing a common plan of action. In this case, ECU 1 decided not to stow the thrust reverser, ECU 2 decided to stow the thrust reverser[3].

Leslie Lamport's Byzantine Generals solution would have prevented this incident. Neither the Airbus article nor the press release from the accident investigators mention the Byzantine Generals Problem.

---

[2] The ECUs only take the computed ground/flight status into account and not the ground speed, which makes the logic even more perplexing.

[3] It is normal for each engine to have its own ECU, but it is puzzling why the thrust reverser stowage logic allows an ECU to ignore a stow command. The incident would have been avoided had both ECUs obeyed the stow command without trying to second-guess whether it was valid. As I write later, it makes sense for an ECU to inhibit deployment of the thrust reversers in flight.

Remember that four generals are required to cope with one traitor. In this case, both lanes in each ECU (making a total of four lanes) would need to co-operate to agree on a single set of input values.

It may well be that in this case, there is a simpler solution that does not require the Byzantine Generals solution. For example, why does the CFM56 Thrust Reverser Stowage Logic use the computed ground/flight status to inhibit stowing of the thrust reverser? It makes sense for the ECU to inhibit deployment of reverse thrust when the aircraft is in flight (there was a fatal accident of a Lauda Air Boeing 767 in 1991 that resulted from the uncommanded deployment in-flight of a thrust reverser (Thailand 1993)). However, it is unclear why the ECU inhibits stowing of the thrust reverser in flight. This incident could have been avoided had both ECUs sent a stow command without checking the computed ground/flight status.

Airbus criticised the flight crew for performing a go-around after they had selected thrust reversers. They pointed out that the Standard Operating Procedure (SOP) for landing requires that the flight crew perform a full stop landing after thrust reverser selection. However, their in-service flight data analysis revealed that an average of one go-around per month is performed after selection of thrust reversers. This data analysis was based on data from 31 operators for 3.4 million flights of A320 family aircraft.

Late go-arounds are risky. There was an accident involving an Emirates Boeing 777 that was attempting a go-around on 3 August 2016 (UAE 2020).

5 Analysis

Airbus claims these events are very rare. But we've seen two instances of Byzantine failures on Airbus airliners in two years.

I'm not aware of any incidents caused by Byzantine failures on Boeing airliners. Are Airbus designs more susceptible to Byzantine failures than Boeing designs? The Boeing 777 was designed to avoid Byzantine failures (Driscoll et al 2003, Rushby 2002, Yeh 1998). This is not true of earlier Boeing designs. Little has been published about the Boeing 787. Boeing may just have been lucky.

COM/MON architectures are particularly susceptible to Byzantine failures. Consider the incident that I described in my SSS'22 paper. This resulted from a cascade of Byzantine failures in a COM/MON architecture. A triplex voting architecture would not have shown the same behaviour.

It is not possible to implement the Byzantine Generals solution with a single COM/MON pair. Remember that four generals are required to cope with one traitor. At least two COM/MON pairs would need to co-operate to agree on a set of input values to use.

6 Conclusion

Airbus is to be commended for publishing the details of this incident. The open and honest approach to incident reporting in civil aviation means we can all learn from incidents such as these.

The Byzantine Generals Problem is a well-known problem in computer science, with a solution that has been mathematically proven to be correct. So why do the airframe manufacturers, certification authorities and accident investigators appear to be unaware of the Byzantine Generals Problem?

Two academic friends (one in the UK, one in the USA) have told me it's an old paper (1982) that is not taught any more. Most of the recent citations of Leslie Lamport's paper on the Byzantine Generals Problem have been from those working on blockchains (e.g., Gramoli 2017), not those working on safety-critical systems.

So, what can we do? We can spread the word at conferences like this. The use of story-telling helps us remember problems like the Byzantine Generals Problem. We could start teaching the Byzantine Generals Problem once again. I believe it ought to be taught on engineering courses as well as on computer science courses. Finally, we could ask at design reviews, "How does this design prevent Byzantine failures[4]"?

References

AIB (2022a) Press release. Serious incident to CS-TNV (Airbus A320) in Copenhagen on 8-4-2022. https://en.havarikommissionen.dk/media/10356/l_2022_alvorlig-haendelse_2022-150_cstnv_motorfly_ekch.pdf. Accessed 9 October 2023.

AIB (2022b) Update. Serious incident to CS-TNV (Airbus A320) in Copenhagen on 8-4-2022. https://en.havarikommissionen.dk/media/10360/l_2022_alvorlig-haendelse_2022-150_cstnv_motorfly_ekch-press-release-2.pdf. Accessed 9 October 2023.

AIB (2023) Status Update. Serious incident to CS-TNV (Airbus A320) in Copenhagen on 8-4-2022. Published 29-3-2023. https://en.havarikommissionen.dk/Media/638235532629917920/L_2022_Alvorlig%20h%c3%a6ndelse_2022-150_CSTNV_Motorfly_Kastrup%20Lufthavn.pdf. Accessed 9 October 2023.

Airbus (2023) Thrust Reverser Selection is a Decision to Stop. Safety First | June 2023 - Airbus S.A.S. https://safetyfirst.airbus.com/thrust-reverser-selection-is-a-decision-to-stop/. Accessed 9 October 2023.

Daniels D (2022) What do Byzantine Generals and Airbus Airliners Have in Common? Proceedings of the Thirtieth Safety-Critical Systems Symposium. https://scsc.uk/rp170.19:1. Accessed 9 October 2023.

Driscoll K, Hall, B Sivencrona H, Zumsteg P (2003) Byzantine Fault Tolerance, from Theory to Reality, Proceedings of the International Conference on Computer Safety, Reliability, and Security (SAFECOMP 2003), Pages 235–248.

---

[4] It is very difficult to test for Byzantine failures, which is what makes them so dangerous.

Gramoli V (2017) From blockchain consensus back to Byzantine consensus, Future Generation Computer Systems 107, September 2017, https://www.researchgate.net/publication/319984012_From_blockchain_consensus_back_to_Byzantine_consensus. Accessed 10 October 2023.

Lamport L, Shostak R, Pease M (1982) The Byzantine Generals Problem, ACM Transactions on Programming Languages and Systems, Vol. 4, No. 3, July 1982, Pages 382–401, https://lamport.azurewebsites.net/pubs/byz.pdf, accessed 9 October 2023.

Menon C, Rainer A (2022) Stories and narratives in safety engineering. Proceedings of the Thirtieth Safety-Critical Systems Symposium. https://scsc.uk/rp170,4;1. Accessed 9 October 2023.

Rushby J (2002) A Comparison of Bus Architectures for Safety-Critical Embedded Systems, CSL Technical Report, SRI International, June 2002, http://www.csl.sri.com/users/rushby/papers/buscompare.pdf. Accessed 9 October 2023.

Thailand (1993) Lauda Air B767 Accident Report. http://www.rvs.uni-bielefeld.de/publications/Incidents/DOCS/ComAndRep/LaudaAir/LaudaRPT.html. Accessed 9 October 2023.

TTSB (2020) Final Report, China Airlines Flight CI202, Report Number TTSB-AOR-21-09-001, https://www.ttsb.gov.tw/media/4936/ci-202-final-report_english.pdf. Accessed 9 October 2023.

UAE (2020) Final Report № AIFN/0008/2016. Runway Impact during Attempted Go-Around. https://www.icao.int/safety/airnavigation/AIG/Documents/Safety%20Recommendations%20to%20ICAO/Final%20Reports/UAE_B777_A6-EMW_3Aug2016.pdf. Accessed 9 October 2023.

Yeh Y (1998) Design considerations in Boeing 777 fly-by-wire computers, Proceedings of the 3rd IEEE International High-Assurance Systems Engineering Symposium, 13–14 November 1998.

Poster: Ensuring SOTIF for Off-Highway Autonomous Vehicles

Paul Darnell, Pavan Kumar, Ross McMurran, Ravindra Sabbella

3SK

Abstract *Unlike traditional safety standards that primarily focus on addressing failures and malfunctions, ISO 21448 for the Safety Of The Intended Functionality (SOTIF) emphasises assessing and mitigating risks associated with functional insufficiencies and user interactions. This poster provides an overview on the practical application of SOITIF to Off-Highway Autonomous Vehicles including adaptations for this domain and practices used to meet the requirements of the standard.*

© Ross McMurran 2024.
Published by the Safety-Critical Systems Club. All Rights Reserved.

Project Bluebird: AI for Air Traffic Control

Richard Everson[1], Edmond Awad[1], Ben Carvell[2], Richard Cannon[2], George De Ath[1], Tim Dodwell[3], Marc Thomas[2]

1 - University of Exeter

2 - NATS

3 - Alan Turing Institute

Abstract *Project Bluebird is an investigation into the feasibility of air traffic control (ATC) using AI agents. It has the potential to provide safe management of the increasing air traffic over UK and worldwide skies. In addition to ensuring safety, AI agents may be able to direct aircraft along more fuel-efficient routes, helping to reduce the environmental impact of air traffic. This talk will describe progress made towards these goals: the construction of a probabilistic digital twin of UK airspace; the development of agents capable of safe routing of aircraft in a sector of airspace; and methods needed to promote successful human-AI cooperation to ensure safe, explainable and trustworthy use of AI in safety-critical ATC systems. The talk will concentrate on an agent based on optimisation of safety and efficiency goals and will show some initial simulations of controlling real traffic.*

© Richard Everson 2024.
Published by the Safety-Critical Systems Club. All Rights Reserved.

Achieving railway resilience to climate change using dynamic system risk assessment

Vincent Ganthy

Futures Lab, RSSB

Abstract *The use of risk models can be difficult when trying to respond to rapid change. This is particularly challenging when such models consider rare events and/or try to assess the wide-ranging impacts of large-scale events, such as those arising from climate change. The railway is a dynamic, complex socio-technical system. Improving its resilience in the face of climate change requires a range of proportionate responses. These need to account for the evolving nature of the hazards themselves, various inter-dependencies in and out of the railway, while targeting both the system vulnerabilities and exposure within a multi-risk environment. The Rail Safety and Standards Board Safety Risk Model (SRM) estimates the underlying safety risk from the operation and maintenance of the Great British mainline railway. A modularised approach reusing established components from the SRM interacting with other tools and techniques, has been applied to provide enhanced multi-risk decision-support capability to the industry. The aim being to develop a flexible process to support the industry's strategic decision making despite uncertain future changes.*

© Vincent Ganthy 2024.
Published by the Safety-Critical Systems Club. All Rights Reserved.

Ensuring Safety and Effectiveness of Medical Devices in the Presence of Electromagnetic Disturbances through Unified EMC Assurance: A Compliance Pattern

Vikas Ghatge[1], Laure Buysse[1], Dries Vanoost[1], Johan Catrysse[1], Rob Kleihorst[2] and Davy Pissoort[1]

1 - KU Leuven, Faculty of Engineering Technology, Department of Electrical Engineering

2 - Philips Medical Systems Nederland B.V.

Abstract *This paper introduces a novel approach to developing a compliance pattern for a unified EMC assurance case, ensuring the safety and effectiveness of medical devices. The Goal Structuring Notation is used as a graphical notation for the technical documentation to support the safety and effectiveness compliance. By adopting this approach, the limitations of conventional text-based methods are overcome by providing a clear and explicit visual summary of claims, arguments, and evidence. Through persuasive arguments, the compliance pattern of the unified EMC assurance case demonstrates the adherence to EMC standards after successful implementation of EMC risk management strategies, achieved through the utilisation of EM-resilience design practices. Moreover, the paper emphasises the inter-relationships among the three sub-cases (compliance case – risk case – confidence case), highlighting their collective significance. The proposed EMC compliance pattern employs the modular extension of the Goal Structuring Notation to link arguments from the risk and confidence cases to the compliance case. The culmination of these elements validates the assurance of compliance with basic safety, essential performance, and the intended use of medical devices in the presence of electromagnetic disturbances. By employing the graphical notation and assurance case methodology, this approach presents a comprehensive EMC process for tackling the unique challenges posed by electromagnetic disturbances. As such, this approach contributes to ensuring the reliability and functionality of medical devices in such environments.*

© KU Leuven 2024. © Philips Medical Systems Nederland B.V.
Published by the Safety-Critical Systems Club. All Rights Reserved.

Table 1. List of abbreviations

Abbreviation	Meaning
A	Assumption
C	Context
DoC	Declaration of Conformity
EM	ElectroMagnetic
EMC	ElectroMagnetic Compatibility
EMD	ElectroMagnetic Disturbances
EMI	ElectroMagnetic Interference
ESD	Electro Static Discharge
EU	European Union
FDA	Food and Drug Administration
G	Goal
GSN	Goal Structuring Notation
GSPR	General Safety and Performance Requirements
HS	Harmonised Standards
IU	Intended Use
IUE	Intended Use Environment
IUP	Intended User Population
IUO	Intended Use Operator
J	Justification
MD	Medical Device
MDR	Medical Device Regulation
NMPA	National Medical Products Administration
Non-HS	Non-Harmonised Standards
OJEU	Official Journal of European Union
QMS	Quality Management System
R-ED	Radio Equipment Directive
S	Strategy
Sn	Solution
S & E	Safe & Effective
SOP	Standard Operating Procedures
TD	Technical Documentation
TR	Technical Recommendations

1 Introduction

The dynamic regulatory landscape of medical devices (MDs) mandates manufacturers to demonstrate assurance of safe and effective (S&E) operation within the intended electromagnetic (EM) environment. MDs such as pacemakers, defibrillators, etc. are safety-critical and should always maintain basic safety, essential performance, and intended use in the presence of Electromagnetic Disturbances (EMD) (IEC 60601-1, 2020) (IEC 60601-1-2, 2020). EMDs pose a risk of Electromagnetic Interference (EMI), impacting the effectiveness and safety of such devices. This may lead to severe safety risks ranging from minor injury to death (ISO 14971, 2019). Therefore, reducing or eliminating the risks of EMI caused by EMD to an acceptable level, often referred to as Electromagnetic Compatibility or EMC, is a crucial requirement for MDs. To put it in terminology of the MD Regulation (Regulation (EU) 2017/745), we can state that EMC is required to maintain the General Safety and Performance Requirements (GSPR) of this regulation.

Typically, the compliance assessment with the GSPR set out in the regulation is demonstrated through Technical Documentation (TD). The part in the overall TD dealing with EMC demonstrates the assurance that MDs are S&E in the presence of EMD. The TD should present objective evidence with underlying arguments - such as EMI risk management, GSPR compliance, periodic safety update reports, and so on. The regulatory authorities typically reviewed TD for moderate-to-high risk MDs such as Classes IIa, IIb, and III is by (Regulation (EU) 2017/745). Only after a successful TD demonstration, regulators approve the MD for the intended market. However, very often, review of the TD causes delays due to some common reasons, like poorly structured argumentation, incomplete submissions, and challenges in identifying and comprehending the reasoning why the MD is S&E in the presence of EMD. To overcome these concerns, regulatory authorities recommend that the TD should be prepared with a focus on clarity, simplicity, transparency, traceability, and explicitness of EMC-related arguments and evidence.

However, despite these recommendations, even well-crafted text-based TD inherently possesses limitations that can make it challenging to interpret and follow. (Hawkins R. et al., 2011). Sometimes concerned stakeholders may lack confidence and trust when it is not trivial to see how EMC is managed, leading to ambiguity about whether the design is S&E or not. This may result in unfavourable implications for MD manufacturers, both in terms of time-to-market as well as reputation.

An approach based on the Goal Structuring Notation (GSN) (ACWG GSN v3, 2021) incorporated with the TD addresses many of the above issues with pure text-based TD (Sujan M. et al., 2007). It has been recommended that healthcare stakeholders should consider the particulars of regulatory practices and delve into safety and effectiveness evidence when crafting goal-based safety cases (Sujan

M., et al., 2015). Adopting the approach of a safety argument along with a confidence argument using GSN has been proven effective in overcoming the lack of confidence in safety evidence (Hawkins R. et al., 2011) for medical devices such as infusion pumps (FDA, 2014). Furthermore, AAMI et al. (2014) and Sherman E. et al. (2014) effectively explored well-structured medical device risk management to develop safety cases.

When it comes to applying assurance cases in the domain of EMC, GSN-based assurance cases were translated for the first time into an EMC assurance case in (Pissoort D. et al., 2017) and later elaborated for EMI risk arguments in (Tishehzan M. et al., 2017). Subsequently, the risk-confidence-compliance argument structure as a unified EMC assurance case was proposed to deal with both medical safety and EMC concerns (Ghatge V. et al., 2023). However, the complete and detailed risk-confidence-compliance argumentation was still missing. To the authors' knowledge, developing an assurance case with complete risk-confidence-compliance argumentation is a very lengthy exercise. Therefore, this paper focuses solely on the compliance argument and is mostly about:

1. Developing EMC compliance patterns to demonstrate S&E MDs; and
2. Highlighting how arguments from the risk and confidence modules interact with the compliance module by using modular extensions of GSN.

The remainder of this paper is structured as follows. Section 2 provides some background information on EMC, safety and GSN. Section 3 discusses an approach to create compliance patterns. Section 4 develops the pattern for the main claim of safety and effectiveness of MDs. Section 5 develops the compliance patterns to demonstrate the fulfilment of the main claim. Conclusions are drawn in Section 6.

2 Background to develop the EMC compliance case pattern

The necessary background information to develop and understand the EMC compliance case pattern is discussed in the below sub-sections, which include the main terminology to be used and the GSN elements to be used within the compliance case.

2.1 Important definitions related to safety and EMC

Many common terms from the safety, EMC, and medical domains are used within the compliance case. Unfortunately, not everyone has exactly the same interpretation of those. Therefore, we clearly define below how this terminology should be interpreted throughout this paper. The terminology is aligned with the medical regulation (EU MDR 2017/745) and the standards IEC 60601-1 and IEC 60601-1-2 (IEC 60601-1-2, 2020) (IEC 60601-1, 2020) (Regulation (EU) 2017/745). This paper's fundamental context for the Table 2 terms is centred on the safety of medical devices concerning EMD or EMI risks.

Table 2. List of important definitions

Term	Definition
EM environment	The totality of EM phenomena existing at a given location. Following IEC 60601-1-2, the intended EM environment for MD is either home, hospital, or special. The special environment has EM characteristics that are different from those specified for the hospital environment and the home healthcare environment. For example, magnetic resonance imaging (MRI) devices are specified for use only in a special environment with a shielded room.
Electromagnetic disturbance (EMD)	Any EM phenomenon that has the potential to degrade the performance of a system, within this paper solely focused on an MD.
EM emission	The phenomenon by which EM energy is emitted from a source. These EM sources can be intentional and unintentional radiators, such as mobile phones, walkie-talkies, electrosurgical knives, etc., within a given EM environment.
Immunity to EMD	The ability of MDs to perform without (unacceptable) degradation in the presence of an EMD. The MDs should be immune against a wide variety of EMDs such as electrostatic discharge (ESD), surges, transients, etc. to uphold the MD's safety.
EMC	The ability of MD to function satisfactorily in its specified EM environment without introducing intolerable EMDs to anything in that environment.
EM resilience	The ability of the MD to adjust its functioning prior to, during, or following an interference event and maintain its (critical) capabilities and services even under unanticipated conditions.[1]

---

[1] Within the IEEE 1848 standard (IEEE 1848, 2018), it is used as the general term for the engineering discipline that describes how to use techniques and measures to manage (functional) safety risks as regards EMD.

Term	Definition
Intended use or intended purpose	The use for which a MD is intended according to the specifications, instructions and information provided by the manufacturer.
Safety	Safety is freedom from unacceptable risk. The safety concerns to be discussed here are those related to EMD.
Risk	Risk means the combination of the probability of occurrence of harm and the severity of that harm.
Risk management	The systematic application of management policies, procedures and practices to analyse, evaluate, control and monitor risk.
Risk analysis	Risk analysis systematically uses available information to identify hazards and to estimate the related risks
Risk assessment	Risk assessment is the overall process comprising a risk analysis and a risk evaluation.
Risk control	Risk control is the process in which decisions are made and measures implemented by which risks are reduced to, or maintained within, specified levels.
Performance	Performance means the ability of a device to achieve its intended purpose as stated by the manufacturer.
Essential performance	The performance of a clinical function, other than that related to basic safety, where loss or degradation beyond the limits specified by the manufacturer results in an unacceptable risk.

2.2 GSN core elements and their extensions

GSN is a standardised graphical argumentation notation that integrates claims, arguments, and evidence in systematically structured assurance cases. Within the

GSN community standard, key GSN elements serve as the framework for structuring an assurance case. Below, we outline the GSN elements utilised in this paper:

1. Six core elements, namely Goal (G), Context (C), Strategy (S), Justification (J), Assumption (A) and Solution (Sn)
2. Two relationships, such as InContextOf and SupportedBy.
3. Structural abstractions for optionality, such as Choice symbols
4. Element abstractions, such as Undeveloped and Uninstantiated element
5. Modular extensions, such as away goal, away solution, away context, away assumption, and away justification, are further discussed in Section 3.2.

For full details on GSN, the reader is referred to the GSN community standard (ACWG GSN v3, 2021).

3 Approach to create a compliance pattern of a unified EMC assurance case

3.1 Unified Assurance Case approach for EMC Compliance

This section briefly elaborates on the concept of a unified EMC assurance case. An EMC assurance case was defined as follows in (Pissoort D. et al., 2017):

> *"A structured argument, supported by a body of evidence that provides a compelling, comprehensible and valid case that an equipment exhibits a level of EMC that is acceptable for a given application in a given operating environment."*

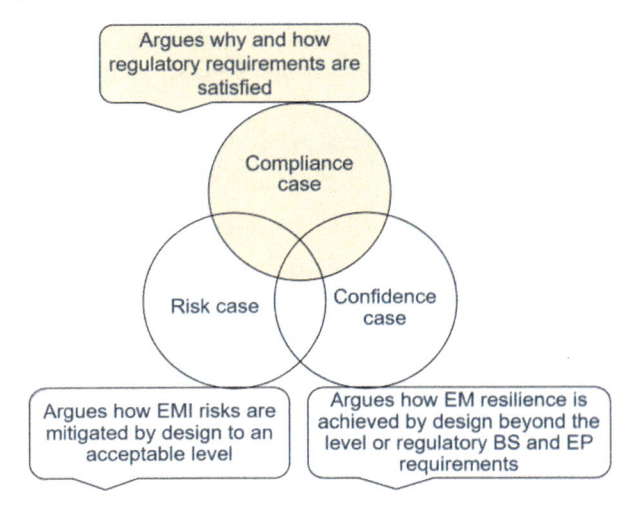

Fig. 1. Risk-confidence-compliance overlapping arguments within a unified EMC assurance case

Inspired by the GSN guidance (ACWG guidance, 2021), which recommends employing risk-confidence-compliance argumentation for comprehensive assurance, Fig. 1 integrates risk-confidence-compliance arguments to create a unified EMC assurance case.

This unified EMC assurance case for medical device safety is a graphical representation of the steps taken to derive solid argumentation for risk, confidence, and compliance claims that are implied by specific goals in given contexts and grounded in certain assumptions during the EMC assessment. Additionally, it provides a rationale or justification for why the selected goals and strategies are considered valid.

The medical EMC standard (IEC 60601-1-2, 2020), which deals with an MD's EMC assessment, provides implicitly the following rationale for the risk-confidence-compliance arguments:

1. The Risk Case argues how EMI risks are effectively identified, analyzed and mitigated to an acceptable level. IEC 60601-1-2 follows the mandatory risk management process set out in ISO 14971 (ISO 14971,2019).

2. The Confidence Case argues how EM resilience is achieved by design, sometimes beyond the level of regulatory basic safety and essential performance requirements. IEC 60601-1-2 refers to the IEEE 1848 standard for additional risk control measures (IEEE 1848, 2018).

3. The Compliance Case argues why and how regulatory requirements are satisfied. IEC 60601-1-2 has detailed compliance requirements.

Fig. 1 shows three overlapping arguments: risk, confidence, and compliance. The paper focuses on compliance arguments and their interrelationship with the risk and confidence arguments, highlighted in color in Fig. 1. The risk and confidence arguments are not fully discussed to avoid lengthy argumentation, but their individual overlaps with compliance arguments are presented using GSN modular extensions. A dedicated compliance argument, incorporating overlapping risk and confidence elements, enhances the clarity of presentation during regulatory compliance submissions and reviews.

3.2 Necessity of modular extensions within compliance patterns

Of course, and as indicated in Fig. 1, the compliance case can never be completely isolated from the risk and confidence cases. Therefore, modular extensions are introduced within the compliance case to show interrelated arguments with the risk and confidence cases from the perspective of the compliance case.

Fig. 2 shows the details of the modular extensions as specified in the GSN Community Standard. The modular extensions use elements such as 'away goal', 'away context', 'away assumption', 'away justification', and 'away solution'. The prefix 'away' signifies that these elements belong to other modules rather than the ones in which they are directly integrated.

The modular extension highlights the compliance module requirements, some of which are influenced by the risk of EMD (risk case) and how they are addressed in the design (confidence case).

Suppose the modular extensions are not appropriately linked within the compliance module where needed. In that case, the absence of the 'away' information may result in inadequate evidence to demonstrate comprehensive coverage of the General Safety and Performance Requirements (GSPR) during the compliance assessment.

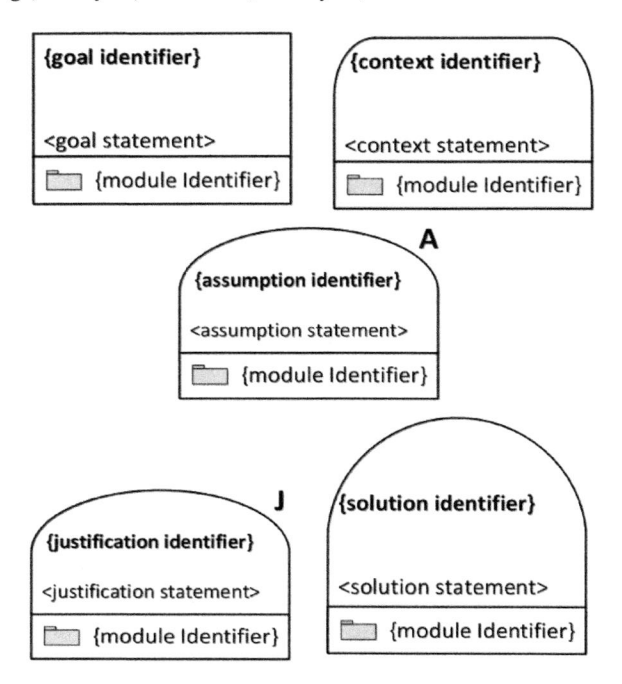

Fig. 2. GSN modular extensions (adapted from ACWG GSN v3, 2021)

3.3 Risk-confidence modular arguments within compliance pattern

Fig. 3 shows how the risk-confidence-compliance argumentation approach and the modular extensions of GSN are used to clarify how risk and design confidence arguments are interconnected with the compliance case pattern.

The modular extensions are used here to argue and identify separate concerns of the risk and confidence cases, but from the viewpoint of the compliance case. For example, identifying regulatory compliance requirements such as GSPR from MDR2017/745 is the concern of the compliance module. However, it is the manufacturer's responsibility to analyse the risk associated with the identified GSPR; this is part of the risk case. Therefore, these details are assigned as an away context to the risk case within the compliance case.

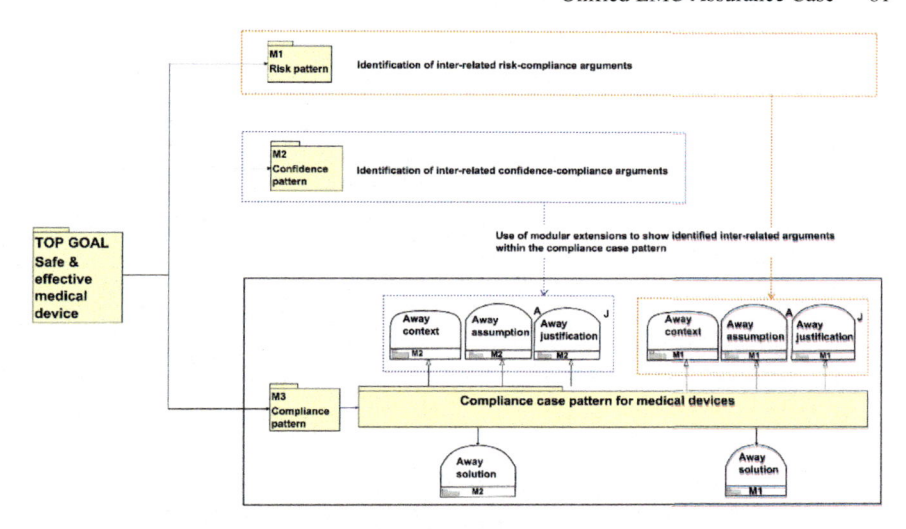

Fig. 3. Modular arguments within the compliance pattern

The use of away extensions themselves presumes that they are available within those away modules. Consequently, if the contextual information and background evidence from the compliance case are not accessible within the risk and confidence cases, the argumentation could be flawed.

4 The main claim of safety and effectiveness of medical devices

Fig. 4 presents the pattern outlining the manufacturer's regulatory strategy for the unified EMC assurance case, which aims to demonstrate the safety and effectiveness of medical devices. Irrespective of the specific regulatory requirements in different countries, various regulations share a common requirement for ensuring the presence of 'safe and effective medical devices throughout their lifecycle, as intended, and in their operational environment.' *TOP GOAL* argues for this generic requirement.

A S&E MD not only contributes to the safety and health of the patient and users but also delivers performance in line with its intended use. This is the rationale for choosing *TOP GOAL* justified within *J1*. Additionally, the contexts *C1* and *C2.1-2.4* limit the scope of the *TOP GOAL* validity.

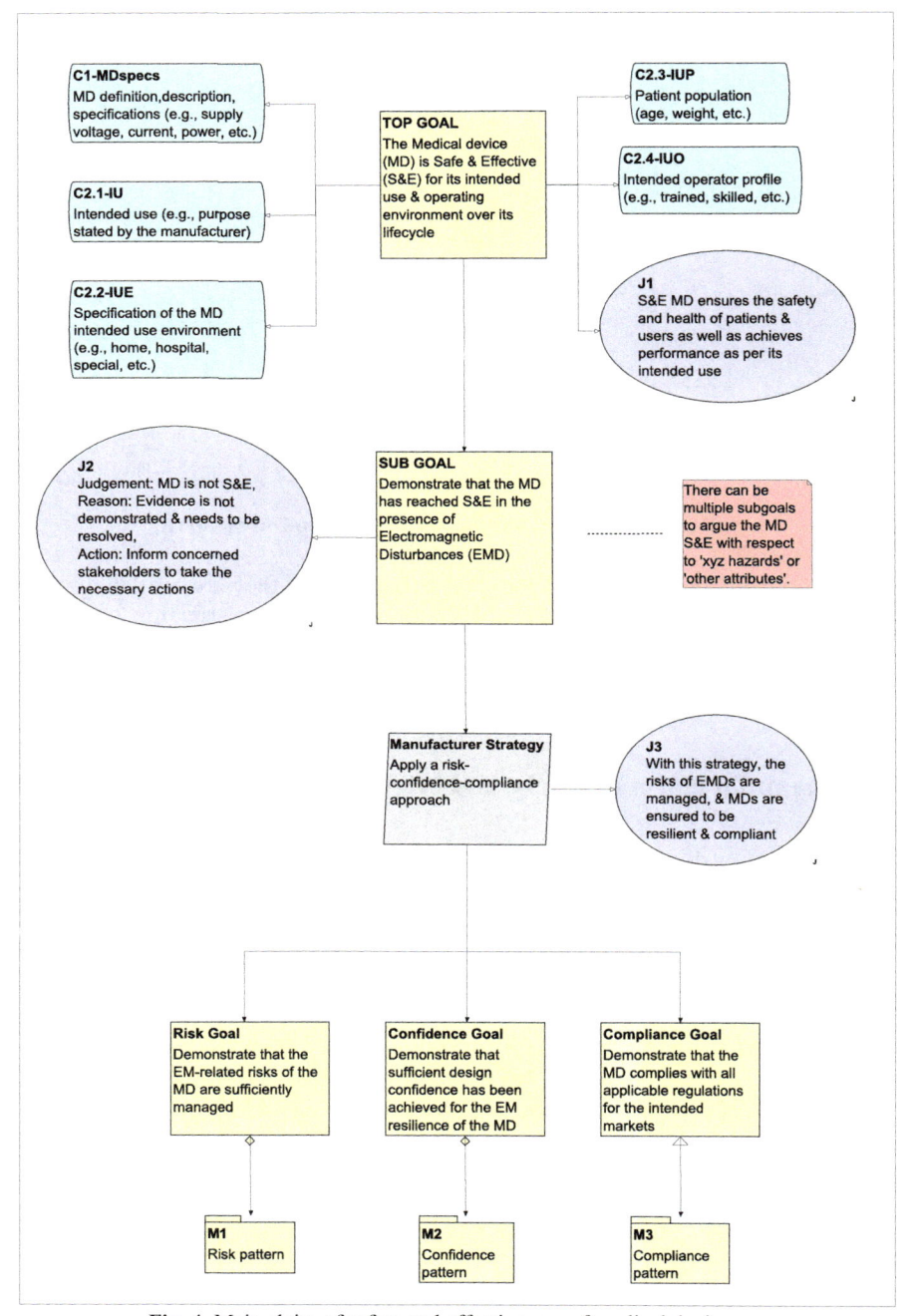

Fig. 4. Main claim of safety and effectiveness of medical devices

C1-MDspecs provides a detailed definition, description and specification of the MD at hand. This includes operating conditions, modes, and configurations in which the MD operates, power specifications, etc.

C2.1-IU (intended use), *C2.2-IUE* (intended use environment, e.g., home or hospital or special), *C2.3-IUP* (intended patient population, e.g., age, weight, etc.), and *C2.4-IUO* (intended operator profile, e.g., skilled, trained, etc.) concretely cover all aspects of the intended use in more detail.

Arguing with a well-defined and specific context is crucial because, without it, the scope in which the goal is expressed can be invalidated. A medical device is considered S&E as long as it aligns with its intended context. For instance, if the designated use environment (*C2.2*) is a hospital, and the device is used in an unintended home environment, for which it is not designed, it may no longer meet the criteria for being S&E.

This paper focuses on hazards related to Electromagnetic Disturbances (EMD), so the *TOP GOAL* is decomposed into a *SUB GOAL* to demonstrate that the MD has reached S&E in the presence of EMD.

The validation of the *SUB GOAL* relies on the objective evidence gathered during the whole assurance process, allowing for an assessment of whether the claim is true or false. As explained in *J2*, if the claim proves to be false, the appropriate action is to inform relevant MD stakeholders. Essentially, *J2* justifies the following steps: if the claim is false, return to the TOP GOAL and/or multiple subgoals associated with the 'xyz hazard'; implement the necessary actions to address it, which may include redesigning the medical device, and ultimately demonstrate that the medical device is S&E, ensuring the claim is true.

The *SUB GOAL* is achieved by a '*Manufacturer Strategy*' that explicitly exploits the risk-confidence-compliance approach. As justified in *J3*, this strategy goes beyond the traditional compliance testing approach and guarantees electromagnetic resilient design that effectively mitigate the risks associated with EMDs. The '*Manufacturer Strategy*' falls apart into '*Risk Goal*', '*Confidence Goal*' and '*Compliance Goal*'. '*Compliance goal*' argues that the MD complies with all applicable regulations for the intended market. However, further sections develop a complete '*Compliance Pattern*' showing inter-relationships with the *risk-confidence patterns*.

5 Development of EMC compliance patterns

5.1 Arguing EM emissions and immunity related general safety and performance requirements (GSPR)

Fig. 5 argues '*Compliance Goal*' and emphasises that without adhering to the applicable regulations, it is impossible to put the MD on the market, as justified by *J4*.

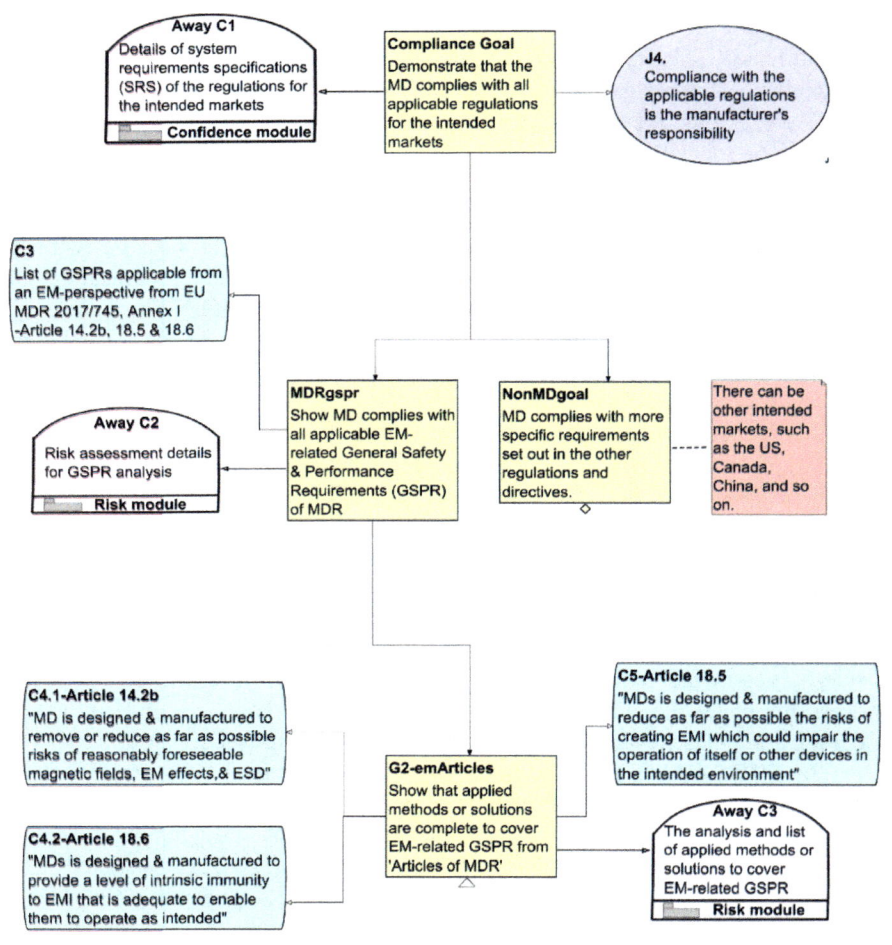

Fig. 5. Main claim of compliance goal

Of course, it is essential to incorporate the regulatory requirements of the intended markets during the design phase itself to prevent unintended design revisions in the future.

Therefore, assigning a *'away C1'* context with applicable system requirements specifications from the *'confidence module'* is wise. The '*Compliance Goal*' is further decomposed into sub-goals related to the applicable regulations, such as:

1. '*MDRgspr*' aims to comply with the EMI-related General Safety and Performance Requirements (GSPR) of the European MDR 2017/745.

2. *'NonMDgoal'* aims to comply with all applicable non-medical legislation's (e.g., Machinery Regulation, R-ED, etc.) for more specific EMI-related requirements. This goal is not argued further and remains undeveloped within this paper.
3. Additionally, there can be sub-goals related to other intended markets, such as the US, China, etc.

The EU changed from the Medical Device Directive (MDD) to the Medical Device Regulation 2017/745 (Regulation EU, 2017). Requirements in regulations are mandatory for all member states. The MDR has an increased number of requirements and has strengthened the requirements for medical device manufacturers and notified bodies. Since the EU MDR is a new regulation, it currently has more extensive and explicit requirements than some regulations from other regions. Therefore, the further focus is on arguing for EU MDR compliance.

The main objective of the MDR 2017/745 is to 'show that the MD complies with all applicable EMI-related General Safety and Performance Requirements (GSPR)' as stated by the '*MDRgspr*' goal. A thorough evaluation of EMI-related GSPR must be conducted within the risk case to make a robust case for compliance with the EU MDR. Objective evidence from the risk assessment is utilised as an *'Away C2'* context to leverage the advantages of this unified argumentation approach. This context also underscores the significance of the specific applicable regulatory requirements, some of which are influenced by the risks associated EMD. *C3* lists all analysed EMI-related GSPRs from articles 14.2(b), 18.5, and 18.6.

From a legal point of view, compliance with the regulation means arguing that each of the applicable requirements within the articles is fulfilled with appropriate solutions and methods. Therefore, the 'MDRgspr' falls into subgoal '*G2-emArticles'* that shows which methods and solutions are applied to cover EM immunity (articles 14.2b/18.6 listed in *C4.1/4.2*) and EM emissions (article 18.5 listed in *C5*). Typically, the regulation prescribes GSPR in generic language (*C4.1*, *C4.2*, and *C5*) without any specific methods or solutions to achieve them. As a result, the process unfolds in two key stages: firstly, the analysis to select appropriate methods is conducted within the *'Risk case'*, as detailed in *'Away C3.'* Secondly, the design implementation in accordance with the chosen methods is documented within the *'Confidence case'*.

5.2 Strategy to split GSPR arguments into safety and performance

At the first level, regulatory GSPR concerns related to emissions and immunity are separated in the above sections using GSN context elements. Now, at the second level, GSPR is further split into 'safety' and 'performance' aspects using GSN strategy elements.

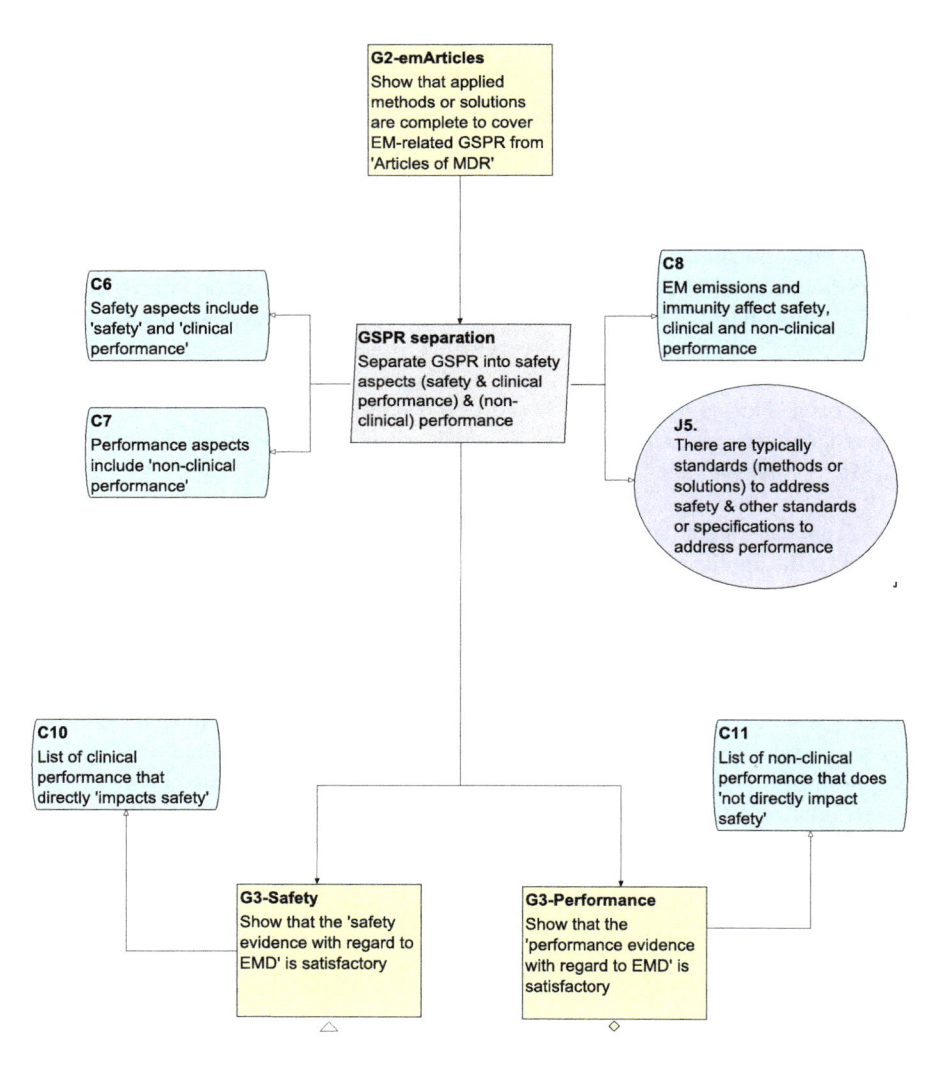

Fig. 6. Strategy to split GSPR into safety and performance

Fig. 6 argues how methods are applied to cover EM-related GSPR claimed by *'G2-emArticles'* This goal is achieved with the strategy *'GSPR separation'* that splits 'General Safety and Performance Requirements' into 'safety aspects' and 'performance aspects' so that methods or solutions are applied separately to address safety and performance aspects. This strategy is considered valid since, typically, separate standards are employed to address safety and performance individually, as substantiated in *J5*.

Within this strategy, the safety aspects cover 'safety' and 'clinical performance,' whereas the performance aspects cover 'non-clinical performance', as detailed in contexts *C6* and *C7*, respectively. Furthermore, EM immunity and EM emissions could affect safety, clinical and non-clinical performance, as detailed in *C8*.

The strategy further decomposes into safety and performance-related subgoals: *G3-safety* and *G3-performance* goals that provide safety and performance evidence with regard to EMD are satisfactory, respectively.

Defining the scope of the term 'performance' itself is quite confusing within MDR. The word 'performance' has different meanings depending on the standard chosen.

Performance in the context (*C10*) of the safety goal (*G3*) is clinical performance (basically the essential performance), and performance in the context (*C11*) of the performance goal (*G5*) is non-clinical functional performance (as this doesn't impact safety). *C10* and *C11* together complete to represent the performance depending on the standard chosen.

Detailed argumentation on how to achieve safety with regard to EMD is explained in the next section. However, to achieve *'G3-performance'* with regard to EMD, the non-harmonised standard, IEC TR 60601-4-2 is used (IEC 60601-4-2, 2018), but this is not discussed further within this paper.

5.3 Strategies to achieve a safety argument with regard to EM emissions & immunity

Up to this point, a clear and consistent argumentation approach has been maintained by moving from higher-level regulations to lower-level standards. The primary focus now shifts towards demonstrating the compliance of 'safety clauses with standards' rather than 'GSPR Articles compliance with regulations.'

Fig. 7 presents strategies to achieve *G3-safety* using applicable methods. *G3-safety* argues that safety evidence 'with regard to EMD' is satisfactory.

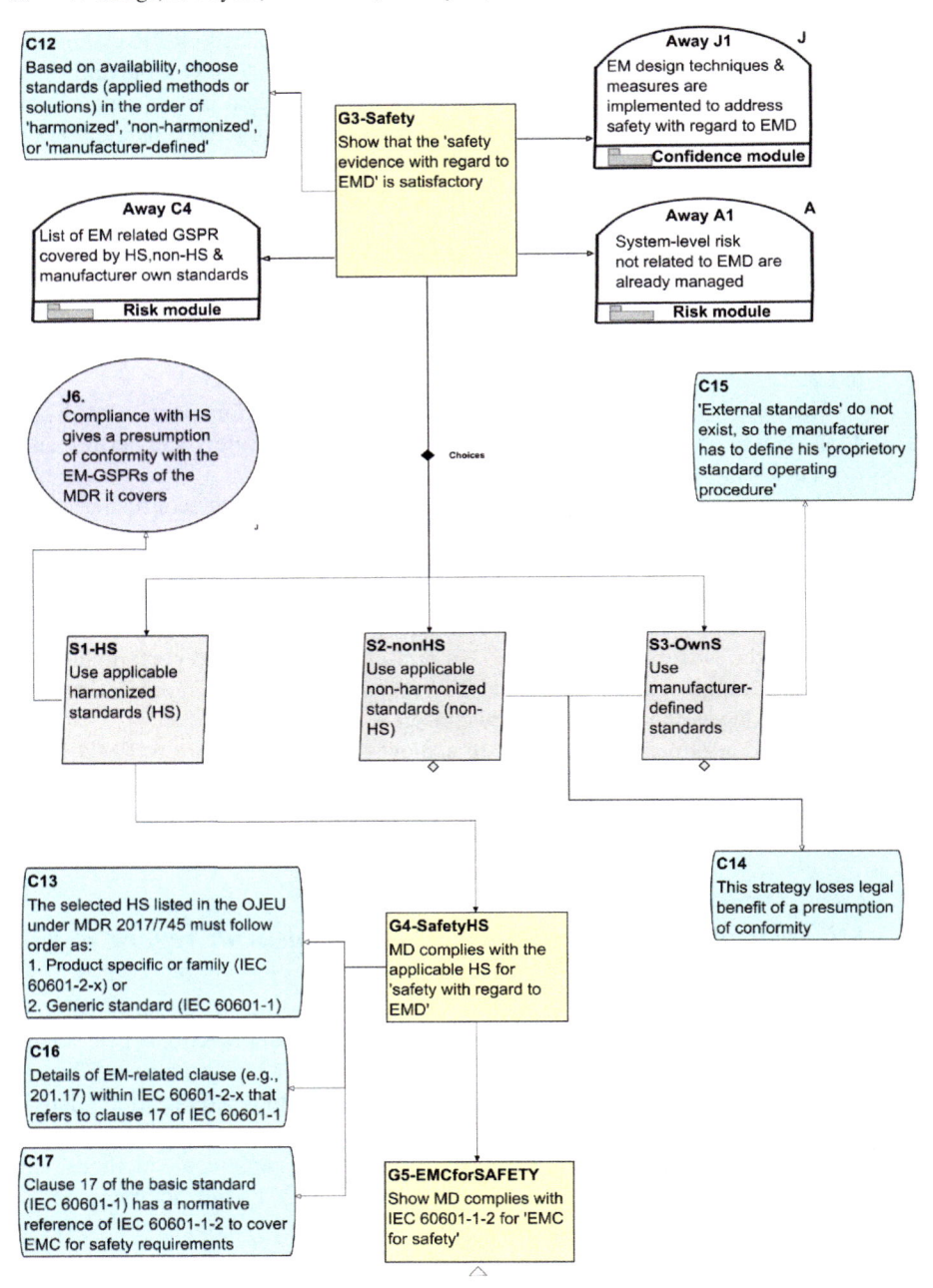

Fig. 7. Strategy to achieve safety with regard to EM emissions & immunity

5.3.1 The rationale behind the choice of strategies to cover safety risks

It is the manufacturer's sole responsibility to choose a specific strategy that covers all identified risks related to EMI-GSPRs as specified in *'Away C2'* of Section 5.1 to achieve *G3-safety*.

The arguments below support the choice argument to decide on applicable strategies:

1. Initially, before choosing a specific strategy, ensure that the safety evidence with regard to other system-level risks has already been managed as specified by the *'away assumption A1'* of the risk module. This assumption should be the baseline of *'G3-safety'*; otherwise, the main claim will be false.
2. Following this, the *'away context C4'* in the risk module analyses and allocates EMI-GSPR related risks, the coverage of which falls within the scope of either harmonised standards (HS), non-harmonised standards (non-HS), or the manufacturer's proprietary standards (OwnS).
3. Following this, the manufacturer needs to check whether design techniques and measures are implemented to mitigate all identified risks related to EMDs, as justified within the confidence module *'away justification J1'*.
4. In the end, the appropriate strategy is chosen as specified within context *C12*. First preference is given to the HS if available and covers the applicable identified risks of *'Away C4'*; and/or, nonHS standards if available and cover the applicable identified risks of *'Away C4'*; and/or, OwnS to cover the applicable identified risks of *'Away C4'*.

The solid diamond below the *G3-safety* indicates choice argument.

The above argumentation immediately shows that solely focusing on external standards (HS and non-HS) is by no means always sufficient to cover all identified risks.

5.3.2 Strategies to achieve safety with regard to EMD

As discussed in above sub-section, to achieve the *G3-safety* goal, the manufacturers have the choice to use one or combinations of the strategies among *S1-HS*, *S2-nonHS*, or *S3-OwnS*.

The strategy (*S1-HS*) of using HS (allocated within *'Away C4'*) should encompass relevant risks (as listed in *'Away C2'* of Section 5.1), which is the manufacturer's default preference. This is due to the legal advantage of a presumption of conformity with the EM-GSPRs of the MDR it covers, as justified in *J6*.

As argued in *C13*, IEC 60601-2-xx is a series of particular standards for MD; preference is always given to this HS if available; otherwise, preference is given to the basic standard (IEC 60601-1).[2]

Based on *C16* and *C17* of *G4-SafetyHS*, the further argument should be a sub-goal claim of *G5-EMCforSAFETY*.

It is crucial to emphasise that achieving '*G5-EMCforSAFETY*' using harmonised standards may not always be sufficient if those lack complete coverage of the EMI-GSPR related risks listed in '*Away C2.*' Therefore, EMC testing based on IEC 60601-1-2 alone will never provide sufficient, comprehensive safety evidence. This realisation underscores the importance for manufacturers to look beyond a rule-based EMC testing approach. Manufacturers should conduct a thorough EMI risk assessment and define their own internal proprietary standards or methods to address the identified risks. Consequently, it is essential and prudent to employ one or a combination of chosen strategies that offer complete coverage of all identified risks related to EMI-related GSPR.

For example, harmonised standards don't address risks related to non-clinical performance, but there exist non-HS IEC 60601-4-2 (IEC 60601-4-2, 2016) that can be used as long as they address all the identified non-clinical performance related risks within *Away C2*. Otherwise, manufacturers have to define the own methods to address these risks.

Additionally, context *C15* further supports using strategy *S3-OwnS*; when both HS and non-HS do not exist, so the manufacturer has to define his 'proprietary standard operating procedure'.

The manufacturer's own standards include his own specifications, proprietary standards, standard operating procedures (SOP), etc.

For example, there may be foreseeable EMI risks, such as surgical noise caused by surgical knives or surgical drills, which are not defined within either the HS IEC 60601-1-2 standard or non-HS standards. These risks need to be independently analysed and mitigated by the manufacturer's own defined methods or standards.

S2-nonHS and *S3-OwnS* are undeveloped strategies in this paper, whereas *S1-HS* has a subgoal '*G4-SafetyHS*' that argues MD complies with the applicable HS as specified in context *C13* for 'safety with regard to EMD'. The legislative obligation for a given standard to be a HS is that it should be listed in the Official Journal of European Union (OJEU) under MDR 2017/745.

---

[2] It's quite hard to argue about how to find the EM-safety clauses of IEC 60601-2-xx due to cross-referencing. The EM-safety clause 201.17 of a particular standard has a normative reference to the basic standard (*C16*), and eventually the basic standards clause 17 has a normative reference to the IEC 60601-1-2 standard (*C17*).

5.4 'EMC for safety' compliance using EMC collateral standard IEC 60601-1-2

The lower level of argumentation simplifies the process of comprehending safety clauses within standards when compared to the higher-level argumentation, which can involve more complex requirements and regulations.

Fig. 8 has a claim of 'G5-EMCforSAFETY' to argue EMC for safety compliance with IEC 60601-1-2 such that the basic safety and essential performance are maintained by managing the risk of EMD (*C18*).

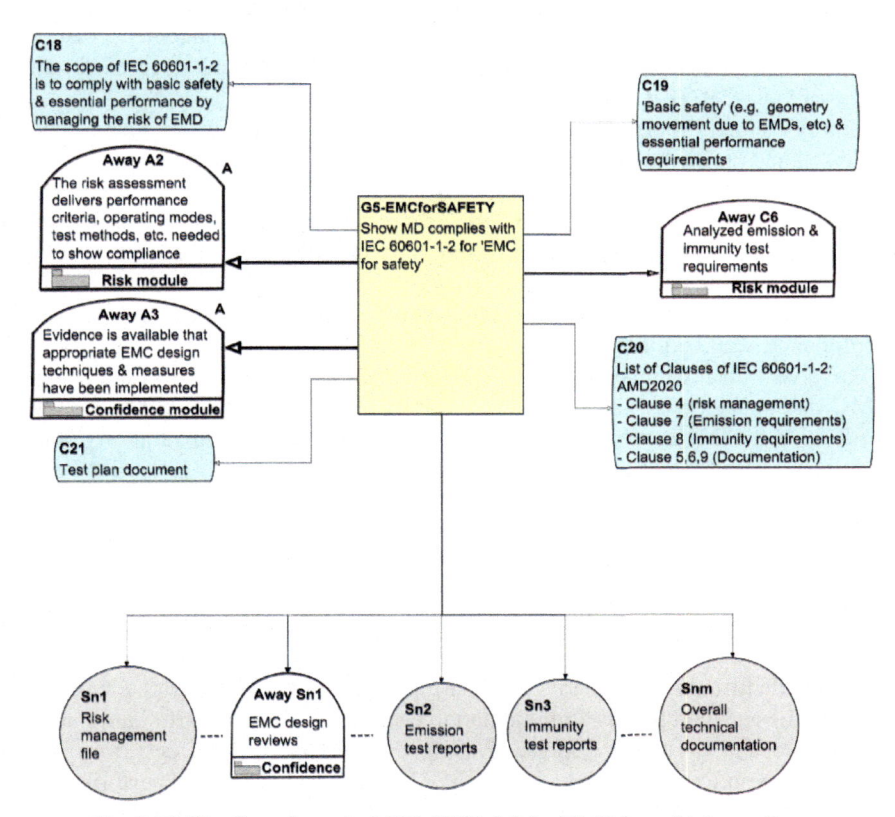

Fig. 8. EMC collateral standard IEC 60601-1-2 for 'EMC for safety' compliance

The contexts *C18, C19, C20,* and *C21* support this claim. Additionally, the modular away assumptions *A2, A3,* and away context *C6* from the risk and confidence module also define the scope of this goal.

While arguing compliance with IEC 60601-1-2, the assumptions are:

1. The risk assessment must have delivered performance criteria, operating modes, test methods, etc. which are the main compliance requirements (Away *A2*).
2. Appropriate EMC design techniques and measures must have been implemented, and evidence should be available (Away *A3*).

If assumed documentation or evidence from risk and confidence modules is unavailable, then the whole argumentation for compliance will fall down with missing information and gaps in documentation.

Context *C19* lists basic safety and essential performance requirements of MD. *C20* lists concrete compliance requirements related to risk management (clause 4), emissions (clause 7), immunity (clause 8), and technical documentation (clauses 5, 6, & 9) (IEC 60601-1-2, 2020).

Away context *C6* provides emission & immunity requirements that have been analysed and defined within the risk module and further validated within compliance module goal *G5*.

Context *C21* provides a detailed EMC test plan referring to the away contexts *C6*. *C21* includes the emission limits, immunity levels, use environment, performance criteria and monitoring methods, list of applicable ports, configuration and operation of the MD in question, resources, sequence of activities during EMC compliance verification and validation, etc.

On a very abstract level, the safety evidence with regard to EMD would be the EMC risk management file (Sn1), test reports of emission and immunity testing (*Sn2, Sn3*), the Declaration of Conformity (DoC), technical documentation (*Snm*) that includes away solutions such as EMC design reviews (*Away Sn1*), EMC design techniques and measures, EMC system-level rationale, etc.

Thus, the modular arguments from the risk module and the confidence module suggest choosing the appropriate strategy for EMC compliance verification and validation. The risk module determines the EMC compliance verification specifications for the intended EM environment based on the (foreseeable) EMI risk assessment. The confidence module implements techniques and measures to mitigate the identified risks effectively, ensuring the design's electromagnetic resilience. In the end, compliance argumentation eventually delivers EMC compliance verification and validation evidence for safety and effectiveness. Regulators provide a presumption of conformity with the MDR general safety and performance requirements (i.e., the presumption that the MD is safe and effective) in the presence of EMD based on a successful notified body review of the necessary objective evidence and rationale.

6 Conclusions

The Goal Structuring Notation and its modular extensions are used to develop EMC compliance patterns that graphically present all arguments on why a medical device is deemed to comply with the EMI-related safety and performance requirements of the MD regulation.

The potential of modular extensions of GSN is leveraged by linking arguments and objective evidence from the risk and confidence cases to the compliance cases. Employing modular risk and confidence arguments in compliance emphasizes that manufacturers must go beyond rule-based EMC testing. This involves managing the risk of EMDs as part of the risk argument and boosting design confidence to ensure sufficient EM resilience. This approach enhances confidence in the safety evidence presented.

The standardised EMC assurance compliance patterns support the executive summary of technical documentation that helps regulatory authorities during the medical device certification stage. With minor modifications, the developed patterns for EU MDR 2017/745 can also be used for other countrywide regulations such as the Food and Drug Administration (FDA), National Medical Products Administration (NMPA), etc., as well as for a broad range of medical equipment. The developed compliance case patterns can be used all the way through from the start of medical device design and development as an EMC process, so compliance case patterns are fulfilled by part of the quality management system (QMS) to develop safe and effective medical devices. This paper presents high-level abstract compliance patterns with a broad scope to separate the regulatory concerns by introducing strategies and goal decompositions from the higher-level regulations to the lower-level standards and developing detailed compliance patterns.

Additionally, the undeveloped goals and strategies related to performance with regard to EMD, more EM-specific requirements from non-medical regulations, and other intended market requirements need further investigation.

Acknowledgments The research leading to these results has received funding from the European Union's Horizon 2020 research and innovation programme under the Marie Skłodowska-Curie Grant Agreement No 955.816 (MSCA-ETN ETERNITY). This publication reflects only the authors' view, exempting the European Union from any liability.

Project website: https://eternity-project.eu/

References

AAMI Technical Information Report (AAMI TIR38:2014), "Medical device safety assurance case guidance"

Assurance Case Working Group (ACWG), "Goal Structuring Notation Community Standard - Version 3", 2021, https://scsc.uk/SCSC-141C

Assurance Case Working Group (ACWG), "Assurance Case Guidance – Challenges Common Issues and Good Practices – version 1", 2021, https://scsc.uk/r159:1

FDA, 2014. Infusion Pumps Total Product Life Cycle: Guidance for Industry and FDA staff. Rockville, MD.

Ghatge, V., Buysse, L., Vanoost, D., Catrysse, J., Kleihorst, R., Pissoort, D. (2023). Unified EMC Assurance Case to Assure Safe and Effective Medical Devices with regard to Electromagnetic Disturbances. In: 2023 JOINT APEMC/INCEMIC, (31-35).

Ghatge, V., Buysse, L., Vanoost, D., Catrysse, J., Pissoort, D. (2023). Applying the Goal Structuring Notation (GSN) to Argue Compliance of Equipment with the European EMC Directive. IEEE Letters on Electromagnetic Compatibility Practice and Applications.

Hawkins R., T. Kelly, J. Knight, and P. Graydon, (2011) "A New Approach to creating Clear Safety Arguments," in Advances in Systems Safety.

IEC 60601-1: Medical electrical equipment – Part 1: General requirements for basic safety and essential performance (2020)

IEC 60601-1-2: Medical electrical equipment – Part 1-2: General requirements for basic safety and essential performance – Collateral standard: Electromagnetic disturbances – Requirements and tests , 2020

IEC 60601-4-2 - Part 4-2: Guidance & interpretation - Electromagnetic immunity: performance of medical electrical equipment and medical electrical systems, 2016

IEEE 1848, Standard on Techniques and Measures to Manage Functional Safety and other Risks With Regard to Electromagnetic Disturbances, 2018

ISO 14971 Medical devices -Application of risk management to medical devices, 2019

Pissoort D., T. Bultinck, J. Boydens, and J. Catrysse, "Use of the Goal Structuring Notation (GSN) as Generic Notation for an "EMC Assurance Case"," in 2019 International Symposium on Electromagnetic Compatibility - EMC EUROPE

Regulation (EU) 2017/745 of the European Parliament and of the council, (2017) https://eur-lex.europa.eu/legal-content/EN/TXT/PDF/?uri=CELEX:32017R0745

Sherman Eagles and Fubin Wu, " Reducing Risks and Recalls: Safety Assurance Cases For Medical Devices ", Biomedical Instrumentation & Technology, February 2014.

Sujan Mark A., Ibrahim Habli, Tim P. Kelly, Simone Pozzi, Christopher W. Johnson, "Should healthcare providers do safety cases? Lessons from a cross-industry review of safety case practices", Safety Science journal 2015

Sujan Mark A., Floor Koornneef, and Udo Voges, "Goal-Based Safety Cases for Medical Devices: Opportunities and Challenges", SAFECOMP 2007

Tishehzan M., M. Nicholson, J. F. Dawson, D. Pissoort, "Providing Assurance that Risks Associated with Electromagnetic Disturbances are Sufficiently Managed"., 2021

System-Theoretic Process Analysis Approach to Analyse EMI-related Hazards and Prioritise Loss Scenarios

Miriam Gonzalez-Atienza[1], Dries Vanoost[1], Rob Kleihorst[2] and Davy Pissoort[1]

1 - ESAT-WaveCoRe, M-Group. KU Leuven Bruges Campus. Bruges, Belgium

2 - IGT Systems. Philips Medical Systems. Best, The Netherlands

Abstract *This study presents a hazard analysis method that uses a systems approach to analyse risks from Electromagnetic Interference (EMI) in complex systems. It builds upon the System-Theoretic Process Analysis (STPA) technique and extends it to EMI hazards by analysing the system control structure and the electromagnetic environment. A real-world case study with an insulin infusion pump illustrates the method's effectiveness in uncovering EMI-related hazards. The method includes a traceability aspect represented as a directed acyclic graph, providing insight into hazards, con-sequences, and factors causing losses. By using this method, we can prioritize EMI scenarios and gain a better understanding of their system impacts, improving our awareness of EMI risks and enhancing decision-making for increased system safety.*

1 Introduction

In recent years, the task of ensuring effective electromagnetic coexistence between devices while maintaining safety and functionality has become increasingly challenging. The conventional method of addressing Electromagnetic Interference (EMI) is known as the "rules-based" approach. This strategy involves identifying relevant standards, implementing appropriate mitigation techniques, and testing for compliance with those standards. However, some of the limitations of this approach involve the potential of standards to become outdated or

© KU Leuven 2024.
Published by the Safety-Critical Systems Club. All Rights Reserved.

insufficient and the high risk that many (electromagnetic) scenarios are overlooked. Consequently, devices that meet the standards might still suffer from EMI in practice.

Electromagnetic Compatibility (EMC) plays a crucial role in ensuring the reliability and safe operation of electronic systems. EMC encompasses principles and practices that enable different electronic devices to coexist harmoniously within a shared electromagnetic environment. It involves managing the potential interactions and interferences between electronic devices to prevent malfunctions, disruptions, and safety hazards. EMI is a potential cause of functional safety issues, as it can compromise the correct operation of systems, potentially leading to unexpected conditions, errors, malfunctions, or faults that pose risks to people or the environment. As a result, achieving a greater alignment between EMC and functional safety domains has become a priority over the last few years (Armstrong, 2006).

As an alternative strategy to the "rules-based" method, the "risk-based approach" focuses on reducing the inherent EMI risks to the lowest possible level. Several studies (Pissoort et al., 2015; Leferink, 2018) have shown the importance of implementing this approach to increase electronic systems' safety, effectiveness, and reliability. The required confidence level in protecting electrical and electronic systems against EMI can only be achieved by applying a systematic risk management process in all system lifecycle phases. Electromagnetic risk management involves identifying potential EMI-related hazards and assessing their impact on the system. The final aim is to find measures to mitigate or prevent their adverse effects.

Over the years, many hazard analysis techniques have been developed. In general, these can be divided into three types, which should be applied together to the analysis of a system to ensure sufficient "failure coverage". Those are:

- "Brainstorming" methods, such as DELPHI or SWIFT (IEC 31010, 2019).
- "Inductive" or "bottom-up" approach, such as FMEA (IEC 60812, 2006) or Event Tree (Genender et al., 2014).
- "Deductive" or "top-down" approach, such as Fault Tree Analysis (Genender et al., 2011) or HAZOP (IEC 61882, 2016).

Unfortunately, there are very few specific methods for analysing EMI-related hazards. Therefore, selecting and adapting the existing hazard analysis techniques to address EMI issues is urgently needed (Devaraj et al., 2020).

In most traditional hazard analysis techniques, the basic approach is to divide the system into components and assume that component failures cause accidents. However, emergent properties such as safety or security arise from the interactions between system components. Especially when the complexity increases, such interactions can only be analysed and understood by looking at the system as a whole instead of the sum of its parts. STPA (System-Theoretic Process Analysis) is one of the hazard analysis tools of STAMP (System-Theoretic Accident Model and Processes) conceived by Nancy Leveson in 2012. STPA is performed in four steps, and its goal is to identify scenarios leading to hazards and define safety constraints for the system in the design stage.

STPA (Leveson, 2012) combines principles of systems thinking with a structured process for analysing and evaluating the safety of complex systems. Although just a decade in existence, these methods have already proven more effective in pinpointing safety hazards within complex systems when compared to traditional approaches like FTA or FMEA, by comprehensively uncovering the contributing factors behind a hazard while offering precise direction regarding the control structure leading to that hazard (Sulaman, 2019). Recent studies have applied STPA in the medical domain (Yamaguchi and Thomas, 2019), robotics (Bensaci et al., 2018), or autonomous ships (Utne et al., 2019). However, to the author's knowledge, resilience against EMI has not been looked

at with STPA, nor have EMI-related risks been identified with this technique. Therefore, this paper proposes a methodology to extend STAMP/STPA to include EMI-related risks.

2 System-Theoretic Process Analysis (STPA)

STAMP (Systems-Theoretic Accident Model and Processes) is an accident causality model based on systems theory and systems thinking. According to STAMP's principles, safety is an emergent property of the system, and accidents can also occur due to unsafe interactions between system components that remain operationally intact.

STPA (System Theoretic Process Analysis) is a hazard analysis technique based on STAMP. It involves identifying the system's components, functions, and control structures, analysing the interactions between components, and evaluating the potential impact of these interactions on the system's performance and safety. The goal of STPA is to identify hazards and design measures to mitigate or eliminate them to ensure the safe and reliable operation of the system. STPA follows a structured process involving four steps (Leveson and Thomas, 2018).

1. **Define the losses/accidents that must be prevented and the system-level hazards.** A loss involves something of value to stakeholders. Losses may include loss of human life or injury, property damage, loss of mission, or any other loss unacceptable to the stakeholders. System-level hazards are system states or conditions that will lead to a loss in some worst-case environments. Hazards must describe states or conditions to be prevented.

2. **Model the general control structure to capture the functional relationships and interactions within the system.** These interactions are modelled as a (set of) closed control loop(s), which includes (i) a controller responsible for initiating the Control Action (CA), (ii) actuators for updating the CA, (iii) the controlled process, and (iv) sensors responsible for delivering feedback to the controller.
3. **Identify Unsafe Control Actions (UCAs).** An Unsafe Control Action is defined as a control action leading to a hazard in a particular context and worst-case scenario. There are four ways a control action can be unsafe:
    a. Not providing the control action leads to a hazard
    b. Providing the control action leads to a hazard
    c. Providing a potentially safe control action but too early, too late or in the wrong order
    d. The control action lasts too long or is stopped too soon (only for continuous control actions)
4. **Identify loss scenarios.** A loss scenario describes the causal factors that can lead to the UCAs and hazards.

Once the scenarios are identified, they can be used to create additional requirements, make design recommendations and new design decisions (if STPA is used during the initial design), evaluate/revisit existing design decisions, and identify gaps (when STPA is applied during design iterations) or develop leading indicators of risk. STPA also includes software and human operators in the analysis, enabling traceability from requirements to all system artefacts. However, STPA has some limitations, including the following (Abidi, 2017):

- Subjectivity. The approach heavily relies on the expertise and experience of the person performing the analysis, which can introduce biases and inconsistencies. Additionally, it may not consider all possible scenarios and may overlook some potential hazards.
- Complexity handling. It might not be easily scalable for highly complex systems.
- Data availability. Lack of data or incomplete information can reduce the effectiveness of the analysis.
- Time-consuming if applied to very complex systems with many loss scenarios identified.

3 Proposed methodology

Although EMI does not affect the hazards directly, it can affect their likelihood of occurrence or severity, which is why EMI must be included when trying to achieve acceptably low-risk levels. In our approach, we propose a modification of STPA that includes EMI-related hazards and considers EMI as a contributing factor to UCAs. After identifying loss scenarios (output of STPA), a directed acyclic graph can be constructed that represents the dependences between the loss scenarios, UCAs, hazards and losses.

3.1 Hazard analysis based on STPA

The hazard analysis of the system based on STPA includes the following steps:

1. Identify losses/accidents and system-level hazards.
2. Characterise the electromagnetic (EM) environment. The first step in any EMI risk analysis technique is to identify the potential EMI sources in the operating environment of the target system, as well as the propagation of the EM environment towards the system. EMI sources can be characterised by their possible location, distance to the system, operating frequency, bandwidth, duration of exposure, and likelihood of occurrence.
3. Model the system's control structure.
4. Identify Unsafe Control Actions.
5. Identify loss scenarios. EMI is included as a causal factor that can lead to the UCAs. EMI can lead to unsafe control actions in the following cases:
   - Input to the controller, actuator, sensor, or controlled process is corrupted due to EMI disrupting the communication path between these modules.
   - EMI disrupts the normal functioning of the controller, actuator, sensor, or controlled process, resulting in either misinterpretation of the received input or incorrect execution.

3.2 Loss scenarios prioritisation

Applying STPA to analyse a complex system may result in identifying several loss scenarios, each resulting in one or more UCAs. In some cases, not all of these scenarios lead to a significant loss. Hence, it is necessary to prioritise scenarios that may cause substantial losses (Tsuji et al., 2020). One of the critical elements of STPA is traceability, which refers to the ability to trace the flow of information and decisions through a system, from identifying hazards to implementing control measures. The traceability in STPA includes:

a. Link between system-level hazards and losses

b. Link between UCA and hazards
c. Link between loss scenarios and UCA

Therefore, the link between losses, hazards, unsafe control actions and loss scenarios is established. The next step consists of representing these connections in a direct acyclic graph (Zeleskidis et al., 2020; Xu et al., 2022), in which the nodes are defined by the four categories given by the STPA results (losses, hazards, UCA and loss scenarios), and the connections between them represent its causal relationship. An additional group of nodes is connected to the loss scenarios, representing the EMI causal factors. This generic graph is shown in Figure 1.

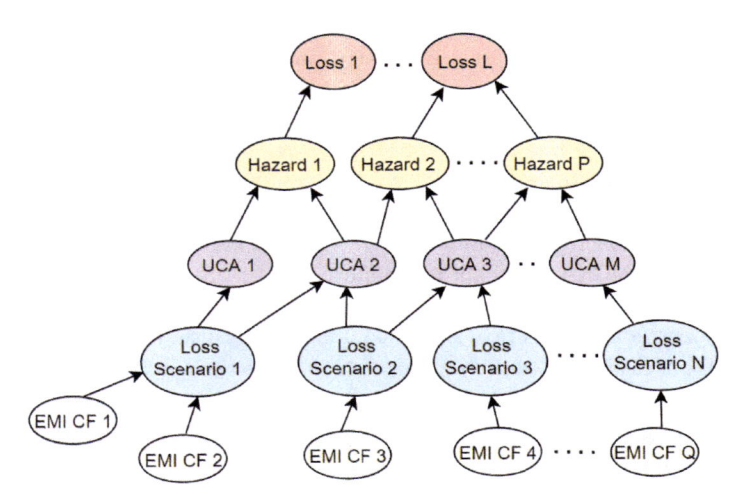

Fig. 1. Traceability diagram based on STPA results

Based on this graph, the following analysis can be done:

- Starting with any loss (top event), identify the hazards that might lead to the top event, as well as the UCAs and their corresponding causal factors.
- Starting with the loss scenario (and linked causal factors), identify the effects on the system (UCAs, hazards and losses).
- Importance analysis. The node importance measures the node's influence in the network. It can be calculated as the number of connections with its parent/child nodes divided by the total amount of nodes. This analysis can then identify the most critical UCA/loss scenario.

This analysis can help determine the weakest links in the system, on which additional mitigations should be implemented. In the next section, the proposed methodology is applied to the use case of an insulin infusion pump.

4 Use case: Insulin infusion pump

An insulin infusion pump (see Figure 2) is a medical device that delivers insulin to people with diabetes. It is typically attached to the body and uses a small tube to deliver insulin subcutaneously. The pump is programmed to deliver insulin continuously throughout the day, and extra insulin to cover meals or correct high blood sugar levels. Traditional insulin pumps are battery-powered and contain an insulin reservoir, a pumping mechanism, and buttons or touch screens to program insulin delivery. The failure or malfunction of the pump can have serious consequences, including hypo- or hyperglycemia, which can be life-threatening for the patient if the failure is not detected and corrected on time. Several reports about medical problems are attributed to using a mobile phone near an infusion pump (Calcagnini et al., 2004; Irnich and Tobisch, 2003).

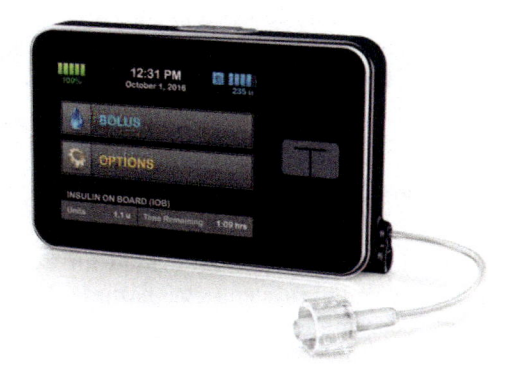

Fig. 2. Insulin infusion pump

Armstrong (2010) reported the following malfunctions in infusion pumps:

- Infusion pump with over-infusion, with the rate changing during the patient's infusion. The patient's cell phone rang, and the nurse at the bedside noticed that the rate of Pitocin[1] was displayed at 120 ml/hr rather than the prescribed rate of 20 ml/hr. The change was noticed in less than one minute, and the patient was not harmed.

---

[1] Pitocin is a synthetic hormone that can help induce labour. Pitocin is delivered through an IV in the patient's arm and the nurse will gradually raise the level of Pitocin received until the patient is having regular contractions about every 2 to 3 minutes.

- Pump stopped infusing during patient use. The pump was infusing heparin[2], at which time the patient's family member used a cell phone close to the pump. The pump then stopped infusing. There was no patient injury or medical intervention.
- An electrostatic discharge damaged a patient-coupled infusion pump, but thankfully, the alarm system was not affected, and a nurse was alerted.
- Infusion pump caused interference with patient monitors.
- An infusion pump changed the rate when a cellular phone was placed on the instrument stand.
- Infusion pumps were prone to alarms and error messages and even reversal in pump direction when phones were less than 1 m away.
- Interference of RFID readers and tags with infusion pump was observed at five different frequency bands at a maximum distance of 136 cm. RFIDs are on the rise in healthcare, helping identify patients, and reveal the location of equipment. There are two types of RFID, one which transmits information, and another, "passive", device which can be "read" by a powered machine when it is held nearby. Implantable medical devices can be susceptible to interference from radio frequency sources, including RFID tags, resulting in malfunctions and even device failures.

4.1 EMI hazard analysis based on STPA

Step 1: Identify losses/accidents. The first step is to identify the losses on which the analysis will be focused, and the system-level hazards. The losses are ranked based on their severity, according to standard ISO/TR 24971:2020 for medical devices (see Table I). Table II and III show the losses and hazards linked to the presented use case.

Table I. Loss severity classification

Severity	Effect on patient
Critical	Death, injury with a risk of death or permanent disability
Moderate	Reversible injury without risk of death
Negligible	Absence of injury

---

[2] Heparin is an organic compound used to prevent blood from clotting in the heart or blood vessels during and after surgery, and for initial treatment of various heart, lung, or circulatory disorders in which there is an increased risk of blood clotting.

Table II. Loss outcome list

[Loss]	Effect on patient	Severity
Hypoglycemia [L-1]	Blood glucose between 70 and 54 mg/dL	Moderate
Clinically significant hypoglycemia [L-2]	Blood glucose below 54 mg/dL	Moderate
Severe hypoglycemia [L-3]	Mental confusion, convulsions. The patient needs external help	Critical
Hyperglycemia [L-4]	Blood glucose between 180 and 250 mg/dL	Moderate
Clinically significant hyperglycemia [L-5]	Blood glucose above 250 mg/dL. Requires immediate action	Moderate
Severe hyperglycemia [L-6]	Blood glucose above 250 mg/dL. May induce coma and even death	Critical
Loss of insulin infusion [L-7]	Insulin infusion interruption results in hyperglycemia	Critical

Table III. High-level hazards

[Hazard]	Link to loss
Over infusion rate of insulin [H-1]	[L-1], [L-2], [L-3]
Under infusion rate of insulin [H-2]	[L-1], [L-2], [L-3]
Reversal in pump direction [H-3]	[L-7]
Infusion interruption [H-4]	[L-7]

Step 2: Characterise the EM environment. To identify the potential EMI sources, the first step is to characterise the intended environment of the device. In the presented use case, some insulin infusion pumps are designed mainly for stationary use at patient's bedside, while others are designed to be portable or

wearable. In the case of stationary use at patient's bedside, the following potential EMI sources can be considered (non-exhaustive list):

- RFID tags and readers.
- Bluetooth or Wi-Fi applications which are integrated in smartphones and headsets for audio communication. Medical staff or the patient's family members may use those in the patient room.
- Base stations. Base stations for mobile communications can be in relatively close proximity to the hospital room.
- Implanted devices/defibrillators. Defibrillators can be placed at the patient's bedside in case of cardiac arrest and may also have Wi-Fi communication with a base station or access point.
- Patient monitoring devices. Such as blood pressure monitors, they can transmit patient information wirelessly to their healthcare provider or other monitoring systems.
- Imaging systems (X-ray, CT scans, MRI).

Regarding the EMI not coming from medical devices, a typical situation is using a mobile phone (e.g. GSM and UMTS) inside medical facilities. Some of the reported cases of EMI due to mobile phones were listed in the introduction of this section.

Step 3: Model the control structure. The generic control structure of the considered insulin infusion pump is shown in Fig. 3.

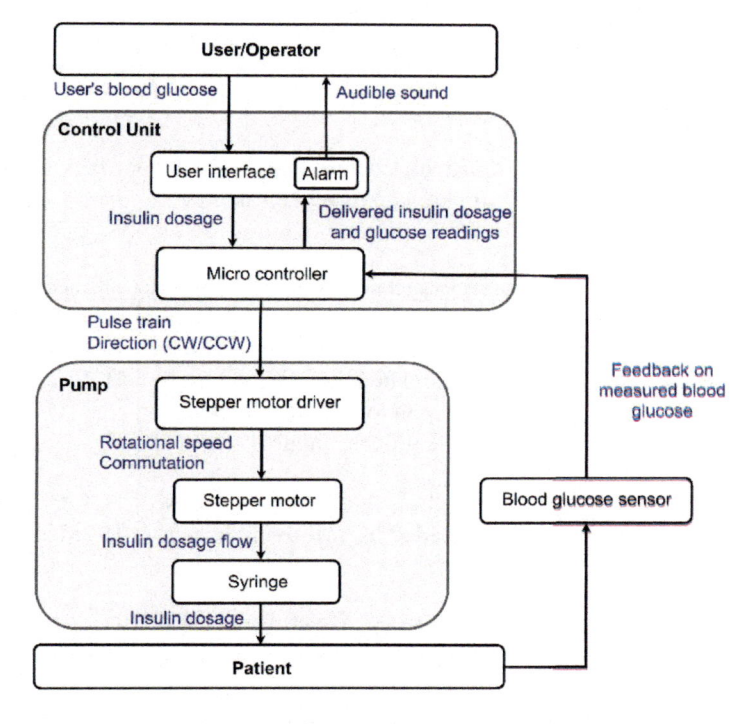

Fig. 3. Control structure of insulin infusion pump, based on Martinazzo et al., 2021

The process works as follows:

1. The user provides their glucose level via the user interface, which calculates the required insulin dose. Bedside devices are operated by nurses, while portable pumps are user-managed. Many pumps have built-in insulin dose calculators for dosage determination.
2. The microcontroller commands the stepper motor for insulin delivery.
3. The motor driver receives signals for speed (pulse train) and direction from the microcontroller.
4. Each pulse causes the motor to move one step.
5. The mechanical transmission converts the motor rotation into syringe plunger movement. The syringe serves as the interface for subcutaneous insulin delivery.
6. The blood glucose sensor measures patient's glucose levels and provides feedback to the microcontroller for speed adjustments in insulin delivery.

The pulse train and the stepper motor's direction, which control the flow of insulin delivered to the patient, are the most critical actuator signals in the system. Any disturbance that affects their normal operation might pose a risk to the user's health.

Step 4: Identify Unsafe Control Actions. Some of the identified unsafe control actions from the control structure are listed in Table IV.

Table IV. Control responsibilities and identified unsafe control actions

Control responsibility	Unsafe Control Action	Link to Hazard
User interface calculates the insulin dose needed based on the patient's blood glucose	UCA-1.1: The insulin dose is calculated based on the user's or microcontroller's inaccurate glucose input.	H-1: Over infusion H-2: Under infusion
	UCA-1.2: The insulin dose needed is incorrectly calculated	H-1: Over infusion H-2: Under infusion
	UCA-1.3: The insulin dose is correctly calculated but there is a problem in transmitting the dosage information to the microcontroller.	H-4: Infusion interruption
Blood glucose sensor measures the patient's blood glucose and gives feedback to microcontroller	UCA-2.1: Blood glucose sensor provides incorrect readings	H-1: Over infusion H-2: Under infusion
	UCA-2.2: Readings are correct but communication to the microcontroller fails	H-1: Over infusion H-2: Under infusion H-4: Infusion interruption
	UCA-2.3: Feedback is delayed or not correctly updated.	H-1: Over infusion H-2: Under infusion H-4: Infusion interruption
Pulse train and direction signal is transmitted from the microcontroller to the stepper motor driver	UCA-3.1: Pulse train and direction signal are lost during transmission	H-1: Over infusion H-2: Under infusion H-4: Infusion interruption

Control responsibility	Unsafe Control Action	Link to Hazard
	UCA-3.2: Direction signal is inverted, causing the stepper motor to move in the opposite direction than intended	H-3: Reversal in pump direction
	UCA-3.3: Both signals experience a delay, causing a lag in the stepper motor's response	H-1: Over infusion H-2: Under infusion
	UCA-3.4: Change in frequency of pulse train	H-1: Over infusion H-2: Under infusion

Step 5: Identify loss scenarios. Table V presents the results of the STPA. The loss scenarios are the conditions in which the UCA can occur, and the EMI causal factors are pre-requisites for the occurrence of the scenarios.

Table V. List of loss scenarios and EMI causal factors

Unsafe Control Action	Loss scenario	EMI Causal factor
UCA-1.1: The insulin dose is calculated based on incorrect glucose input.	EMI disrupts the communication between the microcontroller and the user interface, leading to incorrect readings received by the user interface.	Mobile phones working within close proximity to the user interface at the same time that the insulin dose is received by the user interface.
UCA-1.2: The insulin dose is incorrectly calculated	The user interface experiences temporary glitches. The interface briefly displays incorrect readings from the patient's glucose level input, and this corrupted data is used in the insulin dosage calculation	Mobile phones working within close proximity to the user interface at the same time that the insulin dose is being calculated Wireless communication devices such as pagers used by hospital staff Nearby medical equipment (patient monitors, defibrillators, etc.)

Unsafe Control Action	Loss scenario	EMI Causal factor
UCA-2.1: Blood glucose sensor provides incorrect readings	The patient's bed is located close to a nursing station where several wireless communication devices, such as mobile phones, tablets, and pagers, are frequently used by healthcare personnel. The patient's bed is within range of these devices, and the electromagnetic radiation emitted by the wireless devices causes EMI.	Mobile phones working within close proximity to the sensor

EMD generated from the Wi-Fi access points in the hospital room. |
| UCA-3.2: Direction signal is inverted, causing the stepper motor to move in the opposite direction than intended | The patient's hospital room has various electrical devices, such as electronic beds, patient monitors, and IV pumps. As the patient receives care, the electronic devices in the room are in use, emitting electromagnetic radiation as they operate. These disturbances interfere with the microcontroller that is transmitting the direction signal to the stepper motor driver. | Medical equipment operating at the same frequency as the microcontroller |

Once the STPA is finished, the analysis can be used to create a traceability graph to represent these results, as shown in Fig. 4, in which each group of nodes is defined by the four categories given by the STPA results.

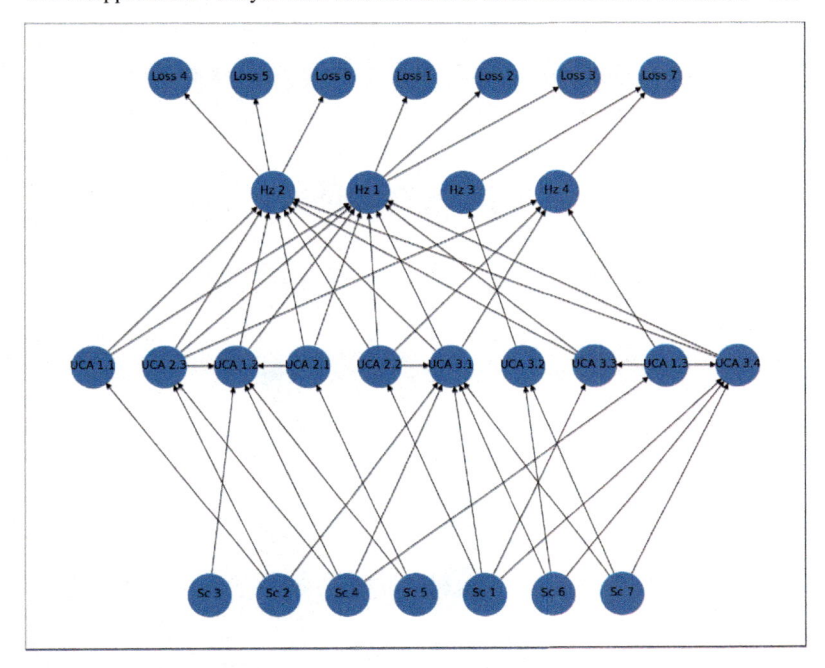

Fig. 4. STPA results for the insulin pump.

As an example, we can perform the traceability analysis for the UCA 2.1: Blood glucose sensor provides incorrect readings. When the blood glucose sensor is disturbed, it fails to provide accurate feedback on the patient's blood glucose levels. Consequently, this inaccuracy affects the calculation of the required insulin dose for the patient (UCA-1.2: The insulin dose is incorrectly calculated). If this error is not detected or notified by the alarm system (for example, SC3: EMI from mobile phone cause alarm failure), the insulin dose that the controller receives might cause an increase in its speed. This, in turn, could lead to over-infusion of insulin or result in oscillatory behavior (Hazard 1: Over infusion).

Based on these traceability results, the following analysis can be done:

- **Importance analysis to identify the most critical components/functions.**
  The significance of each node can be determined by calculating the in-degree centrality (number of connections from lower-level nodes). This metric reflects the node's contribution to the overall network. For instance, we can calculate the in-degree centrality of each UCA node in the following manner:

$$C_{in}(uca_n) = \frac{D_{in}(uca_n)}{N-1},$$

where N is the total number of *Loss scenarios* nodes, and $D_{in}(uca_n)$ is the number of incoming edges to the node uca_n from the *Loss scenarios* nodes.

For example, for UCA 3.1: *Pulse train and direction signal are lost during transmission,*

$$C_{in}(uca_{31}) = \frac{D_{in}(uca_{31})}{7-1} = \frac{6}{7} = 0.71.$$

Figure 5 shows the results of the normalised degree centrality for the *UCA* nodes.

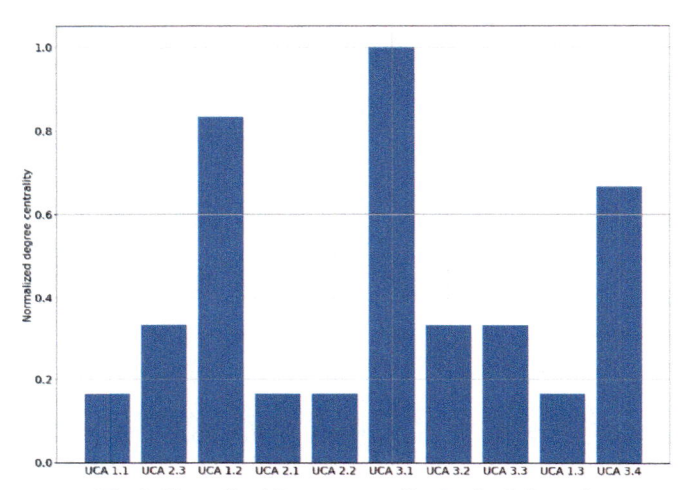

Fig. 5. Normalised Degree centrality for the *UCA* nodes.

Based on these results, we can conclude that the UCA with the most influence on the network is *UCA-3.1: Pulse train and direction signal are lost during transmission.* Therefore, we could determine that one of the most critical parts of the system is the transmission of the pulse train and direction signal to the microcontroller. These signals determine the insulin dose that is delivered to the patient. When the pulse train is affected by the EMD, the sensor will detect this, potentially resulting in a high dose that can lead to overdoses, underdoses, oscillations, or even unstable behaviour. Additionally, any problem in the dose transmission might lead to the incorrect calculation of the dose needed, or the infusion to stop. If these errors are not noticed (either by the alarm system or by the patient/nurse), they might pose a health risk to the patient.

- Select the most critical loss and the linked UCAs. For example, consider the loss "severe hypoglycemia'" (Loss 2 in Figure 5). Starting from this loss, we can trace back to the Hazard linked to it (Hazard 1: over-infusion rate of insulin) and the UCAs and causal factor that might lead to this loss.

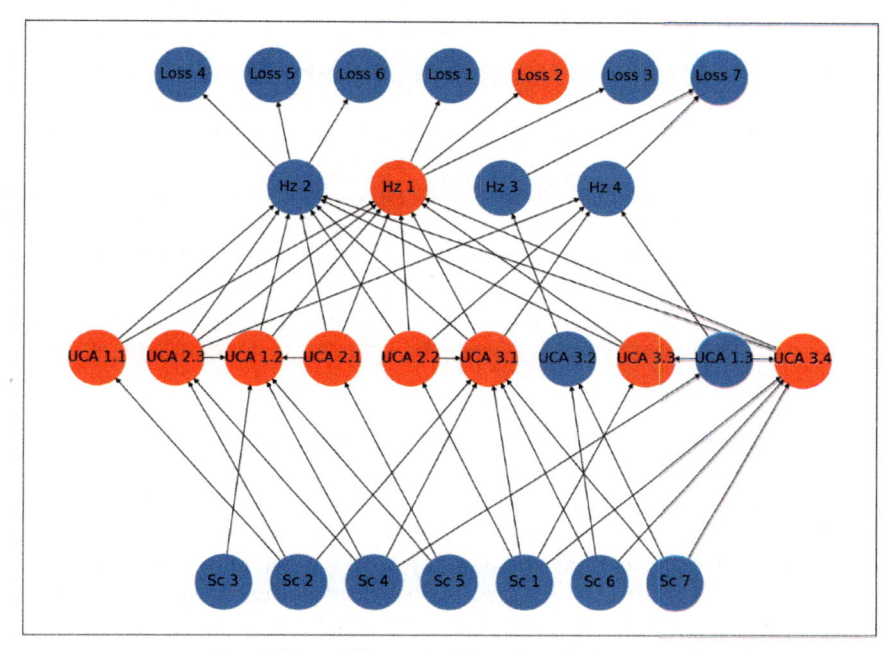

Fig. 6. Traceability analysis based on the STPA results

Once this traceability analysis is performed, the critical UCAs identified can be used to create safety requirements or mitigation techniques to avoid or minimise their occurrence. All the red-colored UCAs in Fig. 6 lead to the Hazard *over-infusion rate of insulin*. Additionally, most of these UCAs are related to a failure in the blood glucose sensor or a disruption in the communication between the sensor and the microcontroller. Thus, we can derive the following safety requirements to minimise the occurrence of these UCAs:

- The blood glucose sensor should provide updated values every few seconds, by continuously monitoring the quality of the transmitted feedback signal, and if deviations from the expected parameters are detected, trigger appropriate corrective actions.
- Ensure that the pulse train and direction signal transmission from the microcontroller to the stepper motor driver is robust, reliable, and minimally affected by external factors to prevent signal loss or delay. For example, implement redundant signal transmission pathways to ensure that even if one pathway experiences signal loss or delay, the backup pathway can provide uninterrupted signal transmission.
- Integrate error-detection and error-correction mechanisms into the signal transmission process to identify and rectify any errors that may occur during transmission.

- Ensure that the user interface provides clear indications of any signal loss or delay and guides the user on appropriate actions to take in case of such occurrences.
- Alarms should be provided to identify over- and under-infusion, failure on the stepper motor, or a mechanical transmission failure.
- The stepper motor should not provide a speed that leads to an inverse insulin flow, or the speed direction should be fixed in the hardware design. Additionally, the alarm should notify when there is a change in pump direction.
- Define safe states for the stepper motor and insulin delivery system in case of signal loss, signal delay, or any unexpected interruption. Ensure the system transitions to these safe states to prevent unsafe motor movements.

5 Conclusions

In this study, the hazards analysis technique STPA was extended to include risks related to EMI. The proposed methodology involves identifying losses, hazards, and possible EMI sources and modelling the system's control structure. Unsafe control actions, underlying EMI-related reasons, and EMI loss scenarios are identified. The technique's outcomes are used to build a directed acyclic graph that facilitates prioritising EMI scenarios based on potential critical losses and recognising system vulnerabilities. Additionally, a node importance analysis can be performed to measure the influence of each unsafe control action/loss scenario/hazard on the overall graph.

The proposed methodology was explained and demonstrated using an insulin infusion pump. The analysis highlighted the impact of EMI disruptions on the alarm system's function and the significance of EMI-induced blood glucose sensor failure in accurate insulin dosing. Some of the advantages of the presented methodology are listed below:

- Identifying weak parts in the design: Traceability allows for a comprehensive understanding of how hazards, loss scenarios, and UCAs are interconnected, enabling the identification of potential weaknesses in the system's design.
- Prioritizing loss scenarios: Tracing causal relationships makes it easier to prioritize loss scenarios that could lead to significant or critical losses, ensuring that resources are allocated to address the most critical losses.
- Improved decision-making: Traceability enhances decision-making by providing a clear and logical flow of information and decision points within the system, facilitating the implementation of appropriate control measures.

- Risk mitigation: Understanding the connections between UCAs, hazards, and loss scenarios enables more effective risk mitigation strategies, reducing the likelihood of adverse events.

However, applying STPA to cover EMI-related hazards comes with certain limitations. Some of them are listed below:

- Subjectivity: STPA heavily relies on the expertise and experience of the analyst, making it susceptible to subjectivity and potential biases. Different analysts may identify EMI-related risks differently. This is why teamwork is always important.
- Lack of specialized knowledge: Effective EMI risk assessment often requires specialized knowledge in EMC.
- Data availability: EMI analysis relies on comprehensive data regarding electromagnetic fields, electronic components, and system vulnerabilities. Incomplete or inaccurate data can limit the effectiveness of the analysis.
- Changing EM environment: EMI risks can vary with environmental conditions, equipment configurations, and other factors. STPA may not account for all scenarios and dynamic EMI risk changes.

To address these limitations, it is highly recommended to complement STPA with additional risk analysis methods and consultation with experts in EMC to ensure comprehensive EMI risk management.

Acknowledgments This project has received funding from the European Union's Horizon 2020 research and innovation programme under the Marie Skłodowska-Curie grant agreement No 955816. This publication reflects only the author's view exempting the European Union from any liability. Project website: https://eternity-project.eu/.

References

IEC 31010:2019, Risk Assessment Techniques – Delphi technique.
IEC 31010:2019, Risk Assessment Techniques – Structured what if technique (SWIFT).
IEC 60812:2006, Analysis Techniques for System Reliability – Procedure for Failure Mode and Effects Analysis (FMEA).
IEC 61882:2016, Hazard and operability studies (HAZOP studies) – Application guide.
ISO/TR 24971:2020 - Medical devices - Guidance on the application of ISO 14971, Geneva, Switzerland: ISO Std., 2020.
Abidi S. (2017), "Advantages and disadvantages of STPA and ISO 26262-3" in document "Application of the STPA methodology to an automotive system in compliance with ISO26262", pp. 40-45.
Armstrong K. (2006), "Why EMC testing is inadequate for functional safety— And what should be done instead," in Proc. 1st IET Int. Conf. Syst. Safety, London, U.K. pp. 179–183
Armstrong K. (2010), "EMI Stories 571 – 665", [Online]. Available: https://www.emcstandards.co.uk/emi-stories-7-571-to-665

Bensaci C., Zennir Y., and Pomorski D. (2018), "A comparative study of STPA hierarchical structures in risk analysis: The case of a complex multirobot mobile system," in 2018 2nd European Conference on Electrical Engineering and Computer Science (EECS), pp. 400–405.

Calcagnini G., Bartolini P., Floris M., Triventi M., Cianfanelli P., Scavino G., Proietti L. and BarbaroV. (2004), "Electromagnetic interference to infusion pumps from GSM mobile phones," in The 26th Annual International Conference of the IEEE Engineering in Medicine and Biology Society, vol. 2, pp. 3515–3518.

Devaraj L., Ruddle A.R., and Duffy A.P. (2020), "Electromagnetic risk analysis for EMI impact on functional safety with probabilistic graphical models and fuzzy logic," in IEEE Letters on Electromagnetic Compatibility Practice and Applications, vol. 2, no. 4, pp. 96–100.

Genender E., Mleczko M., Doring O., Garbe H., and Potthast S. (2011), "Fault tree analysis for system modeling in case of intentional EMI," in Advances in Radio Science, vol. 9, pp. 297–302.

Genender E., Garbe H., and Sabath F. (2014), "Probabilistic risk analysis technique of intentional electromagnetic interference at system level," in IEEE Transactions on Electromagnetic Compatibility, vol. 56, no. 1, pp. 200–207.

Irnich W., and Tobisch R. (2003), "Mobile phones in hospitals," in Biomedical instrumentation technology / Association for the Advancement of Medical Instrumentation, vol. 33, pp. 28–34, 01.

Leferink F. (2018), "Risk-based vs Rule-based Electromagnetic Compatibility in Large Installations," in IEEE 4th Global Electromagnetic Compatibility Conference (GEMCCON), pp. 1-4.

Leveson N.G. (2012), "Engineering a Safer World: Systems Thinking Applied to Safety". The MIT Press.

Leveson N.G. and Thomas J. (2018), "STPA handbook".

Martinazzo A., Martins L. E. G., Aredes S. V. and Cunha T. S. (2021), "Risk management of a low-cost insulin infusion pump: A case study with a brazilian company," in IEEE 34th International Symposium on Computer-Based Medical Systems (CBMS), pp. 336–341.

Pissoort D., Degraeve A. and Armstrong K. (2015), "EMI Risk Management: A necessity for safe And reliable electronic systems!," in IEEE 5th International Conference on Consumer Electronics Berlin (ICCE-Berlin), pp. 208-210.

Sulaman S., Beer A., Felderer M. and Host M. (2019), "Comparison of the FMEA and STPA safety analysis methods–a case study," in Software Quality Journal, vol. 27, pp. 1–39.

Tsuji M., Takai T., Kakimoto K., Ishihama N., Katahira M. and Iida H. (2020), "Prioritising Scenarios based on STAMP/STPA Using Statistical Model Checking," in 2020 IEEE International Conference on Software Testing, Verification and Validation Workshops (ICSTW), Porto, Portugal, pp. 124-132, DOI: 10.1109/ICSTW50294.2020.00032.

Utne I.B., Rokseth B., Sørensen A. and Vinnem J.E. (2019), "Towards supervisory risk control of autonomous ships," in Reliability Engineering & System Safety, vol. 196, pp. 106757.

Xu J., Tian W., Kan L., Chen Y. (2022), "Safety Assessment of Transport Aircraft Heavy Equipment Airdrop: An Improved STPA-BN Mechanism," in IEEE Access, vol. 10, pp. 87522-87534.

Yamaguchi S. and Thomas J. (2019), "A system safety approach for tomographic treatment," in Safety Science, vol. 118, pp. 772-782.

Zeleskidis A., Dokas I.M., Papadopoulos B. (2020), " A novel real-time safety level calculation approach based on STPA", in MATEC Web Conf, vol. 314.

Red Cars are Killing Left-handed People!

Paul Hampton

CGI.

Exeter, UK

Abstract *The old adage that there are "lies, damn lies, and statistics" warns of the perils of relying on statistics but yet our safety and reliability arguments are often underpinned by statistics such as component failure frequencies, service history, accident rates and numerous distribution models. How do we really know we can trust what we draw from these figures? Statistics and importantly, their perceived conclusions and implications drawn from them, are readily published in the media and readily proliferated mostly unquestioned through social media and other outlets, but as we shall see, publications, even from reputable and learned authors can turn out to be flawed. If even experts can make mistakes, then we need to look carefully at the reliance we place on 3rd party interpretations of data, and of course, be very careful with our own data and the wisdom we draw from it. Through the use of real-life examples, this paper highlights the typical pitfalls that arise from the interpretation of statistical data and will conclude that it is often the data that we don't see, the 'dark data', that can fundamentally undermine the conclusions we draw from seemingly compelling data.*

1 Introduction

As someone who is left-handed, I've always wondered whether this characteristic imbues any advantages, or indeed, disadvantages in life. There are certainly many and sometimes contradictory reports of significant differentiators. Reilly (2023) reported in an article to mark National Leftie Day (yes there is such a thing!) that "lefties score higher when it comes to creativity, imagination, daydreaming and intuition. They're also better at rhythm and visualization". But MacMillan (2015) reported that "it doesn't make you more creative" and "it doesn't mean you're artsy" so it's difficult to know what to believe, well, from reading the Internet anyway.

Surely research published in respected journals such as "Nature" and the "The New England Journal of Medicine", might be a better source of fact; and around about 1990, one remarkable statement was being made – that right-handers outlive left-handed people by anything up to 9 years! Researchers proposed that this

© Paul Hampton, 2024.
Published by the Safety-Critical Systems Club. All Rights Reserved.

was due to left-handed people having to operate in a world designed for right-handers and in 1991 Halpern & Coren (Halpern & Coren 1988, 1991) suggested that car accidents were often to blame.

This year I also came across an article by carVertical (Bareckas 2022). Their research stated that red is the most dangerous car colour, as 60% of vehicles checked in their vehicle history database have been involved in an accident and they reported that white and grey were the safest colour of vehicle to drive.

I don't think anyone else has spotted the connection yet, but surely there's a remarkable conclusion here:

> *"red cars are killing left-handed people!"*

Perhaps the 1983 film based on Stephen King's novel "Christine" about a murderous red 1958 Plymouth Fury was not entirely based on fiction?!

Fig. 1. Plymouth Fury
(image ©Randomshots dreamstime.com, id: 32428032)

2 Correlation and Causation

Well, of course, I'm not seriously making that claim, but it does illustrate a common pitfall in the world of statistics: "Correlation does not imply causation". That is, just because two events occur together, it does not necessarily mean there is a cause-and-effect relationship. There are many obvious examples of these, for example, "consuming ice creams causes shark attacks". Consumption of ice cream and shark attacks are highly correlated but of course one does not cause the other – there is a 3rd factor that is hidden from the equation in that people consume ice cream and get in the ocean when it is warmer outside.

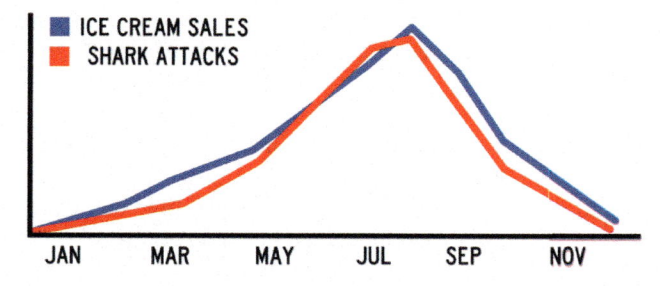

Fig. 2. Ice Cream Sales v Shark Attacks
(image: ©Alain Lacroix dreamstime.com, id 37904189)

This 3rd hidden variable drives the other two and hence gives the impression of causation. This hidden cause can be considered "Dark Data"[1] (Hand 2020) – data that we weren't aware of but nevertheless has a significant influence on the conclusions you draw from the data.

The ice cream example is of course obvious, but this is not always the case and some can be a lot more subtle. In 1991, a paper was published in the Preventative Medicine Journal (Stampfer & Colditz 1991) that showed, from observational studies, a strong correlation between Hormone Replacement Therapy (HRT) and Coronary Heart Disease (CHD). The paper suggested that there was a relative reduction of 50% of CHD in those women taking HRT and claimed that:

> *"overall, the bulk of the evidence strongly supports a protective effect of oestrogens that is unlikely to be explained by confounding factors".*

Confounding factors are effectively "dark data" that might have an unknown but influential role in giving the illusion of causation. This seemed compelling; not only had the researchers found a strong correlation that suggested causation, but also, they claimed there was no dark data lurking in the background to skew the results.

Observational studies by their nature are about observing what happens in the field so there is less control over how the population under study is selected. Another method is a Randomised Controlled Trial (RCT), where the population is, as the title suggests, selected by random. Later RCT studies came up with a much different picture of the relationship between HRT and CHD; randomised trials

---

[1] In his book "Dark Data: Why What You Don't Know Matters", David Hand explores the many ways in which we can be blind to missing data ("Dark Data") and how that can lead us to conclusions and actions that are mistaken, dangerous, or even disastrous. He examines many real-life examples, such as the Challenger shuttle disaster, where it was the data that *wasn't* made available that was ultimately critical to the safety of the decision making. David also provides a practical taxonomy of the types of dark data that exist and the situations in which they can arise to help us learn to recognise and control them.

among both women with established CHD and healthy women found HRT to be associated with slightly increased risk of CHD or null effects (WHI 2002). This of course led to considerable debate, but the most plausible explanation is that women who participated in the randomised trials were *demographically different* from those who participated in the observational studies, or that the observational study results were actually influenced by confounding factors.

Lawlor, Smith & Ebrahim (2004) suggested at the time that women who use HRT tend to come from higher socioeconomic strata and receive better quality of diet and exercise – a hidden explanatory relationship for which the observational study failed to fully account. Despite the denial of dark data, it was still potentially lurking and who knows how many women were wrongly informed about the risks and benefits of HRT during those early years[2].

As well as a cautionary tale on drawing conclusions on correlations from data, it does show how pernicious and elusive dark data can be. Even when experts are aware of the concept of confounding factors, they can still fail to eliminate its influence. However, this example does provide one immediate insight into how we could potentially detect and manage dark data. The presence of dark data was discovered in this case by doing a completely different style of trial and there are parallels in the safety world here with functional independence[3] as a safety mitigation. Could a form of diverse analysis be a means of routing out occurrences of dark data?

3 Artificial "Intelligence" and Machine Learning

If humans and indeed subject matter experts can fail to spot spurious correlations in data then we must be extremely wary of correlations identified by Machine Learning (ML) algorithms. There have been some promising reports on the ability of ML to help or even outdo the performance of clinicians in identifying diseases from scans. A recently concluded study in Sweden (Lancet 2023) showed that a double-reading strategy using a clinician plus AI improved the detection rate of breast cancer from mammograms by 20%, when compared to a double reading with two clinicians.

Other applications of Artificial Intelligence (AI) have however been less successful due to the inadvertent detection of spurious correlations. Jiménez-

---

[2] In case you were wondering, it is now generally accepted that HRT only presents higher risk of cardiovascular disease if they start taking HRT after the age of 60 NICE (2019).

[3] This, to some extent, is what happens when new drugs are introduced through a number of trial phases, typically four (NHS 2021), being undertaken with increasing numbers of candidates and mixtures of controlled, double-blind and randomised testing. This can be a lengthy process – in excess of 10 years – with only 10-20% of candidate medicines ever reaching marketing approval (Yamaguchi, Kaneko & Narukawa 2021).

Sánchez & Juodelyte provide an example of X-ray datasets used to detect if an individual suffers from pneumothorax, that is, the presence of air or gas in the cavity between the lungs and the chest wall, causing collapse of the lung (Jiménez-Sánchez & Juodelyte 2022). The resulting trained algorithm was highly effective with the original training set, but poor in the field when used to detect pneumothorax prior to treatment. The reason for this was that the ML process had found a shortcut; the training data set with positive pneumothorax were generally from individuals undergoing treatment, and so they also had a draining tube that was also showing up in the X-ray. The algorithm was therefore simply differentiating based purely on the presence of the tube and had found the simple but correlation that those undergoing treatment for pneumothorax, suffered from pneumothorax.

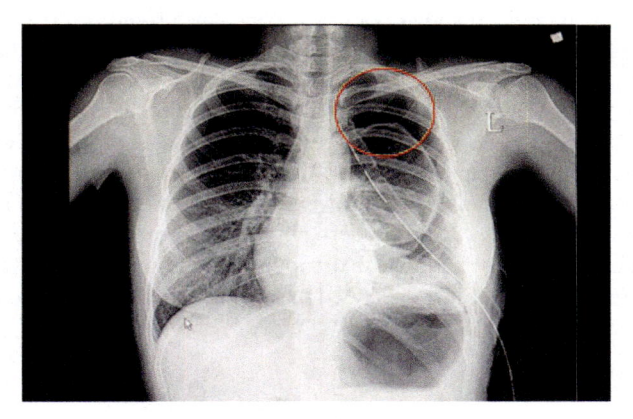

Fig. 3. X-ray Film of Pneumothorax with a Chest Drain
(image © Sopone Nawoot dreamstime.com, id Photo 9890132)

Unexpected correlations in ML training data sets can therefore be seriously detrimental to intended purpose of the algorithm. If these unknown or "dark" correlations go undetected, then it is possible the AI tool may have a detrimental impact on health outcomes. Clearly, we need to ensure the training data does not have these inadvertent correlations, but there then lies the challenge: if we knew our training data set that well, we probably wouldn't be using AI/ML techniques in the first place.

4 The Left-handed Curse

For a left-hander, the claims of Halpern & Coren – the prospect of a much-shortened life – would of course be disturbing. This would reduce the lifespan of a left-handed person as much as a lifetime of moderate smoking (Statistics Netherlands 2017). It took some time, but these results were eventually disproved, and a more recent study (Ganna & Ingelsson 2015) showed relative mortality for left-handers, compared with right-handers, was almost exactly 1.0. While in hindsight it might seem obvious that these results could not be correct, I do have some sympathy with the original researchers as the approach was simple and seemed persuasive at the time.

To summarise, the researchers looked at the records of 2,000 people in Southern California who had recently died. They then confirmed with their families whether their relative was left- or right-handed. The data then showed that the average age at death of the left-handers was about nine years younger than that of right-handers.

The critical underlying assumption in this study was, however, that the proportion of left- to right- handed people is constant through time and indeed, it seems generally accepted that left-handed people represent around 10% of the population. Potentially the largest and most reliable study covering 32 countries was conducted in 1994 and concluded the proportion was on average 9.5% (Perelle & Ehrman 1994). There is also evidence that it has pretty much been this way for a long time – a very long time. An examination of the teeth of around 30 Neanderthals (Volpato et al 2012) showed they also shared the high frequencies of right-handedness found in all modern populations world-wide.

The dark data in this example that tripped up the researchers was societal. Between 1800 and 1900, the left-handed rate was pushed down artificially during this Victorian period (McManus 2019).

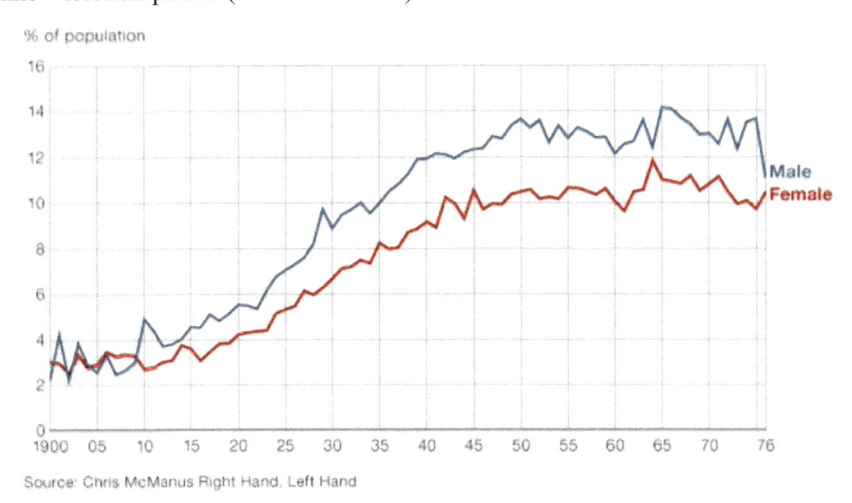

Fig. 4. Left-handedness 1900-1976
(reproduced with kind permission from Chris McManus)

Not only would left-handed people have been encouraged not to be left-handed during this period, life was also pretty difficult for them and they quickly became very conspicuous working in factories using machines designed for right-handers. Furthermore, compulsory schooling came along and they would be obliged to sit in classrooms and try and write with their right hand using an ink pen and they would make a mess. The result of all of this was that left-handers became stigmatised – regarded as "cack-handed", even stupid.

Artificially pushing the natural left-handed rates down during this period would have a significant impact on the findings. From 1900 to 1976, the rate gradually increased from 3% to the rate we have now at around 10%. The easiest way of thinking about how this affects the averages is to imagine that every left-handed forced to be right-handed effectively dies at age 0 – it is no surprise the results were so skewed. Here we see another instance of dark data that the researchers were presumably unaware of, and had a fundamental impact on the results.

Unfortunately, this is not an isolated case with similar research errors being encountered and published, again, in respectable journals such as the Lancet. A Lancet editorial claimed (Lancet 1994):

> "Women doctors die on average 10 years earlier than their male counterparts, the opposite of what happens in the general population. One factor here is the suicide rate among female physicians, which is significantly higher than among male doctors".

It was soon pointed out (McManus 1995) that this suffered from similar problems to the left-handed longevity research. Being a female doctor is a cultural phenomenon more common in the late 20th century than earlier; female doctors are therefore, in general, younger than their male counterparts. McManus also casts doubt on the suicide rate claim – suicide is more common in younger people and so having a younger cohort of female doctors would explain the findings.

A few years later, the same flawed thinking reappeared; based on an analysis of the obituary columns in the British Medical Journal (Wright & Roberts 1996), Milner and Ziegler (Milner and Ziegler 1997) claimed:

> "the average age of death ... of anaesthetists ... [to be] the lowest of all doctors born in the UK. [This] ...gives sobering thought to the profession."

This as pointed out by McManus (McManus 1997) suffered again from the same problem experienced with the research into left-handed longevity in that Anaesthetics is one of the younger medical specialities, having (by the late 90's) developed substantially in the previous four or five decades and indeed its practitioners tend to be somewhat younger.

There are a few insights we can draw from these examples:
- Halpern & Coren initially defended their work with follow-up papers; so perhaps an element of confirmation bias was at play, but it does, to me, show that we could have a concept of "Dark Data Denial", that is, the

persistent belief that there are no confounding elements to one's data-set. It's understandable too: who wants to believe that one's research can be completely invalidated by something they are not even aware of?
- The second insight gives us some initial instruction on how to deal with the risks of dark data and it is simply: to check your assumptions, and not only check they are valid now, but have always been valid for the duration of the dataset's timeframe under consideration.
- The third insight is that we need to remain vigilant; it is still possible to fall into the traps of the past, and even experts can repeatedly make the same mistakes.

5 Vaccines and Car Accidents

As the SCSC Newsletter editor I maintain a 'Safety in the News' column both on the SCSC website and in the Newsletters themselves. For this, I scan online newspaper reports for interesting safety-related news items and add four or five of these in every edition.

In the Feb 2023 edition of the newsletter (Hampton 2023a), I duly reported that Canadian researchers had determined that "People who skipped their COVID vaccine are at higher risk of traffic accidents". This was based on an analysis during the summer of 2021 of government-held records of more than 11 million adults, 16% of whom hadn't received the COVID vaccine. They found that the unvaccinated people were 72% more likely to be involved in a severe traffic crash.

The authors theorised that people who resist public health recommendations might also "neglect basic road safety guidelines". This all seemed fairly plausible at the time and I duly shared the report, but my investigations into dark data now leaves me with a little unease around such a broad claim.

The study called "COVID Vaccine Hesitancy and Risk of a Traffic Crash" (Redelmeier, Wang & Thiruchelvam 2022) published in "The American Journal of Medicine" seems fairly well-considered and as well as the headline results for the entire population (covering 11,270,763 in the Ontario region of Canada) the researchers also considered subgroups such as age group, gender, location (urban/rural), socioeconomic status and other underlying health conditions and found the same results reflected broadly in each subgroup. For example, as we know statistically, young drivers are more prone to accidents than older drivers, considering vaccinated versus unvaccinated in younger drivers yielded the same results. This all seemed reasonable, with the most significant confounding factors being accounted for. However, I did have the following observations:

The "younger" age cohort range was defined as between 18-39 years and accounted for about half the crashes. This is actually quite a broad range and spans several significant statistical groups (Autoinsurance.org 2023), from some of the most dangerous to the safest.

Table 1. Age Range and Crashes

Age Range	% crashes per individual
16-24	0.022%
25-34	0.018%
35-44	0.012%
45-54	0.014%
55-64	0.024%

Polls in Canada around that time noted (Global News 2021) that younger people were more likely to refuse a vaccine so are all these results being contaminated by the simple fact that younger drivers cause more crashes and are more likely to refuse a vaccine? It would certainly be interesting to see if the report's findings still held true when assessed over these much narrower age ranges where there are shared quantified crash rates amongst the cohorts. The fact also that the results themselves show that *vaccinated* 65+ year-olds mean value data indicated *more* accidents not less, suggests some dark data is at play.

Also, the study itself admits that data associated with political affiliation and self-identified ethnicity is absent. Both span all the other subgroups and so bias in these areas would contaminate all the other subgroups and skew the entire analysis. I have not investigated these aspects in great detail but note that in Canada, the uptake in first nation and certain ethnic groups was less than those not part of a visible minority (Government of Canada 2022). This coupled with the knowledge that the vast majority of the foreign-born population live in the nation's largest urban centres where accidents are more likely given the increased volume of traffic, suggests that ethnicity is an important possibly confounding factor.

These points bring some doubt in my mind to the analysis so while it may still be correct, I would be more comfortable if these other dark data aspects were investigated. I also wonder now whether I've inadvertently helped give weight to the findings by simply sharing amongst the SCSC community – if lots of respected media outlets shares someone's findings then "surely it must be true?"

6 The Red Car Curse

Later in the year I came across the article from carVertical (Bareckas 2022), which, you'll recall from earlier, stated that red was the most dangerous car colour, as 60% of vehicles checked in their database had been involved in an accident. They also reported that white and grey were the safest colours with only 50% of those colours being involved in accidents.

I would describe carVertical as a data aggregator taking information from 900+ international databases belonging to national car registries, insurance companies, law enforcement agencies, official garages, and other institutions. This allows them to mine information about the vehicle's history, in particular, if it has been involved in an accident. They operate in 27 markets so while not truly global, they do cover Europe, Australia and the US.

I was faithfully going to reproduce this interesting result in the May 2023 newsletter when I noticed in the same article, another diagram entitled "Colour Distribution by vehicle production year", which showed the volume of vehicle colours produced between 2002 and 2020 held in their database.

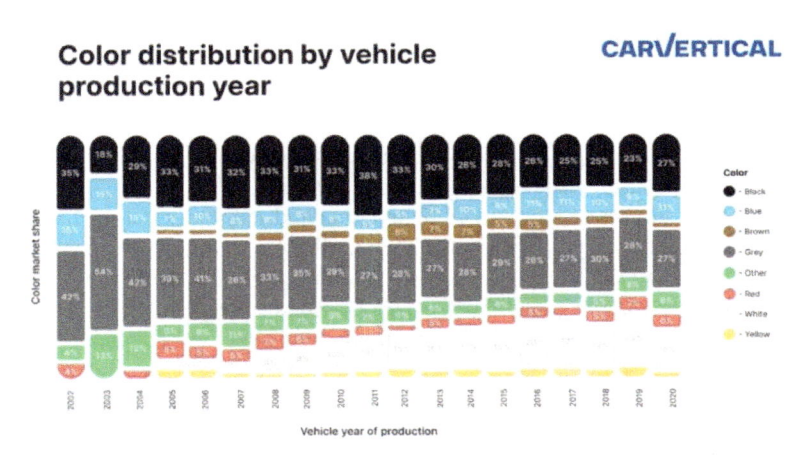

Fig. 5. Colour distribution by vehicle production year (carVertical)
(reproduced with permission from carVertical)

This showed an interesting trend – that there were very few white cars in their database between 2002 and 2007 and the volume has been growing since then, peaking at around 23% of the entries from vehicles manufactured in 2019, less than a quarter of the total population of vehicles. A couple of areas therefore worried me:

- As with the left-handed longevity research, we are seeing changes in volumes over time – so does this analysis suffer from the same issue?
- If white cars only account for a small proportion of the total cars in their database, then surely other colours like black and grey have covered many more miles and therefore have been exposed to a lot more opportunities for accidents than white cars?

Clearly, the number of miles travelled by each colour is an important factor in the crash risk, so a more pertinent metric to calculate is the crash risk for each colour by distance travelled (say every 1,000 miles). To calculate this, firstly we need to know the number of vehicles registered in the database each year, as manufactured vehicles will accumulate miles year on year from first registration.

carVertical very kindly helped estimate this by providing the number of reports requested each year, which can be used as an indicator for the volume of registered vehicles entered into their database in that year[4]. Generally, someone who buys a new car will sell another older vehicle, and the buyer may choose to get an accident report.

We can then use the article's "Vehicle year of production", which shows the percentage of vehicles by colour manufactured in the years 2002 to 2020, to determine the proportion of each colour manufactured per year and hence calculate the average number of miles travelled per colour over the 2002-2020 period.

Using the volume of accident vehicles for each colour, compared to miles travelled for that colour, we can then calculate and plot accident rates per colour per 1,000 miles travelled[5] as follows:

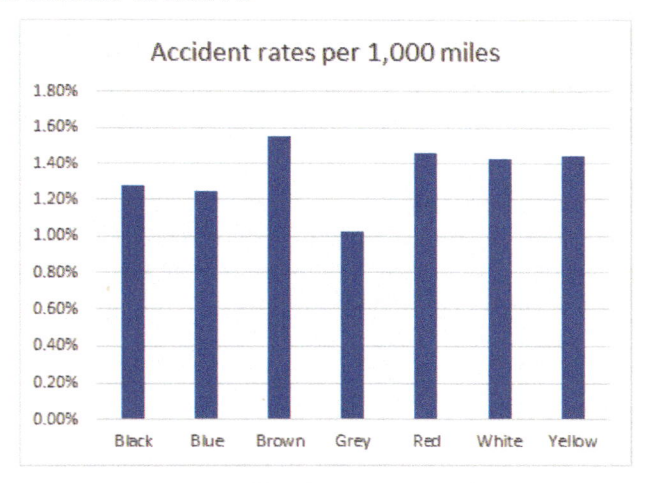

Fig. 6. Accident Rates per 1,000 miles

These results suggest that red is not actually the most hazardous colour to drive with brown being the highest and grey being notably the lowest. Red is a close

---

[4] carVertical also provided other insights such as, at the turn of the millennium, few historical damage records would have been digitised and insurance was not even mandatory in some countries at the time. The number of vehicles registered therefore increases over time and there is a notable manufacturing downturn in more recent years due to Covid-19.

[5] Slight care needs to be taken as the carVertical database records if the vehicle has had *at least one accident* and we want to ultimately know the per mile risk of an individual colour, so a Poisson distribution ($P(k$ in time $t) = (rt)^k * e^{-rt}/k!$) is applied.

second but white and yellow are not very far behind red. Black and blue seem to be notably safer than the more vibrant colours.

To be fair, I don't think my results are really any much better as I strongly suspect there is dark data lurking. I believe the most significant cause of doubt is whether there is a correlation between age and the colour of vehicle. Do younger people – the highest risk group – tend to prefer more vibrant colours? Are less-vibrant colours the domain of business fleets driven by more middle-aged people with a better safety track record simply through more years and experience of miles travelled? Are there colour preferences among genders? Do colour preferences change over time, that is, are they subject to fashion trends? A report by Youi in 2017 (Youi 2017), an Australian car and home insurance firm, illustrates these aspects providing a number of insights including the following about red cars:

- 7.81% of females have red cars compared to 5.84% of males
- Females born prior to 1960 are nearly 40% more likely to own a red car with 9.45% of them insuring a red car, compared to an average 6.81% across both genders and the whole of Australia

The gender differences highlighted here, coupled with the well-established findings that men are involved in more accidents than woman (Scholes et al 2018) just seems to add to the complexity of the problem and we can't truly be confident in the results unless all these aspects are identified and incorporated into the analysis.

With this I would simply conclude that there is too much dark data lurking to really be confident in any conclusions drawn. However, this is not the first study of the relationship between accidents and car colour so let's see what historical research has been done on this subject.

7 Literature Search

As of Sep 2023, from Internet searches, I found 40 articles and reports going back to 1995 discussing the relative risks of car colour. Many seemed to be reporting very similar findings and so I investigated the provenance of each article to trace it back to the original research.[6]

---

[6] In a sense, I was investigating how information is propagated over time, so perhaps a kind of "information epidemiology".

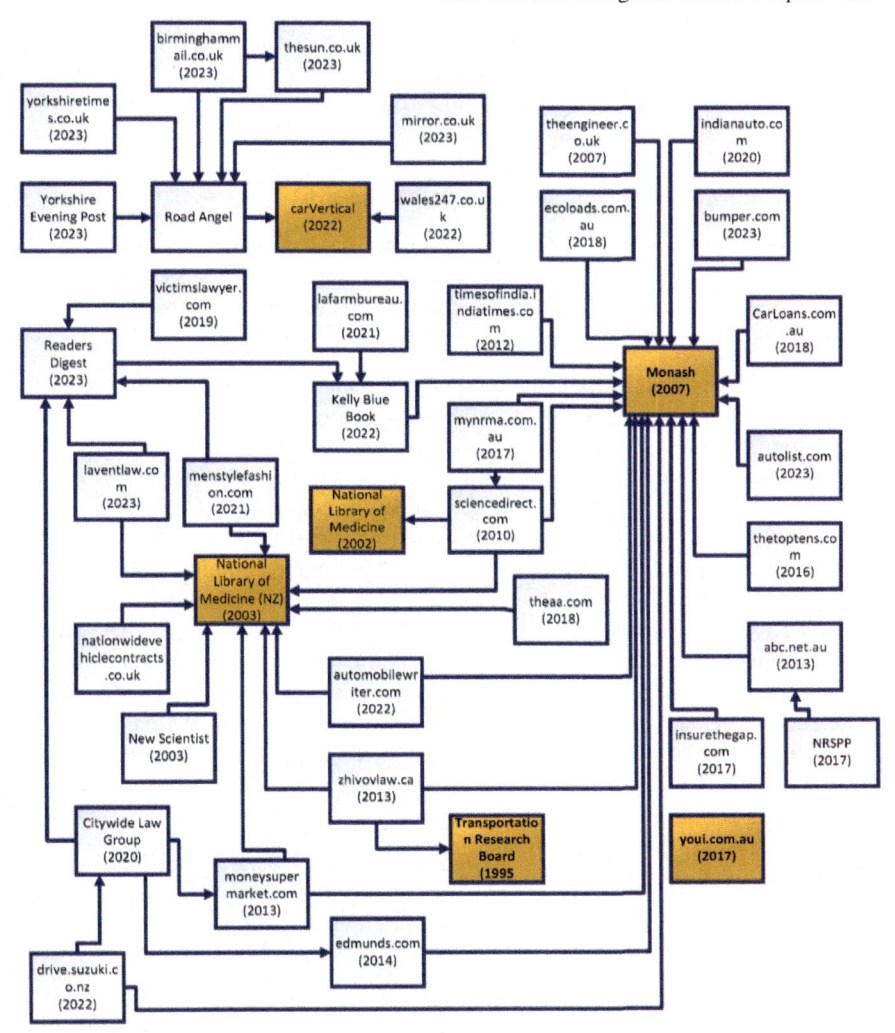

Fig. 7. Propagation of Information

The figure shows how each report traces back to 1 of 6 original studies. One study by car insurance firm Youi is unreferenced elsewhere and simply reports that green cars are the safest, but it is unclear if that is proportionate to miles travelled or simply a reflection that there are very few green cars[7] on the road compared to other colours. Another focusses only on the risks to emergency vehicles like fire engines and concluded that lighter colours like white and lime yellow were safer than the traditional red. This again was rarely referenced and not entirely the information we are looking for.

The 4 main studies that are referenced are:

- A study conducted on a Spanish population (Lardelli-Claret et al 2002)
- A study conducted on a New Zealand population (Furness et al 2003)
- A study based on population in two Australian territories (Monash 2007)
- The carVertical analysis – as already discussed (carVertical 2022)

The Lardelli-Claret study looked at a Spanish database of traffic crashes and selected those collisions from 1993 to 1999 in which only one of the drivers committed an infraction. The violators constituted the control group; the other drivers formed the case group. Information about the colour of the vehicle and other confounding variables was also collected. The study concluded that light colours (white and yellow) were associated with a slightly lower risk of being passively involved in a collision, although only under certain environmental conditions.

The Furness study was restricted to the Auckland region of New Zealand and covered a relatively short period between April 1998 and June 1999. The study population comprised all drivers of cars on public (urban and rural) roads in the region. Cases were all car drivers involved in crashes in which one or more of the occupants of the car were admitted to hospital or died. Controls were car drivers identified by cluster sampling of drivers from randomly selected sites on the road network, at randomly selected times, representative of all time spent driving in the study region during the study. As with the Lardelli-Claret study, this study was conscious of the influence of dark data and considered: age of driver, gender, educational level, ethnicity, alcohol consumption (in previous six hours), use of recreational drugs, seat-belt use, average time spent driving each week, vehicle speed, vehicle age, engine size, registration, warrant of fitness and vehicle insurance, driving licence status, road type, weather, and ambient light conditions (day, night, twilight).

The study's findings were that there was a significant reduction in the risk of serious injury in silver cars compared with white cars. There was a significant increased risk of a serious injury in brown vehicles after confounders had been adjusted for, and the risks for black and green cars were also raised. The risk of a serious injury in yellow, grey, red, and blue cars was not significantly different from that in white cars.

---

[7] If you are bored by "I Spy" on long car journeys, why not play a game I claim to have created called "Apple, Banana, Orange". Green, yellow and orange colour cars are relatively rare and so each player chooses a colour and counts the number of vehicles of their respective colour coming in the opposite direction with the winner being the one with the highest number over a set time period.

The 3rd study was conducted by Monash University's Accident Research Centre and published in 2007. Interestingly, this study was critical of the previous two studies for all the same reasons that I have presented earlier – the influence of confounding factors or dark data as I've been calling it. In particular, Monash criticised the Furness study for not including vehicle type as a factor for consideration; this turned out to be a significant influencing factor for the Monash findings. So how did Monash deal with the problem of dark data?

In my view, they handled it in a remarkable way that can give us great insight into how to manage dark data in other domains. Rather than assessing the data in absolute terms, they took a relative approach. To do this they classed accidents into two groups based on the reported accident type: accidents where vehicle visibility was a potential factor in the accident, and those where it was not, for example:

- In the first group were accidents at intersections and those where vehicles were travelling in the same and opposite directions as well as accidents where pedestrians were struck;
- The second group covered accidents where vehicle colour was unlikely to be a factor, such as, single vehicle crashes, crashes with parked vehicles or other stationary objects.

The study then took the *ratio* of the counts of the two groups for each colour. Using white as the baseline ratio, if colour was indeed a contributory factor in collisions, then the ratios, compared to white, would be higher. This elegant approach means that the effects of confounding aspects, or dark data, are effectively cancelled out and this reduces the risk of some unknown dark data affecting the analysis. To illustrate, imagine some hypothetical dark data is lurking. Suppose anyone who has seen the "Fast and Furious" franchise of movies feels compelled to buy a red car and drive dangerously around the streets to emulate the characters in the film. This unknown dark data would affect the Lardelli-Claret and Furness studies but not the Monash study as increased risk in the accidents for red car-owning "Fast and Furious" enthusiasts will be proportionate between the two groups so the ratio should remain unaffected.

8 The Monash Study in Detail

The Monash study considered police accident reports in two Australian states (Victoria and Western Australia). A much larger data set was assessed compared to other studies and covered accidents in Victoria from 1987 to 2004 and Western Australia between 1991 and 2004. Vehicle manufactured between these dates was 1982 and 2004 in both cases.

The sub-categorisation was much simpler:

- The state: Victoria or Western Australia;
- Light condition: daylight, dawn/dusk or dark;
- Vehicle type: car or four-wheel drive (4x4).

Interestingly, the study excluded commercial vehicles and taxis from the sample for the following stated reasons:

> "due to significant differences in the way these vehicles are often used and the narrower range of environments (typically urban) in which they are used. Furthermore, the relative uniformity of colour of these vehicle types did not allow adequate contrasting in the analysis design".

This was slightly disappointing as arguably, any increased risk between the two groups should be cancelled out irrespective of these specialised uses. It looks like we are not completely free of dark data influences and some selectivity is required.

The findings of the report have been reproduced in a visual infographic by National Road Safety Partnership Programme (NRSPP).

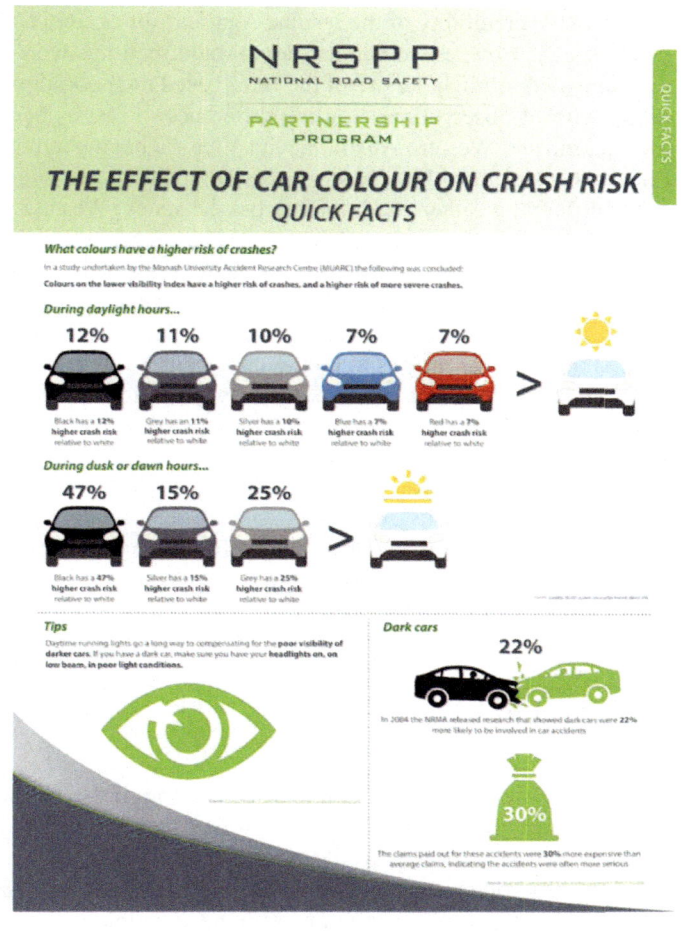

Fig. 8. NRSPP Quick Facts based on Monash Study
(reproduced under NRSSP T&Cs https://www.nrspp.org.au/terms-conditions/)

As can be seen from the figure, black is the highest risk colour peaking at 12% higher crash risk in daylight hours compared to white and rising to 47% during the dusk or dawn hours.

The data relating to vehicle type is interesting as 4x4s seem to be much more dangerous across the board compared to white with 8 of the 14 coloured cars having higher ratios (up to 49% higher). This suggests perhaps a demographic issue. The paper quotes the dynamic handling of the vehicle and says more research is required but I do suspect the relative approach to eliminating dark data is not a complete panacea.

Another interesting result from the data shows that black cars are 15% safer at night than white cars. This result is not brought out in the paper itself but adds a little uncertainty in the credibility of the results. Again, if for example, there was a reluctance of black car owners to venture out at night then this would be proportionately eliminated through the use of the ratio-based methodology.

The final significant observation is on the difference in results between the two states of Victoria and Western Australia with Victoria having a much higher dispersion of crash risk ratios than Western Australia. The paper suggests this could be due to different weather conditions across the states (Western Australia enjoys more sunshine and less rain than Victoria) and also differences in the way the data was collected between the two states (Victoria data was only when someone had been injured and Western Australia also included non-injury accidents).

With this we start to see a few cracks in the analysis; while we thought the ratio approach should be impervious to confounding factors, this might not entirely be the case. Also, if we are seeing significant variations simply between two Australian states, what sorts of variation would we see amongst countries all around the globe?

Nevertheless, in my view, this study is still the most reliable from the set of four. Although it is not without its own set of issues, it seems to tackle the issues of dark data most elegantly, and I believe there is a lot we can learn from this approach of developing a ratio of data sets to help reduce or even eliminate the impact of dark data.

9 Reframing the Question

It is possible that there was just something particular about the dynamics of the Monash study data that leant itself to an application of the ratio-based approach to tackling dark data. The approach would not be very useful if it could not be readily applied in many other situations, so I set myself the task of returning to the ill-fated study of the life expectancy of left-handed people to see if the approach could be used there. I was not optimistic, but thought if it could be applied in such a varied and different case, then this would give some confidence that it could be applied usefully elsewhere.

So, can we in some way reframe the data using this ratio technique to give us more meaningful and trustworthy results?

If you recall, the researchers thought left-handed people's lives were shortened due to the hazards of living in a world designed for right-handed people. I think we can put that to the test in a similar way to the Monash approach, so rather than asking:

"Do left- and right-handed people have an absolute difference in life expectancies?"

let us change the question to:

"Does living in a world designed for right-handed people affect the life expectancy of left-handed people?"

The questions seem very similar but there is a subtlety; a new type of data categorisation is going to be added to the equation much in the same way as the Monash study did by classifying the types of accidents (accident where vehicle colour could have been a contributing factor to an accident, and those where car colour was not important). The extra data that would presumably have been readily available from the death certificates is "cause of death". We then categorise individuals into two groups:

- **Natural**: Those where the cause of death was of natural causes (old age, illness, disease, dietary lifestyle etc.) and
- **Accident**: those where operating in a world designed for right-handed people *might* have influenced matters (car accidents, industrial or mechanical accidents, falls, trips, spills etc.).

We need to remember that the ratio of left to right-handed people changed over the years, but we can circumvent that by simply considering the ratios of death at a particular age. To illustrate, consider looking at all those individuals who died aged 65. We then take the ratio of deaths by **Accident** over those by **Natural** causes. The right-handed ratio represents the baseline, and we can then calculate the same ratio for the left-handed people at the same age and compare. We can compare different ages as long as it is the same age for left- and right-handed people under comparison. If there was a statistically significant difference in the ratios, then it seems reasonable to claim that a right-handed designed world is indeed hazardous for left-handed people. I suspect we would need a lot more than 2,000 test cases to get enough data to make the results statistically significant (and it would be interesting to see what the results would be). Nevertheless, I hope it has illustrated that by reframing the question and using data that was available but might not have originally been considered significant, we have the makings of a technique for combatting dark data that should be applicable in many other situations that we encounter. At the very least, if this technique is used in conjunction with a more traditional technique, it may help show up inconsistencies – the evidence of dark data at play.

10 Information Epidemiology

From the previous sections we see from the 40 or so articles and papers we only have four relevant papers and each one is affected by dark data in varying degrees with the Monash study probably being the least affected due to the relative nature of the analysis. As discussed earlier, the provenance of each article and paper can be traced back to one of these four and the following figure shows the growth of citations from when the first report was published in 2002.

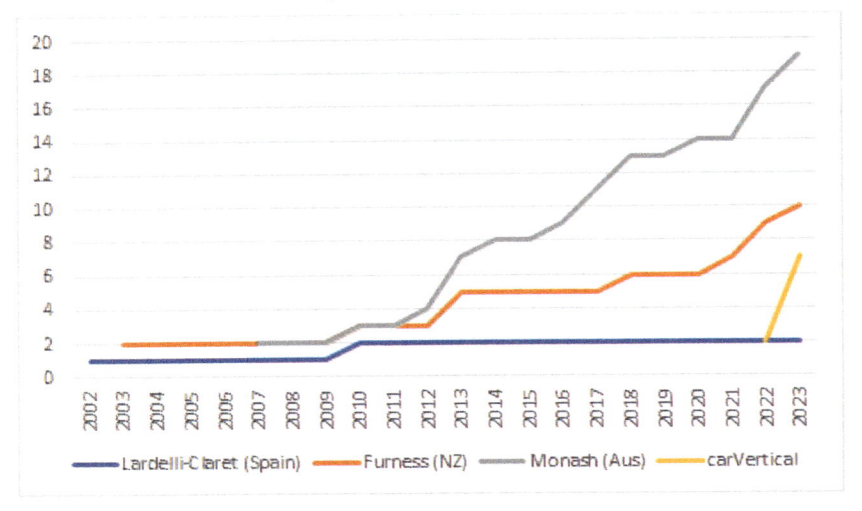

Fig. 9. Growth of Study Citations Over Time

There are some interesting observations to be drawn from this:

- The Monash study is still the most quoted work in this area and that is comforting as I would consider it the best analysis of the four;
- Despite the Furness work being criticised by the Monash study, it is still being referenced and indeed has enjoyed a relatively recent resurgence over the last few years;
- Arguably the weakest study, produced only last year, has already overtaken a study produced two decades ago and looks set to continue the trend in the coming years.

If the level of citation and internet presence is a measure of credibility, then I would suggest more care is required before results are reproduced without investigation and challenge.

11 Summary

We started our journey by looking at research published in respectable journals in the 90's on topics such as the longevity of left-handed people, nurses and anaesthetists all of which were subsequently proved incorrect due to the influences of dark data. We saw how seductive it is to draw causation from apparent correlations, and again, respected experts and peer-reviewed journals have not always detected flaws immediately and AI/ML algorithms are also, if not even more, susceptible to detecting spurious correlations.

We looked at two recent reports on: the propensity of non-Covid-vaccinated individuals to be at higher risk of car accidents and the findings that you are at higher risk driving in a red vehicle than any other colour vehicle. However, armed with our knowledge of the confounding influences of dark data and the pitfalls that have befallen experts in the past, we cast doubt over these findings.

We explored the risk of car colour in more detail, exploring what other research had been conducted over the years and discovered that, despite approximately 40 articles and reports making statements around car colour risks, the findings could be traced back to only a few historic papers, most over 15 years old. All papers seemed to be affected by dark data to varying degrees, but one paper, the Monash paper of 2007, gave us tantalising insight into how to handle dark data – by considering ratios of data sets rather than absolutes, it appears there's a way of "cancelling out" the unknowns and even the unknown unknowns.

12 Conclusion

While our topics of discussion such as left-handedness and car colour have been somewhat removed from the more mainstream system safety consideration, I would nevertheless encourage the reader to give these aspects careful thought and to see what parallels and insights can be drawn into your day-to-day work. Is there some critical statistical analysis that is underpinning your safety case? As we've seen, conclusions around causation can often be wrong due to hidden things and this can critically undermine a safety argument, so:

- Do the results look too good to be true? Do they jar with your instinct or seem too generic, sweeping and broad-brushed?
- Have you checked your assumptions and particularly their applicability over the timeline of the dataset?
- Do you really "know" your data? Is it exactly what you think it is or what it represents? There are many ways in which properties of data can be

inadvertently lost[8] or simply, over time, the provenance of data can be lost[9].

- Have you considered undertaking a different form of analysis on the same data to check the conclusions are consistent?
- Have you considered all the possible sources of dark data that might affect your dataset?
- Have you just said "of course I have!" to the previous question without further deliberation? Might the presence of unknown influences be a rather inconvenient truth and a stone better left unturned? – are you a "Dark Data Denier?"
- Is there an odd non-conforming and unexplained data point in your data set? Are these being argued away as 'statistical outliers' or worse – just glossed over or relegated to "further research is required"? The truth may be that the analysis is not reflecting the whole picture.
- Are you relying on other systems to draw conclusions from identified correlations, such as, those typical of ML training data and AI – are you confident dark data is not distorting outcomes?
- Are you relying on the findings in respected peer-reviewed journals? Are these assumed to be correct without question or would a little due diligence be in order?
- Much of what we do can be based on "expert judgement"; do you promote a healthy culture of challenge and inquiry, even for long-standing beliefs and practices, or is it a case of: "that's just how we do things round here"?

---

[8] The Data Safety Guidance (DSIWG 2023) provides guidance on assessing and managing the risk of losing data safety properties. It enumerates these properties and provides methods and techniques in managing these based on the level of risk.

[9] Work is underway on classifying the many different ways in which data can give rise to safety-related issues, some of which could be quite unexpected, such as "Black Swan Data". Classifying data risk in this way can help articulate the problem and promote the shared understanding of sometimes subtle issues. The use of animal iconography to express these concepts can be powerful and the resulting taxonomy is informally expressed as a "zoo" as we described in the newsletter article "The Data Risk Zoo" (Hampton 2023b).

13 Further Work

Despite the 40 or so articles, papers and infographics declaring that car colour has an influence on accident risk, I remain unconvinced. There is actually relatively little research that has gone into the topic over the last two decades. The research done at a regional level shows that locality is a significant factor so a truly global analysis is required to give a more comprehensive and balanced view. The carVertical database seems a promising source of global data if there was an opportunity to analyse it in more detail, although sadly, I understand the data is anonymised so much of the critically useful demographic data will not be present.

More relevant to the system safety discipline are the insights around techniques to manage the influence of dark data. We saw how using an observational analysis and a randomised control test showed disparities due to dark data's confounding factors. If using diverse analysis techniques yields the same results, then this (as with functional independence in the safety world), gives us confidence in the accuracy of the results. It would be interesting to explore what diverse techniques could complement each other best to identify the presence of dark data. Perhaps, if case studies of existing analyses could be reassessed using a different technique to see if results are indeed the same. The second promising area for future work is to explore the use of relative rather than absolute styles of statistical analysis. As we saw with the Monash paper and the reframing of the left-handed longevity question, many of the confounding issues were elegantly eliminated by using a ratio of key data types compared to a baseline. It would be interesting to find case studies that could be reassessed using a relative approach to see if it yields the same results as the original traditional approach.

Disclaimers All views expressed in this paper are those of the author.

Acknowledgements

I am extremely grateful to Matas Buzelis from carVertical for providing the additional data about the carVertical database and further insights into how it was collected. I would also like to thank Prof Chris McManus for providing the additional cases studies and for reviewing the paper.

References

Autoinsurance.org (2023) What age group has the most fatal crashes? https://www.autoinsurance.org/age-groups-fatal-crashes/, accessed Sept 2023.

Bareckas (2022), Research: Car colors and why they matter, https://www.carvertical.com/blog/car-colors-and-why-they-matter, accessed Sep 2023.

Cairney & Styles (2003), Review of the literature on daytime running lights (DRL), Report Nos. CR 218, ISBN: 0 642 25510 5, October 2003.

DSIWG (2023) Data Safety Guidance (Version 3.5), by the SCSC Data Safety Initiative Working Group (DSIWG), Jan 2023, https://scsc.uk/r127H:1

Furness et al (2003), Car colour and risk of car crash injury: population based case control study, Published in the British Medical Journal 20 Dec 2003, doi: 10.1136/bmj.327.7429.1455

Ganna & Ingelsson (2015) 5 year mortality predictors in 498 103 UK Biobank participants: A prospective population-based study. The Lancet 386(9993): 533–540.

Global News (2021) Nearly 20% of Canadians still hesitant or refusing to get COVID-19 vaccine: poll, https://globalnews.ca/news/7960345/covid-canada-vaccine-hesitancy-poll/, accessed Sep 2023.

Government of Canada (2022) COVID-19 vaccination coverage by ethnicity: Insight from the Canadian Community Health Survey (CCHS) https://www.canada.ca/en/public-health/services/immunization-vaccines/vaccination-coverage/covid-19-vaccination-coverage-ethnicity-insight-canadian-community-health-survey.html, accessed Sep 2023.

Halpern & Cohen (1988) Do right-handers live longer? Published in Nature 333, 213, 19th May 1988

Halpern & Coren (1991) Handedness and life span. The New England Journal of Medicine 324(14): 998.

Hampton (2023a) The Safety-Critical Systems Club Newsletter: Safety Systems, Vol 31. No 1 – Feb 2023.

Hampton (2023b) The Safety-Critical Systems Club Newsletter: Safety Systems, Vol 31. No 3 – Oct 2023, "The Data Risk Zoo"

Hand (2020) Dark Data: Why What You Don't Know Matters, ISBN: 069118237X

Hulley, Grad & Bush et al (1998). Randomized trial of estrogen plus progestin for secondary prevention of coronary heart disease in postmenopausal women. Heart and Estrogen/progestin Replacement Study (HERS) Research Group. JAMA 1998;280:605–13.

Lancet (1994) Volume 344 Number 8937 p1583-1648, originally published as Volume 2, Issue 8937, 10 Dec 1994

Lancet (2023) Volume 5, Issue 10, Artificial intelligence for breast cancer detection in screening mammography in Sweden: a prospective, population-based, paired-reader, non-inferiority study, DOI:https://doi.org/10.1016/S2589-7500(23)00153-X

Lardelli-Claret et al (2002), Does Vehicle Color Influence the Risk of Being Passively Involved in a Collision? Published in Epidemiology 2002; 13:721-724, 2002

Lawlor, Smith & Ebrahim (2004) Commentary: The hormone replacement–coronary heart disease conundrum: is this the death of observational epidemiology? International Journal of Epidemiology, https://academic.oup.com/ije/article/33/3/464/716652

McManus (1995) Increased mortality in women doctors. Lancet. 1995 Mar 25;345(8952):796-7. doi: 10.1016/s0140-6736(95)90676-2. PMID: 7891507.

McManus (1998) Early death amongst anaesthetists: a statistical howler, Anaesthesia. 1998 Jan;53(1):90-1. doi: 10.1111/j.1365-2044.1998.0346a.x.

McManus (2019) Half a century of handedness research: Myths, truths; fictions, facts; backwards, but mostly forwards, Brain and Neuroscience Advance, doi: 10.1177/2398212818820513

MacMillan (2015) 20 ways being left-handed impacts your health https://edition.cnn.com/2015/11/03/health/being-left-handed-health-impact/index.html, accessed Sep 2023.

Milner and Ziegler (1997) Anaesthesia (1997; 52: 797–8)

Monash (2007) An Investigation into the Relationship between Vehicle Colour and Crash Risk, Report Nos. 263, ISBN 0 7326 2333 2, May 2007.

NHS (2021) Clinical Trials, https://www.nhs.uk/conditions/clinical-trials/, accessed Nov 2023.

NICE (2019) Menopause: diagnosis and management https://www.nice.org.uk/guidance/ng23/ifp/chapter/benefits-and-risks-of-hrt, accessed Sep 2019

NRSPP (2017) The Effect of Car Colour on Crash Risk: Quick Facts, https://www.nrspp.org.au/resources/nrspp-quick-fact-effect-car-colour-crash-risk/#resource-downloads, accessed Sep 2023.

Perelle & Ehrman (1994) An international study of human handedness: The data. Published in Behavioural Genetics 24, 217–227 (1994). https://doi.org/10.1007/BF01067189

Redelmeier, Wang & Thiruchelvam (2022) COVID Vaccine Hesitancy and Risk of a Traffic Crash. Published in The American Journal of Medicine 2nd December 2022 https://doi.org/10.1016/j.amjmed.2022.11.002

Reilly (2023) https://www.educationandcareernews.com/early-childhood-education/9-weird-advantages-of-being-left-handed, accessed Sep 2023

Jiménez-Sánchez & Juodelyte (2022) Detecting Shortcuts in Medical Images - A Case Study in Chest X-rays. DOI: 10.48550/arXiv.2211.04279

Scholes et al (2018). Fatality rates associated with driving and cycling for all road users in Great Britain 2005–2013. Published in the Journal of Transport & Health 2018;8:321–33.

Stampfer & Colditz (1991) Estrogen replacement therapy and coronary heart disease: a quantitative assessment of the epidemiologic evidence. Preventative Medicine 1991;20:47–63.

Statista (2023) Estimated worldwide motor vehicle production from 2000 to 2022, https://www.statista.com/statistics/262747/worldwide-automobile-production-since-2000/, accessed Sep 2023.

Statistics Canada (2018) Immigration and Ethnocultural Diversity in Canada, https://www12.statcan.gc.ca/nhs-enm/2011/as-sa/99-010-x/99-010-x2011001-eng.cfm, accessed Sep 2023.

Statistics Netherlands (2017) https://www.cbs.nl/en-gb/news/2017/37/heavy-smokers-cut-their-lifespan-by-13-years-on-average, accessed Sep 2023

Volpato et al (2012) Hand to Mouth in a Neandertal: Right-Handedness in Regourdou 1, Published: August 22, 2012 https://doi.org/10.1371/journal.pone.0043949

WHI (2002) Writing Committee for the Women's Health Initiative randomized controlled trial. Risks and benefits of estrogen plus progestin in healthy postmenopausal women: principal results From the Women's Health Initiative randomized controlled trial. JAMA 2002;288:321–33.

Wright & Roberts (1996) Which doctors die first? Analysis of the BMJ obituary columns. British Medical Journal 1996; 313: 1581–2.

Yamaguchi, Kaneko & Narukawa (2021) Approval success rates of drug candidates based on target, action, modality, application, and their combinations, DOI: 10.1111/cts.12980.

Youi (2017) Study: What Are The Safest Car Colours and Which Are The Most Popular? Accessed Sep 2023.

Poster: Dynamic Risk Assessment in Automated Vehicles: An elaborated Approach to HARA

Nikita Bhardwaj Haupt, Peter Liggesmeyer[1]

RPTU Kaiserslautern

Abstract *Traditional Hazard Analysis and Risk Assessment (HARA) methods for highly automated vehicles (HAVs) predominantly rely on worst-case assumptions about the operational environment. This conservative approach, while ensuring safety, largely depends on the human driver to be the primary element in the control loop. With the advent of increased automation levels, the driving responsibility progressively shifts from the human to the vehicle, rendering the traditional HARA process insufficient and overly reliant on human intervention. To address this gap, our research introduces a systematic approach, elaborated HARA (elHARA), which integrates non-worst-case scenarios into the HARA process. This approach aims to better reflect the dynamic nature of the operational environment and reduce the over-dependence on human drivers for safety assurance in HAVs.*

The elHARA method systematically represents the operational situation by incorporating a variety of scenarios beyond the worst-case. This broadened perspective results in Automotive Safety Integrity Levels (ASIL) that more accurately depict the dynamic and complex nature of the automotive environment. By doing so, elHARA facilitates the identification of situation-specific safety goals and corresponding measures that are less reliant on human drivers, thereby enhancing system availability and performance. Implementing elHARA leads to a more suitable and realistic assessment of risks, reflected in appropriate ASIL values. This shift enables the development of fail-operational safety measures tailored to the varying degrees of vehicle automation. The approach effectively addresses the increased driving responsibility transferred to the vehicle, ensuring a higher level of safety without unnecessary constraints on system performance.

Our research lays the groundwork for transitioning risk assessment from design time to runtime in HAVs. The current focus is on applying the insights gained from elHARA through ontology formalism, which aims to establish a comprehensive knowledge base for real-time risk reasoning. This progression signifies a

---

[1] Chair of Software Engineering: Dependability, RPTU Kaiserslautern, Germany

© Nikita Bhardwaj Haupt, Peter Liggesmeyer 2024.
Published by the Safety-Critical Systems Club. All Rights Reserved.

pivotal step towards adaptive and responsive safety measures in the era of autonomous driving. The elHARA method marks a significant advancement in HARA processes for HAVs. By integrating dynamic, non-worst-case scenarios, it offers a more dynamic and suitable framework for safety assurance in automated vehicles, paving the way for safer, available, and more reliable autonomous driving.

The Safety Case as a Process Driver

Chris Hobbs

Rockcliffe Flight Training Unit
Ottawa, Canada

Abstract *Teaching novice pilots to fly is inherently dangerous as these students necessarily taxi, fly and fuel aircraft by themselves. This paper describes how a particular Canadian flight school integrated a Safety Assurance Case into its operations to justify the claim that the school's processes were adequately safe. Incident reports were then used as "defeaters" of the Safety Case argument and the Safety Case was used to generate a significant part of the school's Safety Management System (SMS). Treating incident reports as "defeaters" to challenge claims and evidence in the Safety Case was particularly useful: consideration of each defeater gave rise to corrective actions and, by this means, the Safety Case was continually updated as processes changed. This ensured that the flight school's procedures could be kept up-to-date and relevant.*

1 Background

The Rockcliffe Flight Training Unit (FTU) operates from the Rockcliffe airport (CYRO) in Ottawa, Canada's capital city: Figure 1. In addition to flight training, the FTU offers sightseeing rides, rents aircraft to qualified pilots and operates a maintenance facility.

Fig. 1. Rockcliffe Airport
(photograph by C. Clark)

1.1 Rockcliffe Airport

Rockcliffe airport has a single east-west runway and is "uncontrolled" (having no control tower and being accessible to aircraft without radios). Because of the proximity of Ottawa's international airport 15 km to the south, Gatineau airport 10 km to the north east and exclusion zones over the Governor General's house and Parliament, the airspace around Rockcliffe is complex as illustrated in Figure 2.

The FTU shares a runway with the Canada Aviation and Space Museum, which operates sightseeing flights in open cockpit biplanes during the summer months. It is also the home of many privately owned aircraft and is a common destination for pilots visiting Ottawa.

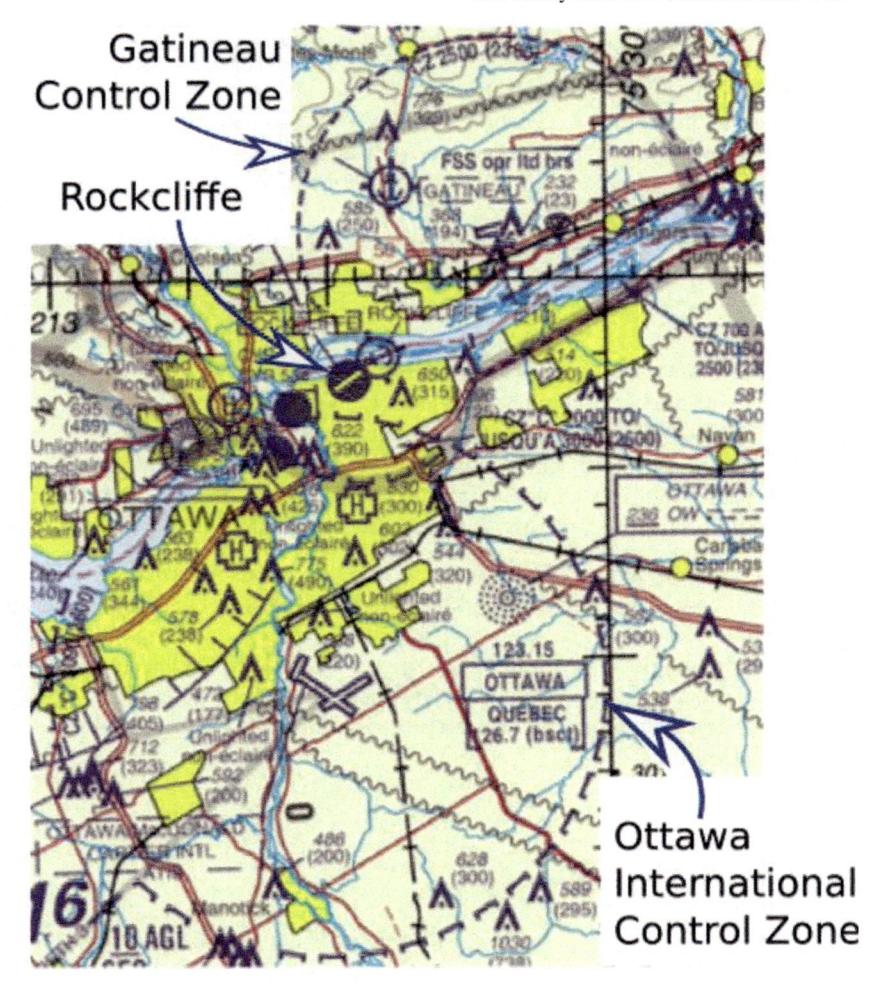

Fig. 2. The Complex Airspace around Rockcliffe Airport

1.2 Flight Training

Initial flight training typically leads to a Private Pilot Licence (PPL) which, possibly combined with a rating allowing flight at night, is normally adequate for a recreational pilot. Pilots intending to find employment in the airlines will add an instrument rating (allowing flight without visibility of the ground), a Commercial Pilot Licence (CPL) and, to build flying hours, a Flight Instructor Rating. The Rockcliffe FTU provides training for all these licences.

To obtain a PPL, a student must be at least 16 years old and must:

- take training with an instructor until the instructor is confident that the student is ready to fly solo: typically after about 20 hours of instruction.
- pass written examinations on air law and the use of the radio.
- obtain a certificate of medical fitness from an aviation medical examiner.
- fly solo (i.e. without an instructor). To do this, the student must be at least 14 years old, and sometimes a student will schedule the dual training so that the first solo flight can be flown on the student's 14th birthday.
- complete additional solo and dual flying lessons.
- fly a solo cross-country of at least 278 km.
- pass a flight test with an independent examiner.
- attend a ground school covering the theoretical aspects of flying and pass a multiple-choice written examination covering navigation, meteorology, human factors, engines, aircraft systems and air law.

Although not strictly part of the course, a student will also learn how to fuel an aircraft and how to perform the "walk-around" before flight: checking the aircraft for defects.

As can be imagined, this training involves risks and an FTU needs to be confident that those risks are reduced to an acceptable level[1]. (Daniels et al 2022) includes a description of a tragedy on a cross-country flight by a pilot working towards a Commercial Pilot Licence.

1.3 FTU Staff

In addition to the flight instructors, an FTU employs other staff whose actions affect the safety of the operation: dispatch staff who check a pilot's licences before handing over the keys of an aircraft, ramp staff who fuel and park aircraft, airport staff who perform runway inspections and operate heavy snow-clearing equipment in the winter, ground school instructors who teach the theoretical aspects of flying and clerical staff who schedule flights. All of these need relevant training and, when acting in a new role, appropriate supervision.

---

[1] In particular, it is often considered odd that in most of Canada, a person cannot drive a car alone before the age of 17 but can fly an aircraft alone at the age of 14.

1.4 Safety Culture

One particularly important aspect of safety culture in an FTU is feeling comfortable in admitting mistakes. A hard landing could damage an aircraft in a way not visible during a cursory inspection, and the safety of the next pilot to use the aircraft depends on the hard landing being reported, allowing the aircraft to be professionally inspected.

The safety culture also has to recognise the commercial pressures of running an FTU: students do not pay in advance for a course; they pay for each lesson after it is taken. This financial pressure could encourage flying when the weather is marginal or when an aircraft's state is suspect. The Rockcliffe FTU is also responsible for the state of the aircraft, employing the technicians who perform maintenance.

1.5 Incident Reporting

A reporting system is available for any pilot, student, instructor, visitor or member of staff to record an incident whenever they feel safety has been affected. An incident may be reported anonymously. Each report is handled first by the Chief Flight Instructor and is then reviewed by the FTU's Safety Committee at its next meeting. The Safety Committee looks particularly for commonalities and trends in the reports. Section 4.3 of this paper describes how these reports can act as "defeaters" in the FTU's Safety Case

2 The Safety Management System

Perhaps surprisingly, the Canadian Aviation Regulations do not stipulate that FTUs must have a Safety Management System (SMS). However, ¶ 3.1.3 of Annex 19 to the Convention on International Civil Aviation recommends that an *"approved training organization that is exposed to safety risks related to aircraft operations during the provision of its services"* should have an SMS in place. That paragraph continues by also recommending an SMS for an *"approved maintenance organization"* of the type operated at Rockcliffe.

Given these recommendations, the Rockcliffe FTU introduced its first SMS in 2010 and this was rewritten in 2023 to interact with the Safety Cases as described in this paper.

The goals of the SMS are defined to be:

1. To protect all ground visitors, visiting pilots, employees, students and other users of the aerodrome from unreasonable risk. Untrained visitors are particularly at risk in an aerodrome environment.
2. To protect those persons outside the aerodrome environment from unreasonable risk caused by aircraft owned by the FTU. Note that this excludes privately-owned aircraft based at the aerodrome and visiting aircraft.

The term "unreasonable risk" is defined to be as in ISO 26262:1-2018: *"risk judged to be unacceptable in a certain context according to valid societal moral concepts"*.

3 Summary of the Dependencies

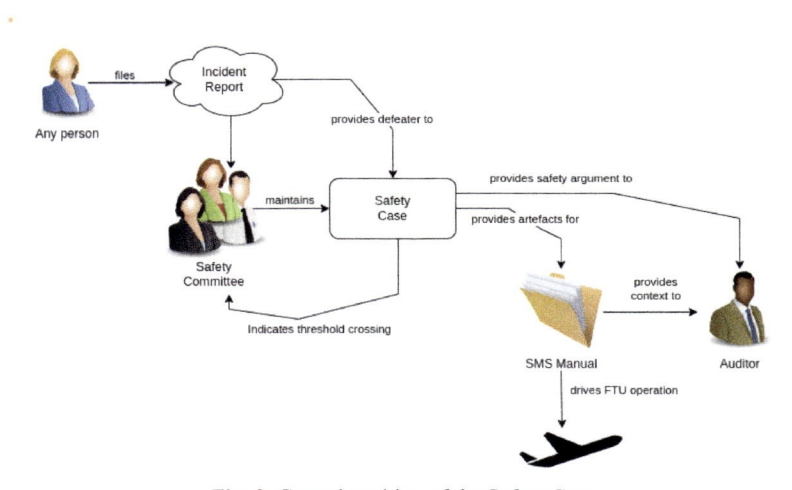

Fig. 3. Central position of the Safety Case

Figure 3 illustrates the main interactions between the various entities. Several of these are described in more detail below, but in summary:

- The FTU's Safety Committee maintains the Safety Case. This contains claims about the FTU, the argument justifying those claims and the evidence supporting the argument.
- The items of evidence listed in the Safety Case become artefacts in the Safety Management System (SMS) Manual that forms the basis of the FTU operations and is available for internal and external auditing.
- Anyone, including visitors, may file a report describing an incident where safety was believed to be adversely affected. This is categorised

by the Safety Committee and often challenges a claim or piece of evidence in the Safety Case: causing a "defeater" to be added.
- The tool used for recording the Safety Case, "Socrates" from Critical Systems Laboratory, allows event counts and thresholds to be maintained. When the pattern of particular incidents exceeds a predefined threshold, the Safety Case informs the Safety Committee of a trend, allowing this to be examined in detail.

4 Creating the Safety Case

The Safety Case prepared for the FTU follows the conventional pattern of defining a context, a top-level claim (goal), an argument and the evidence to support the argument. Following the advice in UL 4600 *("Collection of data before argument has been created is prone to be inappropriately used as evidence for that argument")*, no attempt was made to identify the evidence until the argument structure had been defined and agreed with the stakeholders: in particular the Chief Flight Instructor and the board of directors. As the Safety Case approach does not seem to have been used for an FTU previously, the argument had to be created from scratch and, although the current author was very familiar with preparing a Safety Case for a product, preparing one for a process was breaking new ground.

The top level of the argument of the FTU's Safety Case is illustrated in Figure 4 which shows the primary claim (C0001) that the FTU is adequately safe, backed by four subclaims.

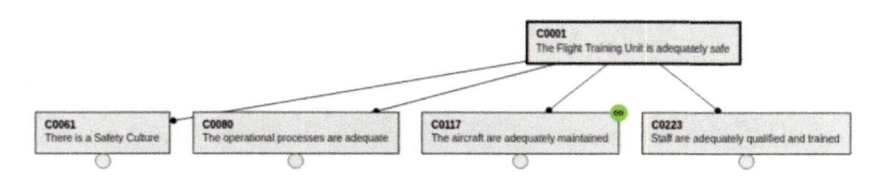

Fig. 4. Top-Level Safety Case Claims

The context (not shown in Figure 4, but included in the full diagram) excludes activities not authorised by the FTU, such as someone breaking into the airport and getting hurt while trying to start an aircraft without permission. "Special Events" such as air shows are also excluded. Given this context, the subclaims shown in Figure 4 claim that the aircraft being adequately maintained, the staff being adequately trained and the operational processes being adequate are sufficient, given a strong safety culture, to support the claim that the FTU is adequately safe.

An FTU is subject to external regulations defined in section 406 of the Canadian Aviation Regulations (CARs), but as with most regulations, while these can form a useful foundation, compliance is inadequate to assure safety. The requirements in the CARs are also general, and do not take into account particular conditions at a specific FTU. To this end, a claim that the FTU is compliant to the CARs is made within the Safety Case; but this is one claim amongst several.

4.1 The Safety Case driving the SMS

Each branch of the argument in the Safety Case is terminated by one or more items of evidence. To support the argument (and thereby the top-level claim), these items must exist and be of suitable quality.

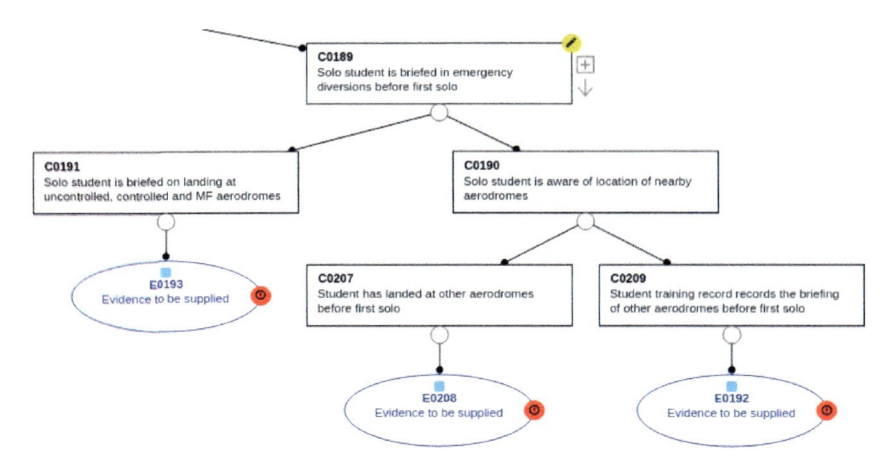

Fig. 5. Example of Supporting Evidence

Figure 5 illustrates some of the items of evidence required to support the claim that, before being sent on a first solo flight, a student pilot is adequately briefed about the options available should the runway at Rockcliffe Airport become unavailable (e.g. because of another aircraft on the runway with a flat tyre). For example, claim C0191 and its supporting evidence E0193 draw attention to the evidence available to show that students are briefed about landing at a controlled airport such as Ottawa International before their first solo.

Each of these demands for items of evidence becomes a policy in the SMS: in the case of evidence E0193 it leads to the policy in the SMS that students be briefed about landing at other airports before their first solo flight. During an internal or external audit, the assessor may use the Safety Case to demand to see the evidence described in E0193: perhaps training records for students recently sent solo.

In this way, the Safety Case becomes the generator for a large part of the SMS Manual and, whenever the Safety Case is updated, those parts of the revised SMS Manual follow without manual effort. Some manual effort is required to keep the remainder of the SMS Manual up to date, but even this is guided by the structure of the Safety Case.

4.2 Defeaters in the Safety Case

(Goodenough et al 2015) introduces the concept of defeaters in a Safety Case. Typically, these are of one of three types:

1. A clear counterexample to a claim (goal). A claim might state that X is true, and this type of defeater would provide evidence of a counterexample indicating that X is not true. For example, it might be claimed that all new staff members are trained in the use of the SMS within two weeks of joining the staff. If evidence were found that Jane Smith had not been so trained, then this would be presented as a counterexample.
2. A doubt thrown onto the quality of a piece of evidence. For example, a technician's report might be presented as evidence that an aircraft having undergone maintenance was again airworthy, but this would be defeated if it were found that the report had not been approved by a certified mechanic.
3. A doubt thrown onto the link between a claim and the supporting evidence. This is in effect saying that the claim may well be true and the evidence may be of high quality, but the evidence does not support the claim. For example, a commercial pilot licence includes the authority to fly at night and a claim might be made that a check is made to ensure someone renting an aircraft after dark is certified for night flying. The evidence presented might be the renter's commercial pilot licence. However, the link between the claim and the evidence can be broken because there is one condition where the possession of a commercial pilot licence does not allow night flying: if the pilot is red/green colour-blind!

Such defeaters are typically found during an audit. As described above, the items of evidence in the Safety Case become supporting artefacts in the SMS and these are audited both internally within the FTU and by an external agency (Transport

Canada). However, incident reports reviewed by the Safety Committee may also be defeaters, as shown in the next section.

4.3 Using Actual Incident Reports as Defeaters

4.3.1 Example 1: Defeater for the Safety Case Context

As described above, the Safety Case was built under the context that excluded activities not authorised by the FTU. This assumption was attached to the top-level claim largely as a formality, but proved to be prescient. When it was written, it was seen as being largely unnecessary, as untrained people do not, in general, break into airports to steal aircraft. However, on 14th September 2023 exactly that happened: a person broke into the Rockcliffe airport, cut the grounding wire on the magnetos of a private aircraft, hand-propped the engine to get it started (he didn't have the ignition key) and attempted to take off from a taxiway, rather than a runway. The aircraft reached about 4 metres above the ground before crashing, damaging two other private aircraft as it did so. See Figure 6. The occupant was not fatally injured.

Fig. 6. The stolen aircraft

This incident led to discussion at the Safety Committee about the safety implications of the assumed context: stealing an aircraft and trying to fly it was a very obvious activity, but what if the person had silently moved along the line of aircraft, subtly damaging each? There are, of course, many other highly unlikely events including a suicidal instructor. This led to a discussion of Principle 4+1 when applied in this area: the amount of analysis should be commensurate with

The Safety Case as a Process Driver 153

the contribution of the context to system risk (Hawkins et al 2013). The Committee needed to determine how often such a security breach occurs at an airport and, at the time of the submission of this paper, that study is ongoing.

4.3.2. Example 2: Defeaters within the Safety Case

One claim in the Safety Case, as illustrated in Figure 7, is that criteria for when a pilot (student, rental pilot or instructor) may be dispatched (given the keys of an aircraft) are defined: claim C0316, supported by evidence E0317. Another part of the Safety Case argument covers staff training and the claim is made there that the dispatch staff are trained to follow the defined criteria before dispatching an aircraft.

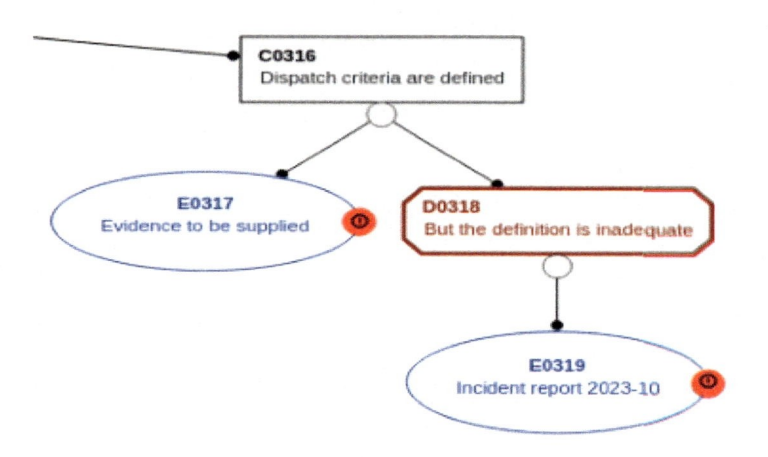

Fig. 7. Example Defeater

An incident report (number 2023-10) was submitted to the FTU in April 2023 indicating that a pilot who had not yet obtained a licence had been dispatched without proper authorisation. The conditions were complex (the student's instructor who would have approved the flight was held up in traffic, and the question of whether another instructor could approve the flight after a telephone call was not fully defined), but this led to a defeater (D0318) being added to the Safety Case as shown in Figure 7. Of course, evidence must be provided to defeat a claim and in this case incident report 2023-10 is the evidence that the definition is inadequate: there was a situation that it didn't cover.

At the time, the Safety Committee identified the corrective action of revising the dispatch criteria and organising a meeting of all concerned with the Chief

Flight Instructor. It was felt that this would be adequate to prevent a similar problem in the future. How to show that a defeater has been defeated (i.e., that the identified problem has been resolved) exercised the group working on issue 3 of the Goal Structuring Notation. It was felt that the fact that a defeater had been raised, even if it was now resolved, was useful information. The notation of putting a large cross through the defeater was agreed. But this can lead to diagrams that are difficult to read.

In this case, the defeater of the defeater was itself defeated when, in June 2023, another incidence report (number 2023-25) was filed, reporting another student pilot being dispatched inappropriately. The circumstances were different, but the outcome was the same. Figure 8 illustrates the updated Safety Case: the additional evidence has been added to the defeater D0318, but, more importantly, a count ("indicator") has appeared on claim C0316 indicating a trend. An investigation into the history of dispatching students uncovered another such incident a year before: now recorded as incident 2023-30.

It would, of course, be possible to record trends and repetitions in another document, but including this information directly (and visually) in the Safety Case, ensures that they come to the attention of the Safety Committee.

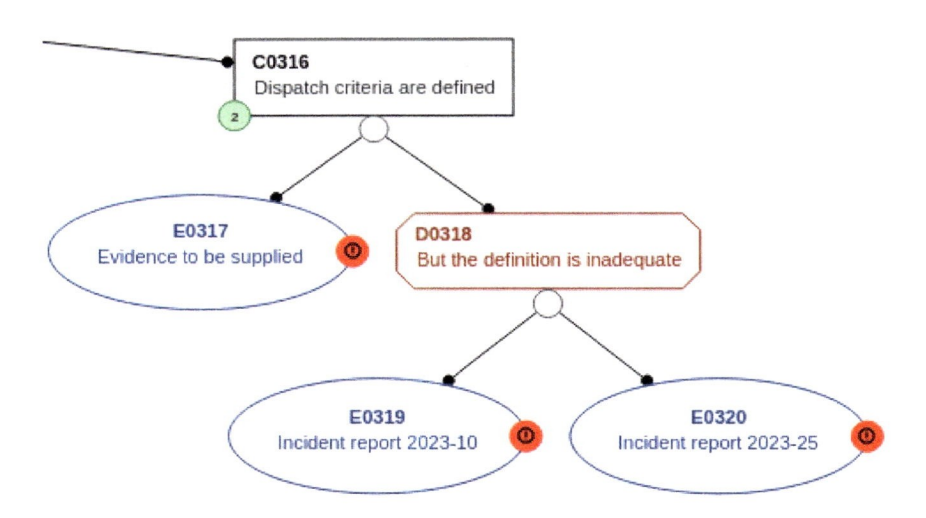

Fig. 8. Indication of a trend

Other examples of defeaters can be found in the incident reports considered by the Safety Committee. For example, incident report 2023-27 describes confusion about the completion of a weight-and-balance calculation before a rental pilot was dispatched. For a flight to be safe, not only must the aircraft be below its maximum gross weight, but the balance point of the aircraft must be within defined limits. This involves knowing the unloaded weight of the aircraft, the amount of fuel on board and the weights of the pilot and passengers. With those data, a calculation can be performed to ensure that the aircraft is within its loading limits. One of the claims within the Safety Case was that the tools (weighing machine, calculation program) for calculating the Weight and Balance are available and are used before the rental pilot is dispatched. Incident report 2023-27 describes a rental pilot being dispatched with an incorrect Weight and Balance calculation, providing a defeater for that claim.

5 Summary

Safety Cases, and other types of Assurance Cases such as Security Cases, are common in many critical industries and are required by standards such as ISO 26262 and UL 4600. However, in the author's experience, applying the Safety Case argument to a process-related claim is less common than applying it to a product-related claim.

Being associated with an intrinsically dangerous organisation — one that teaches novice students to fly light aircraft by themselves — we have applied the argument structure to the processes of the organisation and found that this not only laid the groundwork for the FTU's Safety Culture, it also formed the basis of a large part of the Safety Management System and provided a common repository for tracing trends in incident reports.

Perhaps most importantly, preparing and maintaining the Safety Case has made us think deeply about those aspects of our operation that affect the safety of our stakeholders: instructors, students, passengers and observers.

6 Further Work

The approach outlined in this paper is very much "work-in-progress": at the time that the paper was submitted, the Safety Case and the processes described here were only 8 months old. We are often finding new ways in which the Safety Case can assist with the work of the Safety Committee.

As far as we are aware, Rockcliffe is the only FTU in Canada using a Safety Case as the centre of its safety culture, but we believe that this would be a useful focus, not only for FTUs, but also elsewhere in the aviation industry.

The Transportation Safety Board of Canada is the body that analyses safety incidents from aviation, rail, marine and pipelines in Canada. This body has noted that some commercial aviation operations, such as Air Taxi operations, have more reported incidents than others, such as the Airlines. The board has called on Transport Canada to improve the safety of Air Taxi operations and the current author has proposed the Safety Case approach outlined in this paper to Transport Canada. A generic Safety Case could be prepared that could be modified as appropriate by each Air Taxi operation to form the basis of the operation's Safety Culture, SMS and audits (internal and independent).

Acknowledgments I would like to acknowledge the Rockcliffe FTU's Safety Committee and board of directors. They adopted the unusual approach to safety management outlined in this paper with enthusiasm and collaborated to make it work.

References

Daniels D, Hobbs C, McDermid J, Parsons M, Twomey B (2022) Could the Introduction of Assured Autonomy Change Accident Outcomes? Proceedings of the Thirtieth Safety-Critical Systems Symposium.

Goodenough, J.B, Weinstock, C.B, Klein, A.Z. (2015) Technical Report CMU/SEI-2015-TR-005. Eliminative Induction: A Basis for Arguing Confidence in System Properties, Software Engineering Institute, Carnegie Mellon University.

Hawkins, R, Habli, Ibrahim, Kelly, T. (2013) Principled Construction of Software Safety Cases. Workshop on Next Generation of System Assurance Approaches for Safety Critical Systems (SASSUR)

Driving the Development Process from the Safety Case

Christopher Hobbs[1], Simon Diemert[2], Jeff Joyce[2]

1 - Blackberry QNX, Ottawa, Canada

2 - Critical Systems Labs Inc., Vancouver, Canada

Abstract *The production of a Safety Case is often seen as the "wrapping up" of the safety process – an activity that begins after earlier steps, such as hazard and risk analysis, have been completed. This misses the opportunity to benefit from the critical thinking that underlies a high-quality Safety Case. Especially when using Eliminative Argumentation, an incremental approach to the Safety Case can make the entire development process more efficient. In a range of industries including automotive, aerospace, energy, nuclear and rail, we have witnessed the benefits of starting Safety Case production early. We have used an incremental approach to the Safety Case to help shape the functional safety concept, derive safety requirements, influence system and software architectures, and focus validation and verification in a way that is commensurate with the system and is most likely to yield useful results.*

1 Introduction

As functional safety standards become less prescriptive ("do A, B, and C") and more goal-oriented ("show that your system is adequately safe/secure"), Assurance Cases are becoming important tools for justifying the claim that our product and/or process is adequate. This paper shares real-world experience in support of an incremental approach to Safety Case development that drives the development process from its first steps, rather than being just a "wrapping up" activity. It also describes how Safety Case development helps to de-risk project completion dates and budgets. Two real-world projects are described in use cases below: one where failure to follow the recommendations in this paper led to difficulties, and one where following the recommendation was successful.

This industry experience report speaks directly to a fundamental question about the role of Assurance Cases in the engineering lifecycle of critical systems.

© Blackberry QNX and Critical Systems Labs Inc. 2024.
Published by the Safety-Critical Systems Club. All Rights Reserved.

Should the development of an Assurance Case have a 'front row seat' in the engineering lifecycle, or is it just a documentation exercise that follows behind the design of a critical system? Our two real-world projects provide empirical evidence in favour of having the assurance process be a driving influence as early as possible in the lifecycle.

In addition to the use cases described below, we have also been involved with projects that have benefited from using the Safety Case to eliminate work thought to be essential. In a project to extend a software library to permit formal proofs of correctness, the analysis carried out for the first draft of the Safety Case found that a significant amount of planned verification work was unnecessary and could be eliminated without affecting the safety of the product. In another project, we used Eliminative Argumentation (described below) to identify particular situations that warranted intensive simulation-based testing. By identifying this early in the project, it was incorporated into the project plan rather than being a surprise later.

2 The Safety Case

This paper deals with the safety variant of the Assurance Case, the Safety Case. The traditional definition of a Safety Case is: "*a structured argument, supported by a body of evidence that provides a compelling, comprehensive and valid case that a system is safe for a given application in a given operating environment*" (Defence Standard 00-56). Although this definition contains useful information, for the reasons discussed below, it is now considered inappropriate. It also focuses the Safety Case on a developed and deployed *system*, but a Safety Case can also be used to argue the adequate safety of a *process* or *service*. The system and the process often interact when a new system's deployment leads to changes in operating practices. These procedural changes may also need to be covered in the Safety Case.

One example of a process Safety Case we prepared concerns the processes of a flight school that teaches novice pilots. Early pilot training is intrinsically dangerous (pilots with little experience are necessarily sent to fly by themselves), and it is important to be able to justify that the school's processes adequately reduce the risk (Hobbs 2024).

Many safety standards require the production of a Safety Case, but some (for ex-ample Part 2 of ISO 26262:2018) see this as just a collection of artefacts: the evidence. However, Part 10 of ISO 26262:2018, which is informative rather than normative, describes an argument-first Safety Case.

EN 50129 provides a table of contents for a Safety Case and UL 4600 (Underwriter Laboratories 2022), a goal-based standard, requires a Safety Case as the primary artefact.

It could be said that ISO 26262 and EN 51029 see the Safety Case as a "wrapping up" activity: something to complete just before deployment to demonstrate that the product is adequately safe for deployment. UL 4600, on the other hand, can be interpreted as building the product development on the Safety Case, as argued below.

3 Avoiding Bias in the Safety Case

As humans, we are all subject to bias, and this bias can easily find its way into the Safety Case, rendering it invalid. It was mentioned above that the traditional definition of a Safety Case is considered inappropriate. This is because of the bias it introduces into the Safety Case preparation. As early as 1620, Francis Bacon noted that we are subject to confirmation bias (Bacon 1620):

> "The general root of superstition is that men observe when things hit, and not when they miss, and commit to memory the one, and pass over the other. ... It is the peculiar and perpetual error of the human intellect to be more moved and excited by affirmatives than by negatives; whereas it ought properly to hold itself indifferently disposed towards both alike."

Confirmation bias leads us to notice evidence that supports our existing beliefs and to ignore evidence that contradicts what we already believe. This makes the traditional definition of a Safety Case dangerous: if an engineer is asked to produce an argument that a system is sufficiently safe, then that engineer has been given the implicit notion that the system is safe and will look for evidence supporting that belief, ignoring counter-evidence: "Safety cases tend also to give the answer that the customer or designer wants, i.e. 'that the platform is safe'" (Haddon-Cave 2009).

Eliminative Argumentation, as described below, has been applied very successfully to avoid such bias and perhaps a better definition of a Safety Case would be *an unbiased structured argument, supported by a body of evidence, that provides a compelling, comprehensive, and valid case of whether a system is safe for a given application in each operating environment.*

Bias may also be introduced by collecting evidence too early: the stress on the "structured argument", backed by "evidence", in the definition given above is particularly important — the evidence must back the argument, not drive it. Many sources (for example UL 4600) have pointed out that collecting evidence before the argument structure is formulated and agreed can lead to the argument being built around the available evidence, rather than the evidence being collected to support the argument: "Pitfall: Data collected before argument has been created is prone to be inappropriately used as evidence for that argument. EXAMPLES:

Through cherry-picking and moving the goalposts" (Underwriter Laboratories 2022).

There have been notable occasions where bias in the preparation of the Safety Case has led to disaster: see, for example (Haddon-Cave 2009) which details how a Safety Case was influenced by time pressure and by an assumption that the system was "obviously safe" and that producing the Safety Case reduced simply to a tick-box exercise.

4 Mapping the Safety Case to the Project Lifecycle

We argue that driving the project lifecycle from the Safety Case analysis is natural because the steps in constructing a Safety Case relate to specific phases in product development:

1. Define the boundaries of the product or process being analysed, e.g. should the analysis cover field upgrades? This maps to a project's concept phase.

2. Define the primary claim that is being made about the product or process. This claim determines the risk to be mitigated during testing as defined in ISO 29119, thereby allowing the verification activities to be planned.

3. Without considering the available evidence, build an argument to show whether the primary claim is valid. This consists of assumptions and sub-claims and is often expressed in some form of graphical notation: typically Goal Structuring Notation (GSN) (Assurance Case Working Group 2021b), or as a Bayesian Belief Network (Hobbs and Lloyd 2012). This is where architectural and design decisions are validated.

4. Agree on the argument structure with the stakeholders and rework until all are satisfied: "If I were to provide the evidence to back this argument, would you find it convincing?" This reduces project risk, particularly that associated with certification.

5. Seek the evidence required to back the argument. This again allows project deliverables to be planned: "we will need evidence that X was carried out".

6. Keep the Safety Case alive during the lifetime of the product or process — as redesigns occur or field data become available use these to update the Safety Case.

This flow is augmented using Eliminative Argumentation (see below), but it can be seen that the Safety Case analysis maps cleanly to an agile (e.g. spiral) or even a waterfall development process.

5 Eliminative Argumentation

Eliminative Argumentation (EA) was introduced into the Safety Case production to help counter the bias described above, particularly confirmation bias. EA was initially described by Goodenough et al., and later extended by general guidance (Assurance Case Working Group 2021a). EA is sometimes called "Eliminative Induction" or "Dialectic Argumentation" (Assurance Case Working Group 2021a). EA adds doubt to the Safety Case. As originally proposed by Goodenough et al., three types of doubt (each backed by evidence) are possible (Goodenough et al. 2013):

1. Direct doubt about the accuracy of a (sub-)claim by providing a counter-example. For instance, "you claim that all the identified tests were run, but the test log (evidence) indicates that test 2727 was not executed".

2. Doubt about the quality of a piece of evidence. For example, "you have provided report ABC123 as evidence, but it has never been approved".

3. Doubt about whether the evidence supports the claim. This is the most subtle and, possibly, the most prevalent form of doubt. For example, "You have claimed that the product has been adequately verified and have produced test results as evidence. However, for a multi-threaded system such as this, testing is inadequate to demonstrate correctness." Here the claim may be true and the evidence convincing, but the evidence does not support the claim.

These types of doubt are termed "defeaters" because their purpose is to defeat the safety argument. In its most extreme form, EA's doubting could be applied by requesting that the engineer produce an argument, backed by evidence, that the system is *not* safe for deployment, thus using confirmation bias positively. Then each of those arguments would need to be eliminated in order to demonstrate that the system *is* safe.

A less extreme form has been used successfully by the authors, where EA has been used to identify doubt by inverting the questions. Rather than asking a developer, "Is process X followed?", we now ask, "Can you think of any time when process X was *not* followed?". This has led not only to the identification of gaps that had not been noticed in previous Safety Cases, but also to improved morale in the development teams: "I've always been a little worried about this, but no one ever asked me about it. I feel better now I've mentioned it."

6 Use Case 1: Certified Operating System

Use case 1 describes a project where a Safety Case should have been produced earlier. BlackBerry QNX certified its Operating System (OS) to IEC 61508 at SIL3 in 2010. It has maintained this certification and added IEC 62304 and ISO 26262 certification for the OS, hypervisor, mathematics library and other elements. Each of these certifications has required the production of a Safety Case. For one of the initial releases of QNX OS for Safety, we applied EA for the first time. At this time the Goal Structuring Notation (GSN) standard (Assurance Case Working Group 2021b) had not incorporated dialectics, so we used EA.

The Safety Case, finalized at the end of the project, was quite substantial, containing approximately 200 claims along with numerous unique pieces of evidence and many defeaters (EA nodes). Incorporating EA was a resounding success: it identified some 25 problems that had not been detected in previous Safety Cases. Some of the problems were dealt with without serious effect on the project schedule, but others required larger fixes, typically involving changes to development processes. Had these been found earlier, by using the Safety Case analysis throughout the project, this would have been inconvenient, but could have been handled. As it was, some additional work was needed to prepare and explain concession requests to the certification body. The remedial work was then scheduled and traced.

7 Use Case 2: Certified Bootchain Startup Function

Use case 2 describes a project where the early and continued use of the Safety Case was a positive force in the project.

BlackBerry QNX's Startup Function is the final step in the bootchain, running immediately before control of the processor is passed to the OS kernel. It initialises the memory-management unit, initialises hardware interfaces, and creates the "system page", that provides the OS with details about the hardware platform. The Startup Function is certified to ISO 26262 at ASIL D. The Startup Function comprises a Startup Module and a Startup Verifier that execute in sequence in a classic "doer-checker" architecture (see Figure 1). ISO 26262's ASIL decomposition strategy was used to decompose the ASIL D integrity between the Module, a QM component that performs the initialisation, and the Verifier, an ASIL D component that checks the initialisation was performed correctly. If the initialisation is correct, the Verifier transfers control to the OS kernel; if not, it transitions the processor into a persistent fail-safe state.

Driving the Development Process from the Safety Case   163

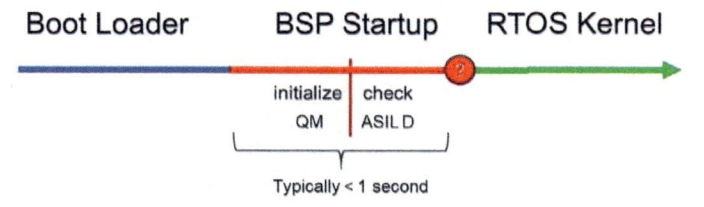

Fig. 1. Startup Function execution sequence (doer-checker pattern).

Using EA, a detailed technical Safety Case for the Startup Function was prepared. The top-level argument (see Figure 2) has been sanitized to protect proprietary data and uses the GSN: a rectangle holds a (sub-)claim, a parallelogram holds a strategy, an oval holds evidence and a rectangle with rounded corners represents a defeater. Shaded boxes indicate that the node is a root of a sub-tree that has nodes underneath.

The top-level claim is focused on the specific function of the system. This claim is supported by an argument whose overall strategy is to show that the ASIL decomposition approach is adequate.

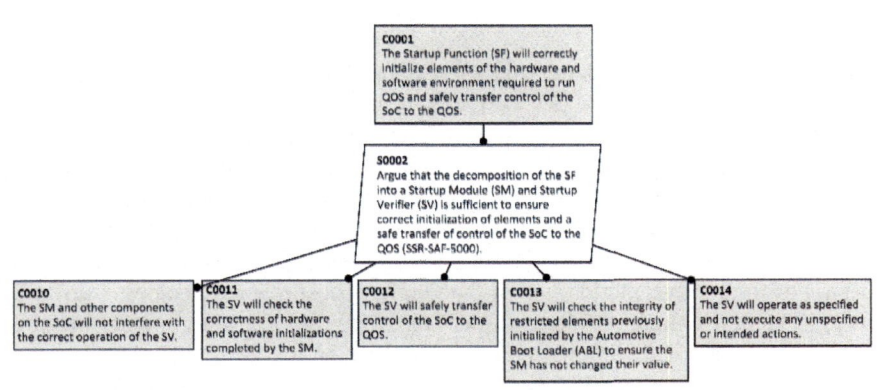

Fig. 2. Top-level argument structure of the Safety Case for Safety Function.

Continuing along one branch of the argument, for example, consider node C0012 which claims that the transfer of control from the Startup Verifier to the kernel is done correctly. Using EA, we identified two sources of doubt: the Startup Verifier could transfer control even if it detects an invalid initialisation or could transfer control to an incorrect address. As shown in Figure 3, these two sources of doubt are explicitly captured in the EA by a pair of defeater nodes, D0024 and D0025, which are children of C0012.

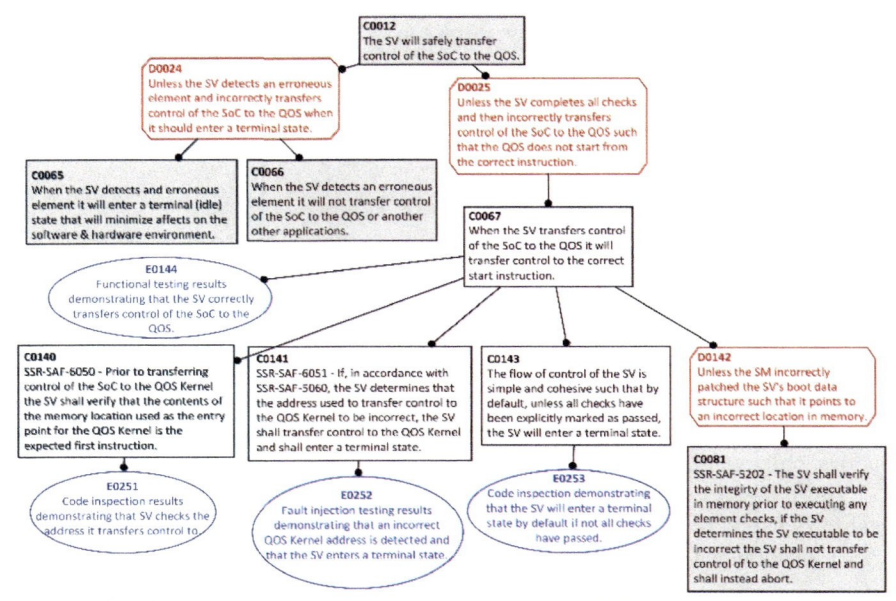

Fig. 3. Detailed sub-argument from Safety Case for QNX Startup Function.

The first of these two defeaters, D0025, is refuted by a pair of sub-arguments rooted at C0064 and C0065 respectively. These sub-arguments refer to various diverse measures used by this safety function to detect erroneous elements. Within these sub-arguments, there are additional defeaters that explore ways in which error checking might be incomplete or otherwise compromised. These defeaters are also addressed by lower levels of argumentation. Like other parts of the overall argument, the development of these sub-arguments largely drove the design of the safety function, rather than being a post-design "wrapping up" activity. The development of the argument including these sub-arguments was the focal point of the critical thinking process for design.

The second of the two defeaters under C0012, namely, D0025, captures a potential source of doubt concerning the destination address of the "jump" instruction that, when executed as the final step of the Startup Verifier, is supposed to transfer control to the entry point of the QNX Operating System kernel. With sufficient technical knowledge, it is possible to imagine a variety of ways in which the destination address might be wrong. For example, some previous step in the execution of the boot chain might have overwritten the location in memory that contains the destination address. The full details of the sub-argument developed in this EA to refute D0025 involve technical details not suitable for discussion here. However, Figure 3 shows a simplified view of this sub-argument including references to static and dynamic evidence, E0144, E0251, E0252 and E0253. The sub-argument also includes examples of claims that embody technical requirements. Such requirements are easily recognized in Figure 3 as "shall" statement prefixed with a unique identifier of the form "SSR-SAF-nnnn". For example, C0140 cites a requirement, SSR-SAF-6050, for a runtime check that the destination address for the jump instruction is in fact the correct value. This branch of the argument is terminated by an evidence node E0251, referring to inspection of the source code.

Other branches of the argument similarly follow a dialectical pattern of critical thinking in which defeaters explicitly capture sources of doubt, which are then ad-dressed by sub-arguments. Substantial portions of the argument correspond closely to the "back and forth" flow of actual discussions within the development team during the design phase of the Startup Verifier. Drawing on the highly specialized knowledge of experienced software developers, numerous "what if?" scenarios were studied. For example, "what if the page tables are corrupted?", "what if the executable code for the Startup Verifier is corrupted?", and so on. Later, during the certification process for this Startup Verifier, some of these "what if?" questions resurfaced when technical experts from the certification authority studied the design. In many cases, their questions were answered by directing their attention to the respective defeater in the argument and its refutation.

Overall, the Safety Case contained 551 nodes, see Figure 4. Of interest is the number of residual doubts ("RESIDUAL"). These are defeaters that could not be resolved by further argumentation or evidence. Residual doubts are a normal and healthy part of a safety analysis (Diemert et al. 2020) and were used to communicate residual risks to management and the end customers, by entries in the product's safety manual.

We began the Safety Case analysis at the beginning of the Startup Function project, focusing initially on establishing high-level safety arguments including why we believed the ASIL decomposition strategy was suitable. Doing so helped us shape the detailed design of the components. We paired this with a Functional Safety Concept, as in ISO 26262, describing our overall safety strategy.

As the project progressed, we regularly reconsidered and elaborated the arguments based on the evolving design and implementation. As the software safety requirements were defined, we included them in the argument: one completeness criterion for the Safety Case being that every safety requirement be in the argument.

We also used EA's defeaters to describe concerns about the design as work progressed. Many of these defeaters arose from the detailed technical analyses (e.g. fault tree and failure modes and effects analyses). Another criterion for completeness was that every leaf from a fault tree and every failure mode be represented in the Safety Case by a defeater (we used abstraction to cover multiple similar failure modes where appropriate). Mitigating requirements resolved these defeaters in the Safety Case.

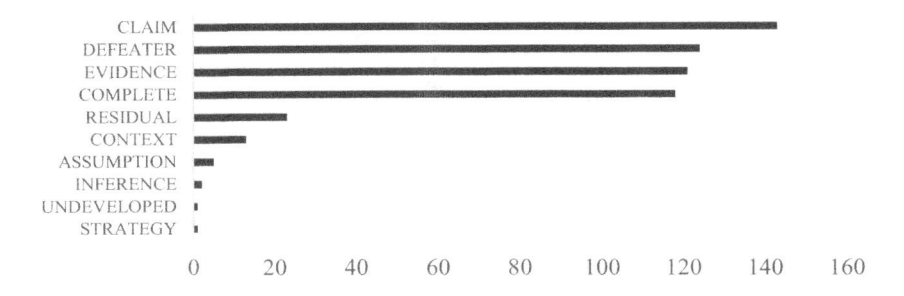

```
    CLAIM ████████████████████████████████████
 DEFEATER ██████████████████████████████████
 EVIDENCE █████████████████████████████████
 COMPLETE █████████████████████████████████
 RESIDUAL █████
  CONTEXT ███
ASSUMPTION █
INFERENCE ▪
UNDEVELOPED ·
 STRATEGY ·
          0    20   40   60   80   100  120  140  160
```

Fig. 4. Breakdown of EA node types.

Finally, developing and maintaining the Safety Case throughout the project allowed us to track the type of evidence needed from the V&V team. We prepared a list of evidence necessary to support the argument and this guided the V&V activities. This ensured that we had the evidence necessary to support our argument, instead of adjusting the argument to fit the available evidence.

We chose this decomposition strategy (Module v. Verifier) because, although initialising of the processor is complex (particularly given the many hardware architectures supported), checking whether the initialisation is correct is much simpler and is suitable for an ASIL D element.

8 Recommendations

Drawing from the experience reported here, as well as experience with the development of structured arguments for "real-world" Assurance Cases across a wide spectrum of industries, we can offer the following recommendations:

1. Start development of the Assurance Case as early as possible, ideally, as part of concept development.
2. Take care in formulating the top-level claim, and re-visit this claim throughout development as understanding deepens.
3. Explicitly represent the strategy of the argument at each level where the argument splits into multiple branches.
4. Encourage dialectical reasoning, i.e. identifying and explicitly capturing doubts in the assurance case.
5. Look for opportunities to refute doubts by introducing safety requirements to eliminate or otherwise control sources of risk.

6. Capture safety and other requirements in the assurance case, either by copying the text of requirements into the assurance case or linking references to requirements to where they are stored in a document or repository.
7. Explicitly reference or link to verification and validation results.
8. Take account of how confidence in various claims within the Safety Case can (and should) increase incrementally during development (Diemert et al. 2023), representing this progression of increasing confidence explicitly in the Safety Case.
9. Take measures to control the technical vocabulary used in the assurance case, both vocabulary unique to the subject of the Safety Case as well as generic words such as "fail", to ensure a common understanding among stakeholders.
10. Use an appropriate software tool to support scalability and modifiability, i.e. not merely a drawing tool.

9 Discussion and Future Directions

As described above, we have informal evidence that the approach outlined in this paper is effective, but it needs to be integrated into the appropriate points in the development process. Reference (Boehm 2000) describes the Life Cycle Objectives (LCO) milestone in the spiral development model used for many developments. At this milestone the following questions must be answered: "If I build this product using the specified architecture and processes, will it support the operational concept, realize the prototyping results, satisfy the requirements, and finish within the budgets and schedules in the plan?" There are similar milestones in other development methodologies: the milestones where the viability of the development is reconsidered. The version of the Safety Case refined for the milestone, can provide answers to several of these questions, particularly the support for the operational concept and the budget and schedule. The levels of maturity of the Safety Case at each such milestone should also be defined. For example, by the milestone where the proposed design has been validated and verified, the Safety Case should contain specific defeaters concerning the adequacy of the verification planned for the implemented product.

In summary, preparing a Safety Case argument should be an intellectual activity that requires a detailed analysis not only of the design of a product, but also of how it is being developed and deployed. Describing this as an intellectual activity is meant to make a distinction from post-design "wrapping up" activities with relatively little need for critical thinking. This activity should begin as early as possible and follow the product through its deployed lifetime. Given this, we have found that preparing the Safety Case early in a project has de-risked the development activity (and, as in Use Case 1 above, when not applied early has added risk to a project). Using EA focuses yet more attention on possible shortcomings of the product's design, development, and deployment. Identifying these shortcomings early can de-risk the project.

References

Defence Standard 00-56 Issue 4 (Part 1): Safety Management Requirements for Defence Systems. UK Ministry of Defence.
UL 4600: Standard for Safety for the Evaluation of Autonomous Products, 2nd edition. 2022. Underwriter Laboratories.
Assurance Case Guidance: Challenges, Common Issues and Good Practice. Version 1. 2021. The Assurance Case Working Group of the Safety Critical Systems Club.
ISO/IEC 15026-1: 2019; Systems and Software Engineering - Systems and Software Assurance Part 1: Concepts and vocabulary
ISO/IEC/IEEE 29119; Software and systems engineering — Software testing.
EN 50129; Railway applications – Communication, signalling and processing systems – Safety related electronic systems for signalling.
John B. Goodenough and Charles B. Weinstock and Ari Z. Klein; Eliminative Induction: A Basis for Arguing System Confidence, New Ideas and Emerging Results Workshop, ICSE, 2013.
Goal Structuring Notation Community Standard, Version 3. 2021. The Assurance Case Working Group of the Safety Critical Systems Club.
ISO 26262-9:2018; Road vehicles — Functional safety — Part 9: Automotive safety integrity level (ASIL)-oriented and safety-oriented analyses.
S. Diemert and J. Joyce; Eliminative Argumentation for Arguing System Safety - A Practitioner's Experience, 2020 IEEE International Systems Conference (SysCon).
Francis Bacon; Novum Organum Scientiarum, 1620.
Chris Hobbs and Martin Lloyd; The Application of Bayesian Belief Networks to Assurance Case Preparation, 2012 Safety Critical Systems Symposium.
Chris Hobbs; The Safety Case as a Process Driver, 2024 Safety Critical Systems Symposium.
Charles Hadden-Cave; The Loss of RAF Nimrod XV230; Final Report, UK Secretary of State for Defence, 2009.
B. Boehm, W. Hansen; Spiral Development: Experience, Principles, and Refinements, Spiral Development: Workshop, 2000.
S. Diemert, J. Goodenough, J. Joyce, and C. Weinstock; Incremental Assurance Through Eliminative Argumentation, Journal of System Safety, vol. 58, no. 1, pp. 7–15, Feb. 2023.

ISO-26262 - The unfriendly, the friendly and the friend-in-need

Islem Jouini, Sai Pavan Kumar Eswara, Mikhail Tchernikov

CapGemini

Abstract In this presentation we give three 'faces' of ISO-26262: The unfriendly, because ISO-26262 series of standards offer comprehensive and conservative guidance to achieve functional safety in automotive E/E systems, which may lead to a cost/benefit imbalance. The friendly, because ISO-26262 series of standards offer relief methods & principles to rationalize the effort to achieve functional safety in automotive E/E systems, which establish cost/benefit balance. The friend-in-need, because ISO-26262 series of standards offer state of the art approaches to address how to achieve functional safety in automotive E/E systems, which ensures moral and legal compliance. Proceeding without the offered relief methods & principles, the entire product development process needs to follow the highest ASIL, determined for the automotive E/E system. During the presentation, we will explore different relief methods & principles which allow an effective and efficient execution of the ISO-26262 series of standards, including: Part 2 Clause 6.4.5 Tailoring of the safety activities, Part 9 Clause 5 Requirements decomposition with respect to ASIL tailoring, Part 4 Requirement 6.4.2.5 ASIL Reduction due to Latent Faults, Part 9 Clause 6 Criteria for coexistence of elements and the Openness of ISO 26262 for state-of-the-art methods.

© Islem Jouini, Sai Pavan Kumar Eswara, Mikhail Tchernikov 2024.
Published by the Safety-Critical Systems Club. All Rights Reserved.

Breaking the Tyranny of Net Risk Metrics for Automated Vehicle Safety

Philip Koopman[1] and William H. Widen[2]

1 - Carnegie Mellon University, Pittsburgh PA, USA

2 - University of Miami School of Law, Miami FL, USA

[The full paper is published in the SCSC Journal, scsc.uk/scsc-191]

Abstract *An inquiry into how safe might be "safe enough" for automated vehicle technology must go far beyond the superficial "safer than a human driver" metric to yield an answer that will be workable in practice. Issues include the complexities of creating a like-for-like human driver baseline for comparison, avoiding risk transfer despite net risk reduction, avoiding negligent computer driver behaviour, conforming to industry consensus safety standards as a basis to justify predictions of net safety improvement, avoiding regulatory problems with unreasonably dangerous specific features despite improved net safety, and avoiding problematic ethical and equity outcomes. In this paper we explore how addressing these topics holistically will create a more robust framework for establishing acceptable automated vehicle safety.*

© Philip Koopman and William H. Widen 2024.
Published by the Safety-Critical Systems Club. All Rights Reserved

Safety and Certification Considerations of eVTOL Aircraft

Benita Lawrence, George Head

Ebeni

Corsham, UK

Abstract *There are significant challenges with the design and related certification of eVTOL (Electric Vertical Take-off and Landing) aircraft. Much of this is driven by the novel aspects and diversity of technical solutions of eVTOL, for example the significantly increased levels of system complexity due to the use of distributed and integrated propulsion and advanced flight control systems. It is perceived that the regulation is lagging behind the development of novel technologies and applications which are rapidly advancing to develop eVTOL. As such, it is clear that aircraft manufacturers and regulators need to work more closely, in effect going on 'a journey' together to ensure certification is achievable. In this paper, typical eVTOL aircraft operating scenarios and design architectures are presented as the certification background. These are then considered regarding risks related to eVTOL certification together with their complex technical solutions and subsequent operation. Safety challenges and considerations are discussed for the future certification of eVTOL*

1 Introduction

1.1 Advanced Air Mobility (AAM)

The definition of AAM, as provided by BAE Systems, is '…an air transport system concept that integrates new, transformational aircraft designs and flight technologies into existing and modified airspace operations[1].' The types of AAM

---

[1] https://www.baesystems.com. Accessed 24 September 2023

© Ebeni 2024.
Published by the Safety-Critical Systems Club. All Rights Reserved.

in development nearly all have all-electric or hybrid-electric power systems, (with some exceptions of hydrogen-powered zero emission aircraft) and are either piloted and/or remotely piloted. Currently, designs can be classified as:

- eVTOL – electric vertical take-off & landing e.g. on-demand air taxis;
- eCTOL – electric conventional take off & landing e.g. short-range trips;
- UAVs – unmanned air vehicles e.g. videography, transfer of medical supplies.

This paper will focus on eVTOLs, which typically comprise of all-electric, low noise level, distributed power propulsion and a battery power supply.

The eVTOL world has expanded recently due to the capabilities of modern electric powertrains and Distributed Electric Propulsion (DEP) technologies. Large batteries supply electrical energy to motors which power the Lift Thrust Unit (LTU)[2].

For an eVTOL to hover, the power required for lift is governed by equation (1):

$$P_h = \frac{W^{1.5}}{\sqrt{2\rho An}} \qquad (1)$$

Where P_h is the power in hover, W is the weight of the eVTOL, ρ is the air density, A is the swept area of a rotor (a circle of radius the same as the rotor) and n is the number of propellers producing lift.[3] Evidently, the power usage is heavily influenced by the overall weight of the eVTOL, making weight saving an area of significant interest for manufacturers.

Improvements in batteries and the ability to have multiple LTUs has allowed eVTOLs to become viable. Vertical flight is an energy intensive operation which requires batteries capable of delivering a significant amount of power for a period of time to encompass all flight phases. This presents an issue for manufacturers: any increase in weight requires more power and therefore more battery weight. This leads to a trade-off between the payload and the range performance an eVTOL can achieve. This means that advances in the battery power to weight ratio (specific power) will give the biggest increases in performance.

---

[2] The Lift Thrust Unit (LTU) is any engine that directly contributes to providing lift or thrust and includes its controller, the controlled effector (e.g. rotor, propeller, fan) and any related actuators (eg. pitch change, tilting, vectoring).

[3] From momentum theory. Reducing power requires less weight, more disc area, or more rotors.

1.2 eVTOL

An 'eVTOL aircraft is a variety of VTOL aircraft that uses electric power to take off, hover, and land vertically.[4]' The technology is based on electric propulsion (motors, batteries, electronic controllers) and the need for new aerial vehicles for AAM that are responsive to environmental challenges, such as low-carbon transport emissions, noise levels and societal acceptance.

Aircraft are required to produce sufficient lift to maintain height and thrust to move between locations. eVTOLs typically provide lift in hover through the use of LTUs positioned vertically, similar to a helicopter. For lift in cruise, some eVTOLs continue to use these same LTUs, whereas others use a wing to fly more like a conventional aeroplane. Forward thrust is provided by either:

- Tilting the full eVTOL, similar to how small drones move;
- Dedicated propellers fitted to the front or back, in a static configuration, similar to traditional aeroplane;
- Rotating the LTU from providing lift to providing forward thrust.

The simplest eVTOLs are small, light passenger aircraft that utilise electric motors to power the propellers with on board batteries to store energy. More complex configurations have been proposed, which are outlined below.

1.2.1 Types

As eVTOLs are a novel concept, manufacturers have developed a wide array of configurations. These all pose different challenges and are tailored to serve specific market needs and operations. Before considering the challenges for certifying eVTOLs, an appreciation of the types is needed.

This paper will focus on battery powered eVTOLs. The following are examples of generic types:

- Multi-rotor (Figure 1) – examples include designs by Volocopter etc. These often use fixed-pitch LTUs with simpler rotor mechanics required for flight control.

---

[4] en.wikipedia.org/wiki/EVTOL. Accessed 24 September 2023.

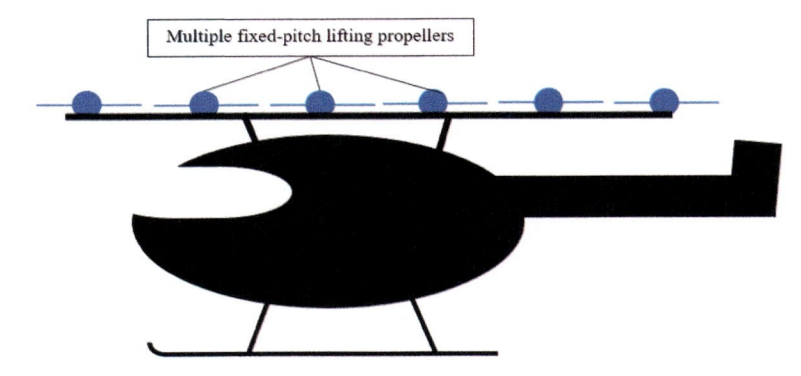

Fig. 1. A multi-rotor type eVTOL

The low speed and optimisation for hover of these configurations means they suit operations at short ranges. Volocopter claim that their VoloCity is an air taxi, designed to transport passengers between hubs. This eVTOL type is best suited to operations involving long periods in hover and low-speed flight, such as small hops within a city. This is an Urban Air Mobility (UAM) operating model. The European Union Aviation Safety Agency (EASA) has also suggested the use of eVTOLs for emergency service applications[5], with Volocopter working with ADAC Luftrettung for air rescue operational testing[6].

- Vectored thrust (Figure 2) – examples include designs by Lilium, Vertical Aerospace, etc. These typically include wings, LTUs, and ducts which affect the direction of thrust. The LTUs rotate for vertical take-off and landing and are horizontal in cruise (conventional forward flight). These tilting components are required to reliably and safely complete the transition from lift to the cruise phase of flight.

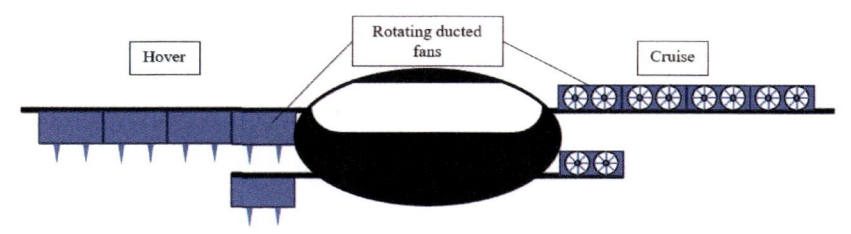

Fig. 2. A vectored thrust type eVTOL

---

[5] Emergency Medical Services by Vertical Take-off and Landing aircraft | EASA (europa.eu), Accessed 06 October 2023.

[6] ADAC Luftrettung to use electric air taxis in winter 2024/25 | AirMed&Rescue (airmedandrescue.com). Accessed 09 October 2023.

The ability to transition from lift provided by LTUs to lift provided by a wing with the LTUs providing thrust allows these vehicles to achieve a greater range than multi-rotors. The LTUs will not be perfectly optimised for hover or cruise. This means there is a compromise, so these designs may be less efficient in hover. They are therefore suitable for medium-distance flights operating between cities. 'Regional air mobility,' flying routes up to 200km between cities, has been proposed for many vectored thrust configurations, such as Lilium.[7]

- Lift & Cruise (Figure 3) – examples include designs by Airbus, WISK, Embraer X etc. These designs often take the properties of fixed wing (longer range) and rotor aircraft (ability to VTOL). Additional mass for different flight modes (as the wing is not used in hover), and some aerodynamic resistance from the LTUs could reduce the effectiveness and efficiency of these designs.

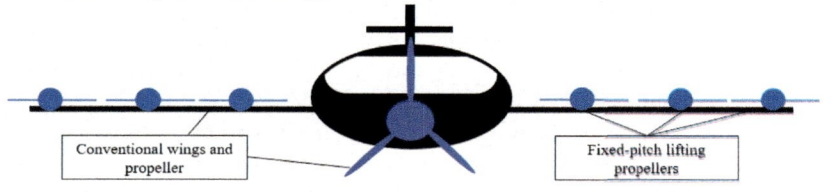

Fig. 3. A lift & cruise type eVTOL

These designs are a compromise between multirotors and vectored thrust, using both fixed vertical propellers for lift and traditional propellers for thrust. They combine the simplicity of multirotors with the ability to turn off the LTU by using a wing and/or pusher prop. Lifting rotors are limited and draggy for forward flight,[8] meaning lift & cruise are potentially faster than a multirotor as the LTU can be turned off. They are also better in hover than a vectored thrust eVTOL, due to the LTU being optimised for hover rather than a compromise. They are also simpler than vectored thrust designs due to having fewer moving parts. However, the vertical LTUs are still an issue in cruise, creating unwanted drag. These designs are suited for both intra- and inter-city flights, though less aerodynamically efficient than a vectored thrust design. The manufacturers believe that simplicity will help with certification. Lift and cruise configurations remain a compromise, however, as the LTUs are still limited in forward flight.

- Hybrid designs (Figure 4) – example include Archer, Vertical Aerospace, Wisk, etc. These designs include some fixed and some tilting LTUs dependent upon when required for which flight phase.

---

[7] Lilium Air Mobility - Lilium. Accessed 09 October 2023
[8] Due to dissymmetry of lift and retreating blade stall.

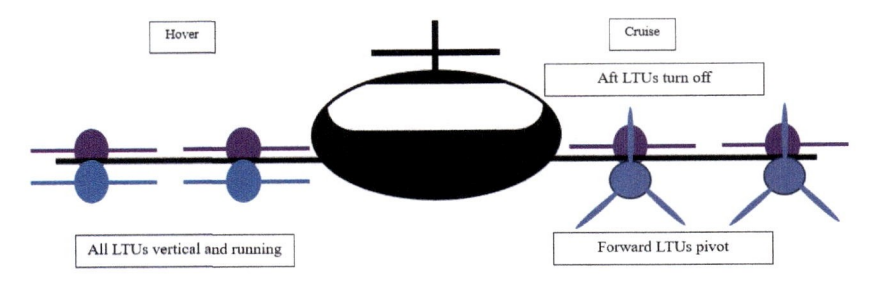

Fig. 4. A hybrid type eVTOL

Hybrids remove some of the disadvantages of lift and cruise by having some of the LTUs pivot to provide forward thrust. These will target use between cities and as air taxis, with greater ranges than multirotors. However, since the LTUs that rotate need to be designed for both lift and thrust, they will be less optimised than lift and cruise configurations, which have static propellers designed purely for either lift or cruise. Nevertheless, hybrid configurations will likely have a greater range since some of the LTUs will pivot, reducing the drag they produce in cruise by contributing to thrust.

Some eVTOL manufacturers have stated the desire to be fully autonomous with pilotless vehicles. WISK aviation is intending to be pilotless from day-one, with VoloCopter stating a desire to begin with piloted flights with a view to eventually produce pilotless eVTOLs.

2 Certification Process

To certify an aircraft, regulatory organisations such as EASA (European Union Aviation Safety Agency), the FAA (Federal Aviation Administration), and National agencies such as the CAA (Civil Aviation Authority) work with manufacturers to establish a set of standards that ensure the safety and airworthiness of an aircraft during design, manufacture, and modification as well as in service and through operations. The manufacturers then must conduct comprehensive analyses and testing programmes to demonstrate that their aircraft complies with these standards. Examples of such EASA standards include (with FAA equivalents):

CS 23 – Normal, Utility, Aerobatic and Commuter aeroplanes
CS 25 – Large Aeroplanes
CS 27 – Small Rotorcraft[9]
CS 29 – Large Rotorcraft

---

[9] Helicopters and autogyros.

There are 4 main steps to achieve Type Certification of an aircraft, always considered in discussion and agreement with the Regulator. These are:

- Technical Familiarisation and Certification Basis
- Establishment of the Certification Programme
- Compliance Demonstration
- Technical Closure and Issue of Approval

The first two phases begin prior to a completed design or a physical aircraft. Various analyses, including computational fluid dynamics, is used extensively to optimise the key performance characteristics of an aircraft, depending on the specific requirements of the project. Presenting the concept and the results of the analysis to the Regulator, the two parties can come to an agreement about the exact nature of the certification process. This will be unique to each aircraft.

Once the certification programme has been agreed, the next stages are Compliance Demonstration, Technical Closure, and Issue of Approval. This is where the manufacturer needs to demonstrate that an aircraft meets the requirements of its type approval.

2.1 Challenges

eVTOLs are a new type of aircraft with technologies and concepts that have not been certified before. Consequently, regulators are collaborating with manufacturers to ensure that certification is achievable. As stated by the CAA 'introducing these new aircraft and their operations involves significant work.[10]' This requires regulatory approval of new powerplants, LTUs etc with high levels of integration, which require potentially new ways to integrate within national and international aviation frameworks.

With AAM a novel industry, manufacturers are constantly developing their concepts to achieve the best performing designs. This has led to a huge variety of concepts, which makes defining a set of standards that are suitable for all designs a real challenge.

EASA for example, reviewed more than 150 VTOL project configurations with limited common characteristics, except for a VTOL capability and distributed propulsion. Despite having design characteristics of aeroplanes, rotorcraft, or both, in most cases EASA was not able to classify these new vehicles as being either a conventional aeroplane or a rotorcraft.

Applying the certification specifications for aeroplanes or for rotorcraft, depending on whether they are an aeroplane or a rotorcraft, and only adding some

---

[10] https:///www.caa.co.uk. Accessed 22 September 2023.

modifications would not ensure equal treatment. The conventional regulations as listed earlier in this paper, for example CS-23 and CS-27 have significant differences, especially in terms of system Safety Objectives and operational aspects. The opinion of EASA was that it would not be fair to treat applicants differently based on the regulatory starting point (CS-23 or CS-27) as it would probably favour some configurations, thus preventing potentially innovative concepts to compete on the market. Instead, EASA produced objective based certification requirements, which provide the necessary flexibility to certify innovative state-of-the-art designs and technology, to establish a common set of conditions for the certification of these new concepts.

With an absence of applicable regulations for eVTOL aircraft, this has led to the production of high-level objective requirements (EASA SC-VTOL-01, July 2019) that do not consider whether the eVTOL concept is a rotorcraft or a fixed wing aircraft. This prevents the introduction of any bias into the regulatory process for such technologies, without penalising a design by imposing requirements that may prevent some concepts achieving certification.

SC-VTOL and its associated Means of Compliance (EASA MOC-2 SC-VTOL, June 2022) will require harmonisation with international regulators to enhance safety and to increase efficiency for Industry and Regulators. In addition to SC-VTOL and to aid the transition from conventional propulsion systems/engines to several electric and/or hybrid propulsion system (EHPS) architectures, EASA introduced SC E19. This is a Special Condition focusing on new and emerging technologies introduced by an EHPS. This is not considered mature enough at this stage to have associated means of compliance, as they would need to encompass all possibilities for several EHPS architectures, therefore it is likely that this will need to be discussed with Regulators on an applicant-by-applicant basis.

A difficulty faced in regulating the eVTOL industry is that there is no uniformity in what operations the proposed aircraft will be performing. Urban Air Mobility (UAM) operating models for eVTOLs have suggested using the aircraft as a means of creating air taxis for inner-city environments, whereas Joby has recently delivered an eVTOL to the US Air Force for testing, demonstrating a military interest in eVTOLs.[11]

Such diverse operations require a diversity of regulations, as the eVTOLs will each be operating in different airspace and under different classifications. EASA has considered this, introducing two categories under SC.VTOL. UAM eVTOLs will need to meet the enhanced classification certification as they fly over congested areas, whereas (non-commercial) VTOLs operating outside of city airspace may only require basic certification.

Following the definition of the general requirements of performance and operation, the certification basis dedicated to specific eVTOL architecture and

---

[11] First Joby eVTOL Delivered to the US Air Force (helis.com). Accessed 09 October 2023.

concept of operations should be determined and agreed. The following section of this paper provides an overview of the safety assessment process, which is an important part of certification as the safety artefacts produced are a Means of Compliance (albeit not the only ones), which will determine whether the risks are acceptable and whether mitigations or redesign is required.

3 Safety Assessment Process

As discussed earlier, eVTOLs are different from conventional aircraft in terms of the use of distributed electric or hybrid propulsion units and advanced flight control systems. Requirements for eVTOLs incorporate objectives and principles of a 'fail-safe' design concept, which considers the effects of failures and combination of failures.

The Safety Assessment Process aims to demonstrate that:

- Systems and components are designed and installed in a way that probabilities of failure conditions are commensurate with their classification; and
- No catastrophic failure condition results from a single failure.

It must be demonstrated that specific criteria have been met/achieved:

- Quantitative and Qualitative.
- Many forms of compliance activities to demonstrate adequate level of assurance, e.g. Analyses, Testing, Safety Assessment, etc dependent upon level of criticality.
- Application of a Safety Assessment Process.

Guidance on how to perform a System Assessment Process is contained within Aerospace Recommended Practice (ARP) 4761A[12], which is closely aligned with ARP 4754A[13] for guidelines on the development process for civil aircraft/systems. The depth and scope of the analyses are dependent upon system criticality and/or complexity.

The Safety Assessment Process contained with ARP 4761A:

- Is an iterative process from Aircraft level decomposed to Systems and Equipment.

---

[12] SAE Aerospace, Aerospace Recommended Practice ARP 4761 Rev. A, (Not yet issued)
[13] SAE Aerospace, Aerospace Recommended Practice ARP 4754 Rev. A, Issued Nov 1996, Revised Dec 2010

- Includes preliminary assessment steps to ensure that the proposed system architecture(s) can reasonably be expected to meet the safety objectives.
- Is used when identifying the aircraft and system functions and classifying the hazards associated with the Failure Conditions. The applicant will have to substantiate the effects of failure conditions with consideration to operational conditions and events.

The following section provides a summary of the ARPs used for the development and safety assessment of aircraft systems.

3.1 Summary of ARP 4761A and ARP 4754A Safety Assessment Process

SAE International's ARP 4761A provides guidelines for conducting the safety assessment process on civil aircraft, systems, and equipment. ARP 4754A provides guidelines for developing civil aircraft and systems. This section will summarise the process that these two documents contain for safety assessments.

The Safety Assessment Process assesses both the functions of the aircraft and the systems which deliver the aircraft functions. The process begins with a top-down functional assessment of the aircraft to identify requirements, decomposing down into functional and safety assessments of each system and again to an item-level requirements identification during the preliminary design phase. These activities identify the required Development Assurance Levels (DALs), both at a functional and item level. Hardware and software for each system is then designed to these DALs. Following hardware and software design the items, systems, and finally the aircraft are verified against the safety objectives identified during the design. Figure 5 shows the development process for aircraft systems design, from ARP 4761A.

The safety assessment begins in concept development, with a top-down analysis of the aircraft functions to identify failure conditions. This is done through an Aircraft Functional Hazard Assessment (AFHA), which is updated throughout the lifecycle as new functions are identified. The outputs of the AFHA are aircraft failure conditions and severity classifications associated with them, as well as setting safety objectives for each function.

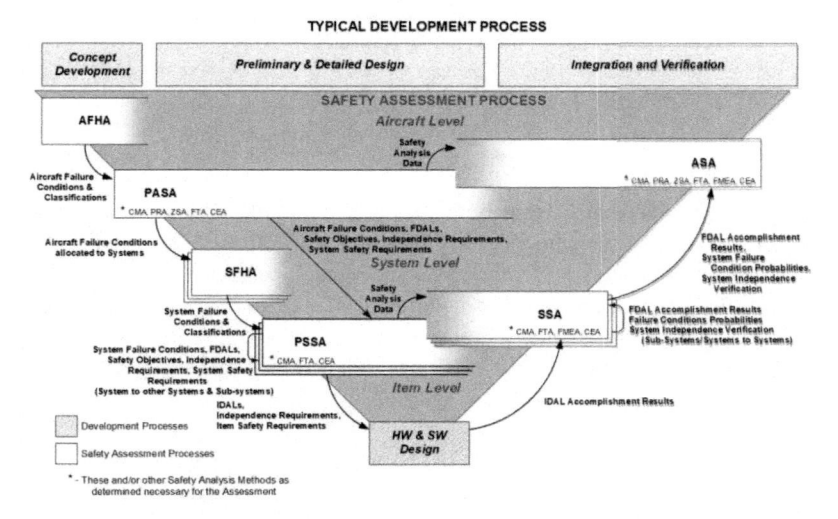

Fig. 5. Aircraft System Development Process, from ARP 4761A

The Preliminary Aircraft Safety Assessment (PASA) is started during preliminary design and assesses whether the proposed aircraft architecture can meet the safety objectives set by the AFHA. The PASA considers common cause failures and allocates aircraft failure conditions to individual systems. During this stage, the PASA also identifies the independence requirements needed for individual systems. For eVTOLs there will be a considerable number of interdependent systems, as all systems depend on the electrical system for power. Failure of an electrical bus could be a common cause failure for multiple aircraft functions. The PASA will identify the need to separate eVTOL functions between multiple electrical systems, to prevent any single point failures. Functional Development Assurance Levels (FDALs) are assigned at this stage in the aircraft design. Table 1 shows the FDAL assignment based on the severity of failure conditions.

Table 1. FDAL assignment based on the severity of failure conditions

Top-Level Failure Condition Severity Classification	Likelihood (Enhanced Category SC.VTOL)	Top-Level FDAL Assignment
Catastrophic	$\leq 10^{-9}$	FDAL A
Hazardous / Severe Major	$\leq 10^{-7}$	FDAL B
Major	$\leq 10^{-5}$	FDAL C
Minor	$\leq 10^{-3}$	FDAL D

Top-Level Failure Condition Severity Classification	Likelihood (Enhanced Category SC.VTOL)	Top-Level FDAL Assignment
No Safety Effect	-	FDAL E

FDAL assignment depends on both the failure condition severity classification and the degree of independence in the Functional Failure Set (FFS). For Functional DALs, the degree of functional independence must be identified at this stage in the design. Functional independence is achieved by having two distinct functions achieve the same outcome, reducing the likelihood of a common requirement error. Examples of functional independence relating directly to eVTOLs may include:

- Separating the provision of lift between LTUs and a wing
- Two means of directional control in the air: vectored thrust and control surfaces

During the preliminary design phase of systems, a Systems Functional Hazard Assessment (SFHA) classifies the failure conditions of system-level functions, including any aircraft-level functions which may be affected by the system. The SFHA identifies the severity of failure conditions for each system function and is used to set safety objectives for the system's design. These system failure classifications influence the Preliminary System Safety Assessment (PSSA).

Item Development Assurance Levels (IDAL) assignment takes place at the item development phase of the design. Electronic hardware and software assurance levels come under IDALs. Item independence, the degree to which items are different to minimise the likelihood of a common mode failure, need to be identified for IDAL assignment. One example of item independence is using different operating systems on computers.

FFS with greater independence allow for a lower FDAL and IDAL to be assigned to each individual item as no single failure will lead to the top hazard materialising. An eVTOL with item independence will not require as high a DAL as one without. For example, if one eVTOL uses multiple computers (each with dissimilar software) to control the thrust vectoring it will not require as high a DAL as another eVTOL which uses a single computer, or multiple computers each using the same software. Hardware and software are designed to meet the IDAL targets set from the PSSA.

Some of the prototype eVTOL designs lack functional independence, such as multirotors that have a single means of providing lift with no other means of delivering this function. Similarly, multirotors depend on one system for directional control. All eVTOLs rely on electrical power for all functions, so there is a functional dependence on delivery of power for all other systems. As such, the IDAL and FDAL for the electrical systems will need to be higher than many conventional aeroplanes. Most elements of the Battery Management System (BMS), including the control systems, battery monitoring and delivery buses will need to be developed to DAL-A, but this is dependent upon the architectural design of the BMS.

Following the preliminary design of the aircraft and detailed design of hardware and software, System Safety Assessments (SSAs) and the Aircraft Safety Assessment (ASA) verify through tests that the systems are integrated correctly and meet the required DAL and failure condition probabilities. System independence is verified at this stage. The ASA is a comprehensive evaluation of the completed aircraft to show that the safety objectives are all satisfied.

A key consideration throughout the Safety Assessment Process is common cause failures. Independence between both functions and systems is required to ensure the level of safety is acceptable and to meet regulatory requirements. For example, SC.VTOL states that a catastrophic failure condition must not result from any single point of failure. Independence principles are established for aircraft-level functions at the PASA and systems-level functions at the PSSA stages of the SAP. Common Cause considerations are used to determine whether the proposed architecture can meet the independence principle that is required.

It is necessary to ensure that independence exists, or that the associated risk is acceptable. 'Particular Risk Analyses (PRAs), Zonal Safety Analyses (ZSA) and Common Mode Analyses (CMA) are methods for the evaluation of independence, or the identification of specific dependencies due to a common cause.' (ARP 4761A) These methods can aid the PASA and PSSA stages in generating independence requirements, whether physical installation requirements or functional requirements. In summary, ZSA examines physical zones of an aircraft to address physical installation & interference between systems, PRAs address hazards that are internal or external to the aircraft which could impact more than one system, for example bird strike, and CMA addresses the independence of functions, for example identical systems susceptible to common development errors.

For eVTOLs, there will be a greater degree of interdependency for both systems and aircraft functions when compared to conventional aircraft. As mentioned earlier, weight saving for eVTOLs is of critical importance even when compared to traditional aviation. There is therefore a desire for eVTOLs to have software solutions rather than traditional hardware redundancy. eVTOLs will have a greater degree of interdependency with electrical power, both for systems and functions, which the eVTOL will not have means of generating in-flight. Common cause considerations are therefore essential throughout the design of a new eVTOL to ensure that sufficient independence is in place, or that the associated risk is acceptable.

At the SSA and ASA stage, these analyses are used to verify that the independence requirements have been implemented into the design.

3.2 Challenges

Many eVTOL proposals have no functional or item independence, which reflects the levels of integration and interdependencies. Hence conventional regulations require amendment and innovative application. Mitigations, evidence, and rationale are required to demonstrate what is considered 'good enough' therefore demonstrating the need for manufacturers to work closely together with Regulators. For example, with multirotors provision of lift is from one source (LTUs) which are all driven by the electric system. eVTOL manufacturers must therefore work with the regulators to ensure that the certification requirements are both suitable for eVTOLs and supported with evidence and rationale for why the proposed architecture is sufficiently safe.

Traditional aviation benefits from decades of evolution, improvements and well-established processes used to build compliance arguments. Since eVTOL designs have little of this experience, there will likely be design errors in the early years of development. eVTOLs will need to demonstrate that each of the novel systems are sufficiently robust and safe to achieve certification.

The proposed scale of eVTOL production has interested parties who view them as a possible 'air taxi.' This is further evidenced by the interest that Uber showed in UAM from 2016 with the Uber Elevate white paper (Uber, 2016). This has produced many eVTOL manufacturers which have experience from the automotive industry. The regulators must therefore work with these companies to ensure that eVTOL certification requirements are clearly understood.

It was briefly mentioned earlier in this paper that some eVTOL manufacturers are exploring self-flying eVTOLs. The regulators will need to establish certification specifications for autonomous eVTOLs. However, many suggest that 'autonomy is a long way from reality' (October 2023 Emerging Technologies Forum in Japan).

3.3 General Safety Issues

Designers of eVTOL systems must consider the complexity of control mechanisms and demonstrate that any failures do not prevent continued safe flight and landing (CSFL). Designers must demonstrate that continued safe flight and landing is possible including emergency landings as part of the safety assessment process.

All eVTOLs must consider the risk of fire as a particular risk. Battery fire or explosion may arise due to issues with charging and protection devices, which must be assessed and mitigated in the event of these failures. Thermal battery runaway constrains safe cell temperatures and pressures that must be maintained during charging or discharging conditions (ICAS 2020 0231paper.pdf). Thermal runaway can result in fire and /or explosion, which can spread to adjacent cells. Containment structures may prevent these effects but can add significant weight, hence presenting a challenge of meeting requirements and weight reduction to enable viability of eVTOLs.

In relation to batteries another concern is the amount of energy the batteries can hold and the power delivery. The batteries on an eVTOL are sized based on the required power draw and the energy needed for the expected range. Presently, Li-Ion batteries have a limited range which will be improved as this technology evolves to increase energy and power densities. An additional battery margin is needed in case of a single battery failure or in case of diversion or delay. Aeroplanes and helicopters are required to carry contingency fuel, alternative destination fuel and final reserve fuel. The regulators will need to introduce contingency energies for eVTOLs, to ensure sufficient energy is available for abnormal occurrences.

Another relevant particular risk is bird strike. Bird strikes are significantly more likely at low altitudes, so the likelihood of multiple bird strikes is increased. The Enhanced Category of SC.VTOL requires continued safe flight and landing (CSFL) after an impact. Potential damage includes windshield penetrations, propeller failure, battery fires, and pitot and angle of attack (AOA) sensor damage. Manufacturers will need to understand the possible effects of bird strikes to ensure eVTOLs can still maintain safe flight for credible damage scenarios when considering size/mass of bird, operation altitude and maximum operating speeds.

As mentioned earlier, many eVTOL configurations lack functional independence. All eVTOLs depend on the integration and interdependencies of the flight control system and electrical related system for thrust, lift, and control. All these scenarios require analysis based on safety requirements and evidence to determine an acceptable level of safety commensurate with the eVTOL and its mode of operation.

Currently, eVTOL manufacturers have developed different configurations and there is not yet an agreement on what a certified eVTOL will look like. The eVTOL industry would benefit from sharing knowledge about errors and lessons learned rather than treating all information as proprietary. This would require a cultural shift that would enable progression of development and certification of such technologies. There have been incidents during early prototype testing of some manufacturers. For example, Vertical Aerospace's prototype had an accident during flight testing. Vertical Aerospace has been forthcoming in sharing what happened and released public statements on the chain of events leading to the accident. Transparency on these accidents is necessary from all eVTOL manufacturers to ensure that lessons are shared about the evolution of eVTOL technology, which may in turn aid a more efficient route to certification.

4 Conclusions

In this paper different types of eVTOL aircraft have been identified. An overview of the Certification process and the System Safety Assessment process have been presented, together with identification of some challenges that such technological advancements may introduce and will need to be addressed to achieve a certifiable product.

Adapting the regulatory frameworks to help with the Certification of eVTOLs by incorporating existing regulations together with objective-based requirements is underway. In parallel with this an increased level of cooperation, consistency, and negotiation between eVTOL manufacturers and regulatory authorities is necessary. eVTOLs represent a significant change from traditional aviation, with significantly increased levels of system complexity due to the use of distributed and integrated propulsion and advanced flight control systems.

The key points within this paper are, the increased integration of systems which means that there will be greater emphasis on specific aspects of the system safety assessment process of ARP 4761A in the production of the Preliminary Aircraft Safety Assessment, increased emphasis on common cause considerations, and the verified Aircraft Safety Assessment to reflect the correctness & completeness of the analysis of interdependencies, and on ARP 4754A to aid the verification and validation of the entire Safety Assessment process.

Abbreviations

AAM	Advanced Air Mobility
AFHA	Aircraft Functional Hazard Assessment
AOA	Angle of Attack
ARP	Aerospace Recommended Practice
ASA	Aircraft Safety Assessment
BMS	Battery Management System
CAA	Civil Aviation Authority
CMA	Common Mode Analysis
CS	Certification Specification
CSFL	Continued Safe Flight and Landing
DAL	Development Assurance Level
DEP	Distributed Electric Propulsion
EASA	European Union Aviation Safety Agency
EHPS	Electric and/or Hybrid Propulsion System
eVTOL	Electric Vertical Take-off and Landing
FAA	Federal Aviation Authority
FDAL	Functional Development Assurance Level
FFS	Functional Failure Set
IDAL	Item Development Assurance Level

LTU	Lift Thrust Unit
PASA	Preliminary Aircraft Safety Assessment
PRA	Particular Risk Analysis
PSSA	Preliminary System Safety Assessment
SC	Special Condition
SFHA	System Functional Hazard Analysis
SSA	System Safety Assessment
UAM	Urban Air Mobility
UAV	Unmanned Air Vehicles
VTOL	Vertical Take-off and Landing
ZSA	Zonal Safety Analysis

References

AirMed&Rescue (2023), ADAC Luftrettung to use electric air taxis in winter 2024/25. ADAC Luftrettung to use electric air taxis in winter 2024/25 | AirMed&Rescue (airmedandrescue.com). Accessed 09 October 2023

BAE Systems, What is Advanced Air Mobility? https://www.baesystems.com/en-us/definition/what-is-advanced-air-mobility. Accessed 24 September 2023

EASA, Emergency Medical Services by Vertical Take-off and Landing aircraft. Emergency Medical Services by Vertical Take-off and Landing aircraft | EASA (europa.eu). Accessed 06 October 2023

EASA, Special Condition Electric / Hybrid Propulsion System, SC-E-19, Issue 1, April 2021

EASA, Special Condition Vertical Take-Off and Landing (VTOL) Aircraft, SC-VTOL-01, Issue 1, July 2019

EASA, Second Publication of Means of Compliance with the Special Condition VTOL, MOC-2-SC-VTOL, Issue 3, Dec 2022

Helis.com (2023), First Joby eVTOL Delivered to the US Air Force. First Joby eVTOL Delivered to the US Air Force (helis.com). Accessed 06 October 2023.

Lilium, Introducing High Speed Regional Mobility. https://lilium.com/?_gl=1*4wl1x9*_up*MQ..*_ga*MTc3MDc0MDk2Ni4xNjk2ODM4NjU3*_ga_9YC7ETNZ98*MTY5NjgzODY1Ny4xLjAuMTY5NjgzODY1Ny4wLjAuMA. Accessed 09 October 2023

SAE Aerospace, Aerospace Recommended Practice ARP 4761 Rev. A, (Not yet issued)

SAE Aerospace, Aerospace Recommended Practice ARP 4754 Rev. A, Issued Nov 1996, Revised Dec 2010

UBER Elevate (2016) Fast-Forwarding to a Future of On-Demand Urban Air Transportation

UK CAA, Advanced Air Mobility challenge. https://www.caa.co.uk/our-work/innovation/advanced-air-mobility-challenge/#:~:text=Introducing%20these%20new%20aircraft%20and%20operations%20involves%20significant,within%20the%20traditional%20national%20and%20international%20aviation%20frameworks. Accessed 22 September 2023

Wikipedia, eVTOL, https://en.wikipedia.org/wiki/EVTOL. Accessed 24 September 2023

Images

Figure 5 – SAE Aerospace, Aerospace Recommended Practice ARP 4761 Rev. A, (Not yet issued)

Towards Formal Verification and Robustification of Neural Systems in Safety-Critical Applications

Alessio Lomuscio

Imperial College London & Safe Intelligence

Abstract *A major challenge in moving ML-based systems, such as ML-based computer vision, from R&D to production is the difficulty in understanding and ensuring their performance on the operational design domain. The standard ML approach consists of extensively testing models for various inputs. However, testing is inherently limited in coverage, and it is expensive in several domains. In this talk I will present novel verification technologies developed at Imperial College London as part of the recently concluded DARPA Assured Autonomy program and other UK-funded efforts. Novel verification methods provide guarantees that a neural model meets its specifications in dense neighbourhood of selected inputs. For example, by using verification methods we can establish whether a model is robust with respect to infinite noise patterns, or infinite lighting perturbations applied to an input. Verification methods can also be tailored to specifications in the latent space and establish the robustness of models against semantic perturbations not definable in the input space (3D pose changes, background changes, etc). Additionally, verification methods can be paired with learning to obtain robust learning methods capable of generating models inherently more robust than those that may be derived with standard methods. In the presentation I will succinctly cover the key theoretical results leading to some of the existing ML verification technology, illustrate the resulting toolsets and capabilities, and describe some of the use cases developed with our colleagues at Boeing Research, including centreline distance estimation, object detection, and runway detection. I will argue that verification and robust learning can be used to obtain models that are inherently more robust, more performant and better understood than present learning and testing approaches.*

© Alessio Lomuscio 2024.
Published by the Safety-Critical Systems Club. All Rights Reserved.

Poster: Towards Trustworthy AI: Legislation, Techniques and Challenges

George Mason and Greg Chance

Frazer-Nash Consultancy

Extended Abstract With continuing increases in compute power, data availability and theoretical advances, Artificial Intelligence (AI) has progressed from being primarily an academic discipline to being a household term. Indeed, the use of AI is becoming ubiquitous in society, ranging from benign tools, such as email spam filters, to assisting with advanced tasks, such as financial analysis.

Recent developments of AI – most notably, deep learning – have transformed it into a highly versatile technology, able to carry out a variety of complex activities; however, this has sparked concerns that its utilisation may have a disruptive effect on society (Gillespie et al., 2023). For example, foundation models, trained to perform a wide range of tasks, have the potential to make entire careers redundant; generative models, capable of creating convincing yet false information, could lead to confusion and conflict; and black box models, whose decisions may have life-changing consequences yet cannot be justified. Furthermore, there is growing apprehension that future forms of AI – more advanced and capable of affecting society in deeper ways than current forms – may unintentionally be trained to learn behaviours that do not align with human preferences (Russell, 2022).

These concerns, and others, bring rise to the concept of 'trustworthy AI'. Although there isn't yet a widely accepted formal or legal definition for what qualifies as trustworthy AI, across the literature (including academic and governmental), recurring qualities that constitute trust in AI include safety, fairness and transparency; and governance to ensure that it is used ethically, accountably and contestably (Chance et al., 2023).

To realise trustworthy AI, jurisdictions globally have begun drafting legislation on the responsible use and development of AI: regulatory frameworks, AI-specific laws, general IT laws that can apply to AI and guidelines have all been proposed (IAPP, 2023). Furthermore, the research community has responded by developing techniques to assess the risks of AI systems and to ensure that such systems incorporate the appropriate qualities that inspire trust (Li et al., 2023).

Of the legislation under development, it is regulatory frameworks that offer the greatest safeguards to ensure trust in AI. These frameworks, currently being developed in the UK (Department for Science, Innovation & Technology, 2023), Canada (Innovation, Science and Economic Development Canada, 2023), Brazil

© George Mason and Greg Chance 2024.
Published by the Safety-Critical Systems Club. All Rights Reserved

(OECD, 2023) and the EU (European Commission, 2023), are designed from the ground up to account for a wide range of AI uses and developments – including efforts to future-proof against new forms of AI. China has also developed and enforced several AI regulations; however, whilst these regulations do include various rules for trustworthy AI, they are generally formulated to suit Chinese national interests (China Law Translate, 2022).

Across the regulatory frameworks still under development, the key principles for trustworthy AI outlined in each are broadly similar yet not identical. Common principles include safety and accuracy (AI will behave as it is expected to), transparency (how has AI made its decisions), fairness and equality (AI is free from racial, gender or other forms of discrimination), accountability (who is responsible for the use and development of AI systems) and human oversight (decisions made by AI will align with human values). Themes of other principles that are featured in some regulations include environmental conscientiousness, respect for labour rights and democratic values.

AI-specific laws, such as those proposed in the US, focus on particular instances of using and developing AI; for example, US law mandates that federal government employees who work with AI must undergo training to learn its capabilities and risks (AI Training Act, 2022). General IT laws that can apply to AI, such as New Zealand's Algorithm Charter (New Zealand Government, 2020), could prove helpful in mitigating its risks; however, they may fail to accommodate the inherent characteristics of AI that distinguish it from other classes of technology (importantly, its adaptable nature to potentially learn behaviours beyond those that were assessed). Guidelines, for example, those created in Japan (Ministry of Economy, Trade and Industry, 2022), offer only weak safeguards: adherence to them is not mandatory.

Whilst legislation prescribes what trustworthy AI must or must not do, or how it can or cannot be used, it does not provide the means to achieve it. Therefore, in parallel with legislative efforts, researchers are devising techniques for both assessing risk and assuring trust.

Risk assessment is the process of evaluating the trustworthiness of an AI system; various metrics have been developed to accomplish this. Assessing risk includes the preliminary step of determining which metrics are relevant to stakeholder values; for instance, an autonomous vehicle may require rigorous evaluation of its safety and accuracy, but less so its fairness and equality. Metrics used for risk assessment range from subjective to objective: subjective metrics, such as those used to assess how ethical a system is, include questionnaires and polls – debate is increasingly required (Chance et al., 2023). Oppositely, for functional properties, objective metrics can be used, such as AI-specific standards (The Alan Turing Institute, 2022).

The principles of trustworthy AI require different classes of techniques to be assured. For safety and accuracy, formal methods using mathematical analyses and proofs can be employed to monitor and shape behaviour (Mason et al.,

2017), simulations can be done to evaluate a system's performance (Singh et al., 2021) and testing of the system's code can identify implementation errors (Braiek and Khomh, 2020). For transparency, there is explainability to justify why AI has made a decision (Hassija et al., 2023) and traceability to examine all the factors that created the AI (Mora-Cantallops et al., 2021). For fairness and equality, data should be representative and free from errors (Clemmensen and Kjærsgaard, 2023) and appropriate models should be selected to mitigate bias (Ferrara, 2023). For accountability, there is redress to contest unjust decisions by AI (Fanni et al., 2023) and auditing for assessing the overarching process of developing AI systems (Falco et al., 2021). For human oversight, human-in-the-loop AI architectures require a human to always be included in the decision-making process; similarly, human-on-the-loop architectures ensure that a human can always intervene with an otherwise fully autonomous system (Nahavandi, 2017).

Despite advances in legislation and research, and even though current AI can be trusted in certain contexts, trustworthy AI in a general sense remains a goal; it is not yet the status. Although progress is being made with legislation, most of it is still in the drafting stage; moreover, its effectiveness is yet unproven. Furthermore, whilst many techniques to provide assurances of trustworthy AI have been developed (and continue to be developed), some offer only vague assurances, are too restrictive or have limited applicability (Hassija et al., 2023); and others are vulnerable to attack, such that they could be manipulated into giving assurances for systems that are not actually trustworthy (Noppel et al., 2022). More development is needed for trustworthy AI techniques so they are mature enough to be applied widely and effectively.

An additional challenge, as outlined in the UK's proposed AI regulations (Department for Science, Innovation & Technology, 2023), is that efforts to ensure AI trustworthiness should not stifle innovation. Unreasonably high expectations of trust, excessive legislation and overly restrictive techniques may dissuade people from using or developing AI in systems where it could otherwise flourish.

Acknowledgments We thank all of our colleagues in the Digital Systems Assurance group at Frazer-Nash Consultancy for their valuable expertise and feedback throughout this project. Particular thanks go to Rose Gambon, the group leader, and Lee Ramsay for their support that went beyond technical advice and leadership.

References

AI Training Act (2022). Public Law 117–207, § 136 Stat. 2238. United States.
Braiek, H. B. and Khomh, F. (2020). On testing machine learning programs. Journal of Systems and Software, 164, pp. 1–24. doi: 10.1016/j.jss.2020.110542.
Chance, G., Abeywickrama, D. B., LeClair, B. et al. (2023). Assessing Trustworthiness of Autonomous Systems. arXiv:2305.03411v2 [cs.AI].
China Law Translate (2022). Provisions on the Management of Algorithmic Recommendations in Internet Information Services. https://www.chinalawtranslate.com/en/algorithms/. Accessed 18th October 2023.

Clemmensen, L. H. and Kjærsgaard, R. D. (2023). Data Representativity for Machine Learning and AI Systems. arXiv:2203.04706v2 [stat.ML].

Department for Science, Innovation & Technology (2023). A pro-innovation approach to AI regulation. Great Britain. (CP 815).

European Commission (2023). The Artificial Intelligence Act. [online]. https://artificialintelligenceact.eu/. Accessed 5th October 2023.

Falco, G., Shneiderman, B., Badger, J. et al. (2021). Governing AI safety through independent audits. Nature Machine Intelligence, 3, pp. 566–571. doi: 10.1038/s42256-021-00370-7.

Fanni, R., Steinkogler, V. E., Zampedri, G. et al. (2023). Enhancing human agency through redress in Artificial Intelligence Systems. AI & Society, 38, pp. 537–547. doi: 10.1007/s00146-022-01454-7.

Ferrara, E. (2023). Fairness and Bias in Artificial Intelligence: A Brief Survey of Sources, Impacts, And Mitigation Strategies. arXiv:2304.07683v1 [cs.CY].

Gillespie, N., Lockey, S., Curtis, C. et al. (2023). Trust in Artificial Intelligence: A Global Study. The University of Queensland and KPMG Australia. doi: 10.1426/00d3c94.

Hassija, V., Chamola, V., Mahapatra, A. et al. (2023). Interpreting Black-Box Models: A Review on Explainable Artificial Intelligence. Cognitive Computation, pp. 1–30. doi: 10.1007/s12559-023-10179-8.

IAPP Research and Insights (2023). Global AI Legislation Tracker. [online]. https://iapp.org/resources/article/global-ai-legislation-tracker/. Accessed 4th October 2023.

Innovation, Science and Economic Development Canada (2023). Artificial Intelligence and Data Act [online]. https://ised-isde.canada.ca/site/innovation-better-canada/en/artificial-intelligence-and-data-act. Accessed 5th October 2023.

Li, B., Qi, P., Liu, B. et al. (2023). Trustworthy AI: From Principles to Practices. ACM Computing Surveys, 55(9), pp. 1–46.

Mason, G., Calinescu, R., Kudenko, D. et al. (2017). Assured Reinforcement Learning with Formally Verified Abstract Policies. In: Proceedings of the 9th International Conference on Agents and Artificial Intelligence. Science and Technology Publications, pp. 105–117. doi: 10.5220/0006156001050117.

Ministry of Economy, Trade and Industry (2022). Governance Guidelines for Implementation of AI Principles. [online]. https://www.meti.go.jp/shingikai/mono_info_service/ai_shakai_jisso/pdf/20220128_2.pdf. Accessed 5th October 2023.

Mora-Cantallops, M., Sánchez-Alonso, S., García-Barriocanal, E. et al. (2021). Traceability for Trustworthy AI: A Review of Models and Tools. Big Data and Cognitive Computing, 5(20), pp. 1–14. doi: 10.3390/bdcc5020020.

Nahavandi, S. (2017). Trusted Autonomy Between Humans and Robots: Toward Human-on-the-Loop in Robotics and Autonomous Systems. IEEE Systems, Man, and Cybernetics Magazine, 3(1), pp. 10–17. doi: 10.1109/MSMC.2016.2623867.

New Zealand Government (2020). Algorithm charter for Aotearoa New Zealand. [online]. https://www.data.govt.nz/toolkit/data-ethics/government-algorithm-transparency-and-accountability/algorithm-charter/. Accessed 5th October 2023.

Noppel, M., Peter, L. and Wressnegger, C. (2022). Backdooring Explainable Machine Learning. arXiv:2204.09498v1 [cs.CR].

OECD (2023). Brazil's path to responsible AI. https://oecd.ai/en/wonk/brazils-path-to-responsible-ai. Accessed 18th October 2023.

Russell, S. (2022). Artificial Intelligence and the Problem of Control. In: Werthner, H., Prem, E., Lee, E. A. et al. (eds) Perspectives on Digital Humanism. Springer, Cham. pp. 19–24. doi: 10.1007/978-3-030-86144-5_3

Singh, V., Hari, S. K. S., Tsai, T. et al. (2021). In: Proceedings of the IEEE/CVF Conference on Computer Vision and Pattern Recognition Workshops. pp. 122–128.

The Alan Turing Institute (2022). AI Standards Hub. [online]. https://aistandardshub.org/. Accessed 5th October 2023.

RAFIA - Using open-source software in an Automotive safety application - a case study

Gavin McCall

Codethink Ltd

Abstract *The size, complexity and integration of automotive software has increased beyond the point that bespoke software can be developed for each application, and there is a growing need to leverage existing software bases. This paper describes a Safety Software Engineering process called RAFIA (Risk Analysis, Fault Injection, Automation), which enables system developers and integrators to directly incorporate suitable open-sourced software components into safety applications. This process considers the properties of systems and subsystems as a whole rather than breaking them down into their smallest units. It uses System Theoretic Process Analysis (STPA) to identify critical interactions and specify safety requirements, and to derive tests and fault injections to verify these. The method is therefore suitable to design and identify issues in larger complex systems without needing to analyse each existing component in detail. This paper will present an overview of the process and present a case study describing its application in the development of a combined safety-related rear-view camera system and non-safety infotainment system. The case study has been developed as a safety element out of context (SEooC) and we have worked with an independent safety assessor to ensure a result that can be certified to ISO 26262.*

© Gavin McCall, 2024.
Published by the Safety-Critical Systems Club. All Rights Reserved

System Analysis on Driver Monitoring System for Mainline Railway

Niki Mok

TÜV Rheinland UK Ltd

Extended Abstract *Driver alertness and attention are factors in nearly 50% of Signal Passed At Danger (SPAD) events that could lead to railway accidents. Due to their shift work nature, train drivers need to overcome drowsiness and being distracted during operation. More than half of UK train drivers uses caffeine drinks, or even tablets to deal with fatigue. To ensure drivers are fit to work, the current Driver Safety Device (DSD) has been used in UK railway for decades. A DSD requires periodic pressure applied on a Deadman's pedal, handle or button for the vigilance system to reset. However, the current system can lead to routine action, or even be tricked or isolated. The delay time is 60s with action time typically 5-7 seconds that allows the driver to react and reset, or else an emergency brake applies. The timeout is much longer compared to the required reaction time for drivers to acknowledge other controls such as a train protection equipment. Moreover, a train runs hundreds of metres just within a few seconds nowadays, compared to a few decades ago when high-speed trains had not been introduced.*

Based on the multitude of problems that the current system possesses; the aim of this presentation is to introduce a system analysis to increase the capability of the existing vigilance system for UK mainline passenger trains to provide functionalities on detection and actuation based on driver's attentiveness.

This research looks at previous studies and different sensing and actuating technologies. Using Capability Systems Engineering approach, the purpose and understanding of stakeholder's needs is identified, high level performance requirements are established, and an operational concept that enables the capability of the vigilance system to be enhanced in a way that satisfies the requirements is developed.

An operational concept is proposed for a driver monitoring system with enhanced capability. A camera-based sensor emits infrared light that is able to capture images in dark environments and can accommodate drivers wearing sunglasses.

© TÜV Rheinland UK Ltd, 2024.
Published by the Safety-Critical Systems Club. All Rights Reserved.

When a driver experiences drowsiness including increase in eye closure speed to above 0.5s or an increase in percentage of eye closure over time to more than 30%, a fatigue event is triggered. A sensor also detects the driver looking away for more than 1.8s as a distraction event. These occurrences are perceived by a processing unit fitted on the driving cab which activates to produce either an audio warning or seat vibration to alert the driver. Triggered by consecutive fatigue events, a message is sent to the control centre. A staff member then verifies the situation to eliminate any false-positives. The monitoring team seek action through mutual verbal agreement with the driver on whether driving operation should be continued.

This new capability is efficient in reducing the reaction time of detection on driver's falling asleep by 97% from 65s to 2s for drivers who cannot be woken by audio alarm, and by 93% for drivers from 30s to 2s who can be woken up by a beeping sound.

Additional functionalities of the proposed design include detecting early signs of falling asleep, microsleep and eyes-off-road, both intentional and unintentionally. For drivers who become incapacitated or die, the reaction time remains at 65s with no improvement in those cases which still need to rely on traditional DSD.

The new monitoring system is suggested to be deployed alongside the existing vigilance system. It does not need to interface with safety-critical functions such as the braking control circuit to support automatic emergency brake function if run in parallel with the old system. No interface issues are identified regarding ringing of both the old and new audio alarm that could potentially lead to confusion.

This research conducted for the vigilance device reflected the criticality of demand for the enhanced functionalities because of the inherent shortcomings of the traditional system. These improvements can be achieved by monitoring eyes and head movement of drivers using the re-designed capability. If implemented successfully, this new vigilance system can reduce up to 22.9% of overall fatal train accidents in UK under general assumptions.

Implementation of such a monitoring system still faces many challenges in the wider UK railway context. Concerns over data privacy need to be addressed via a robust and secure software model, and detailed negotiations with representatives from driver unions are needed to assure drivers that the system is not for surveillance purpose, nor performance judgement by the employer.

Fatigue prediction technologies available nowadays are largely based on research and development in the road driving sector. Railway operation is different in which its working environment and safety regulations are more complex. It is therefore recommended that future work should involve both a psychologist and software engineer to integrate expertise for such a monitoring system. Once the requirements are refined as the system evolves, the product will become more sophisticated on meeting both functional and non-functional requirements.

When staged implementation is completed with defects resolved, the goal is to establish a continuous improvement programme through identifying 'near misses' of fatigue and distraction events, not only to raise awareness of employees of their own fatigue level, but to strategically plan fatigue management and shift schedules more effectively. This system analysis allows the railway undertakings to understand the technical concerns and requirements associated with the usage of such a monitoring system within the railway context and give the train operating companies (TOCs) an option to explore train services that they can provide to be even safer and more reliable.

Implementing autonomy in nuclear robotics: an experience-informed review of applying SACE

Phillip Mulvana[1], Lacey-Jo Marsland[2], Tom Boden[1], Guy Burroughes[1], Richard Hawkins[3], Matt Osborne[3]

[1]RAICo, UK Atomic Energy Authority

[2]AtkinsRéalis

[3]Assuring Autonomy International Programme, University of York

Abstract *Nuclear decommissioning is a complex, hazardous, and time-consuming process that requires highly skilled and trained operators. To address the work-force bottleneck and the growing inventory of nuclear materials, a Robotic Glovebox with AI capability that can assist in the preparation and processing of nuclear material is being developed. This innovative solution can enable safer, more efficient, and continuous decommissioning operations. To support the adoption of this new technology it is necessary to develop a safety case for the system. In this paper we describe how we have used an autonomous system safety case process (the SACE approach) to generate confidence in our initial AI glovebox design. This safety case example is being provided as input it into the Office for Nuclear Regulation (ONR) regulatory innovation sandbox and should help to establish a new paradigm in safety cases for autonomous systems in nuclear environments.*

© UKAEA RAICo 2024.
Published by the Safety-Critical Systems Club. All Rights Reserved.

1 Introduction

Gloveboxes are sealed containers that allow safe manipulation of hazardous materials in a controlled atmosphere. They are widely used in the nuclear industry for various tasks involving radiological samples. However, gloveboxes differ in their design, material, and number of operators, depending on the specific tasks and requirements. This also affects the safety risks and challenges of glovebox operations.

The operators who work in gloveboxes are highly trained and skilled professionals who follow strict procedures and protocols. However, their training is costly and time-consuming, and their demand often exceeds their supply. This creates a backlog of work and increases the risk of human error and fatigue. Therefore, there is a need for automation of glovebox processes to reduce human-related inconsistencies, enhance safety performance, and increase productivity.

Automation of glovebox processes can provide several benefits for the nuclear industry. It can improve the safety of operators by minimizing their exposure to radiation and other hazards. It can reduce the environmental impact of glovebox operations by preventing the spread of contamination and ensuring proper waste management. It can increase the speed and efficiency of glovebox tasks by enabling continuous and consistent operation without human intervention. It can also facilitate the decommissioning of legacy nuclear sites by accelerating the processing of hazardous materials.

Systems that use AI can exploit its capability to infer desired options in new, unseen settings. This is enabled by training the machine on a large corpus of media showing the target in known settings, so that it can 'understand' what the target is in new settings. The application of AI in this case seeks to train a system to identify a radiological sample in the glovebox environment. This allows the system to take the sample through a process of identifying, cutting, cleaning, and packaging, while accounting for dynamic environmental variables such as size, shape, and material properties.

This capability allows the system to continuously process samples without the constraints highlighted previously (e.g. operator availability, fatigue, training). This is an essential part of managing current and future demands in nuclear decommissioning.

However, autonomous decision-making introduces significant system complexity, which leads to potential hazards with causes that do not exist in conventional systems, such as:

- Object misclassification leading to execution of unsafe actions.
- Unintended interactions with the environment leading to unsafe outcomes.
- Failure to identify an unsafe system state.
- Exploitation of the desired process leading to unsafe outcomes.

AI elements of the system cannot presently lead directly to harm, but they can act as a secondary cause in ways that differ from the automated software that they replace.

These hazards and their root causes are predictably of concern to regulators, industry, and the public alike. The success of this project therefore depends on its ability to assuage the concerns of these parties.

Much like the hazards themselves, there are a defined number of secondary factors for the onset of these hazards, which include challenges such as insufficient/unrepresentative training, skewed/tampered training data or poor goal specification.

At time of writing there is no mature regulatory regime for autonomous systems in the nuclear environment. The Office for Nuclear Regulation (ONR) has clearly identified the same benefits and challenges as the RAICo technical leadership and has made space within their 'regulatory sandbox' environment to explore the challenges of developing safety assurance arguments for AI in the nuclear environment. This resulted in the formation of a panel of experts and stakeholders who stood to either shape or become a recipient of these autonomous systems.

This paper explores the process of a creating a safety case for a robotic glovebox utilising AI to process nuclear material (referred to as the "Robotic Glovebox" hereafter). The development of the Robotic Glovebox aims to reduce risk to operators by eliminating the need for them to be present in high-risk areas and perform manual operations. This paper accomplishes this by hypothesising the addition of goal-oriented AI to a real-world system that is currently trialling robotic decommissioning. This Safety Case has been developed in line with the Guidance on the Safety Assurance of Autonomous Systems in Complex Environments (SACE) (Hawkins, et al., July 2022), which relies on the non-autonomous aspects of the system design and safety assurance running concurrently to produce a complete safety case for an autonomous system.

The paper is structured as follows:

Section 2 considers the background and context of AI and robotics in nuclear applications.
Section 3 discusses the use cases, application and expected deliverables.
Section 4 outlines the selection of the safety case approach.
Section 5 details the implementation of SACE.
Section 6 draws conclusions on the nature of the approach in this context.
Section 7 details potential improvements to the approach.
Section 8 considers possible future opportunities.

2 Background

2.1 AI in the nuclear context

The nuclear domain moves with incredible intentionality with a relatively concrete position on risk acceptance, favouring technologies that have been tried and tested for a given application over minor increases in performance at the expense of adding novelty. Both the RAICo programme and the regulator, however, recognise the expansion of AI into all domains, whether through the automated generation of technical literature or through system design itself. In multiple workshops held with regulators, site license companies and supply chain It was recognised that assessing the impact of highly innovative technologies in AI would be proportionate to the benefits it may yield.

This panel of experts ultimately agreed that creating an exploratory safety case could test the limits of existing technical and governance regimes in the context of AI. This group pursued the RAICo proposal to create a quasi-real-world test case representative of real hardware and nuclear use cases with the notional application of goal-oriented AI.

3 Use Case

3.1 Use Case Description

This goal-oriented AI system would make use of two types of cameras to identify objects within the glovebox; wide field-of-view cameras attached to the glovebox and an object-focused camera situated on the end of the robot arm. The system will first use these to locate the target in its environment, then make decisions which allow the sample to move through the process.

These capabilities would be based on existing capabilities that RAICo possess in deep learning for machine vision which are currently used for research-based pick and place tasks. This capability has been created from a human-labelled training set which allows the system to learn the shape, size, and characteristics of several objects found in a nuclear-industrial environment and would thus be carried forward into the strawman.

3.2 The RAICo Strawman Glovebox

For the purposes of the strawman glovebox, this AI layer would be theoretically applied to an existing hardware project built to test remote sample processing using a modified glovebox fitted with two collaborative robot arms (Figure 1). This was done intentionally to reflect a generic glovebox in industry and ensure that this could serve as a base for the implementation of an autonomous system in the context of SACE.

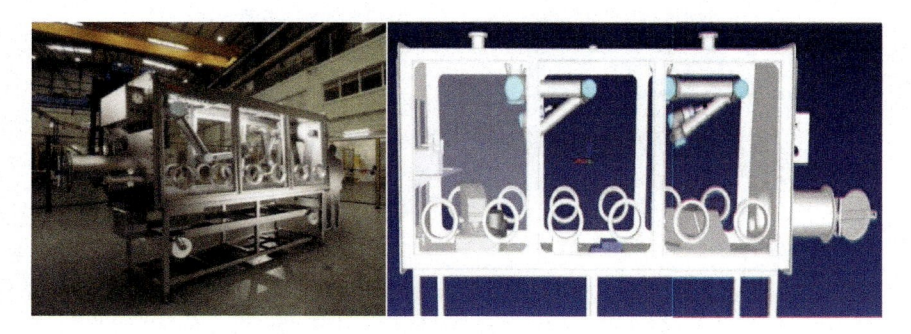

Fig. 1. CAD Renders of the RAICo Strawman Glovebox

This setup proved the ideal vehicle for a strawman safety analysis, allowing safety engineers to build upon its outputs without causing any real-world project or safety risk that may result from the experimental nature of the project. The credibility of the safety case is strengthened owing to its ability to make use of a genuine bill of materials, conduct real analyses of the conventional elements and leverage the expertise of a real combined project team, as illustrated in Figure 3. This conventional glovebox will operate in an environment that has been designed for representative operations to handle the processing of low-activity nuclear samples which lay below a threshold that requires strong nuclear diligence; this uniquely positions the project to conduct safe research and development while retaining the authenticity of the strawman.

The degree to which this project is abstracted from a true deployment does, however, bring challenges; simplifications such as a high degree of control over the environment and object shape/size may not be representative of a final deployment of this system. Despite the potential limitations, it is believed this still offers a strong opportunity to both template safety case approaches for AS and demonstrate a credible regulatory position for the deployment of a complex system.

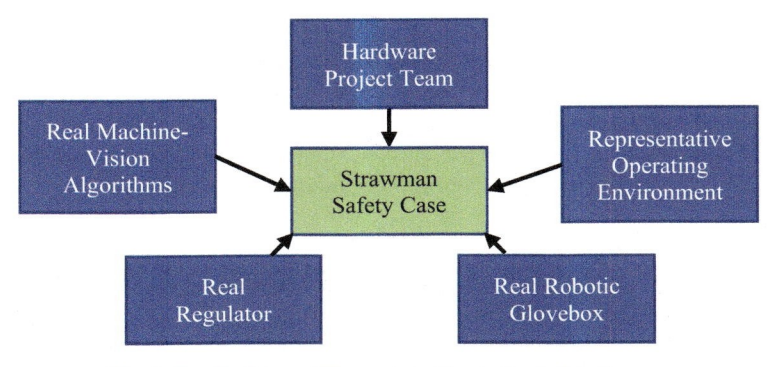

Fig. 2. Synthesizing of Elements to Create the Safety Case

3.3 Expected deliverables

This project offered the ability to assess a number of technical and governance approaches, here primary aims included:

- Evaluating a safety case approach for AI systems in nuclear and other safety-critical environments.
- The assessment of safety and regulatory considerations for autonomous systems in nuclear applications.
- Developing a safety case model for future autonomous systems within the RAICo programme.
- Investigating compatibility with current nuclear operational practises.

Secondary aims include:

- Identifying technical limitations and risk tolerance for autonomous systems in nuclear settings.
- Discovering opportunities for creating new safety assessment tools for autonomous systems in nuclear contexts.
- Building expertise in this emerging field of safety engineering.

4 Selecting an Appropriate Safety Case Approach

The project began by analysing regulatory and standards frameworks for ensuring the safe development of AI systems in high-integrity contexts. This analysis included a review of safety development lifecycles, comparing approaches such as

UL4600 (Standards, 2023) for automotive development and *SCSC Safety Assurance Objectives SCSC-135B for general AI safety guidance*.

Evaluation of these options focussed on three key criteria:

- The extent to which they offered a comprehensive development lifecycle for the autonomous elements of a system, with an emphasis on compatibility with existing safety practices and the ability to provide robust safety decision-making processes.
- Independence from industry-specific biases, ensuring a fair assessment of risk reduction potential irrespective of the approach's origin.
- Compatibility with existing approaches, with the intent of managing challenges related to organisational inertia such as those which may make organisations inclined to remain within existing domain frameworks.

In summary, SACE emerged as a strong, independent framework suitable for building a safety case. It demonstrated adaptability to different systems and implementations, with a track record in various safety-critical domains such as medical, aerospace, and automotive. SACE's development was guided by respected institutions and backed by the Assuring Autonomy International Programme, making it the optimal choice for this project.

SACE (*Hawkins, et al. 2022*) is a methodology that provides detailed guidance on the creation of a compelling safety case for an autonomous system (AS). It comprises a set of safety case patterns and a process for systematically integrating safety assurance into the development of the AS and for generating the evidence base for explicitly justifying the acceptable safety of the AS. SACE builds on existing established system safety assurance processes and defines modifications, enhancements and additions to specifically deal with the safety assurance challenges of an autonomous system operating in a complex environment. As such, SACE is intended to complement activities undertaken as part of existing systems engineering and safety assurance processes.

5 Application of SACE

The safety case project has initiated the SACE process (Figure 3) and, at time of writing, has completed the Operating Context Assurance and Hazardous Scenarios Identification stages.

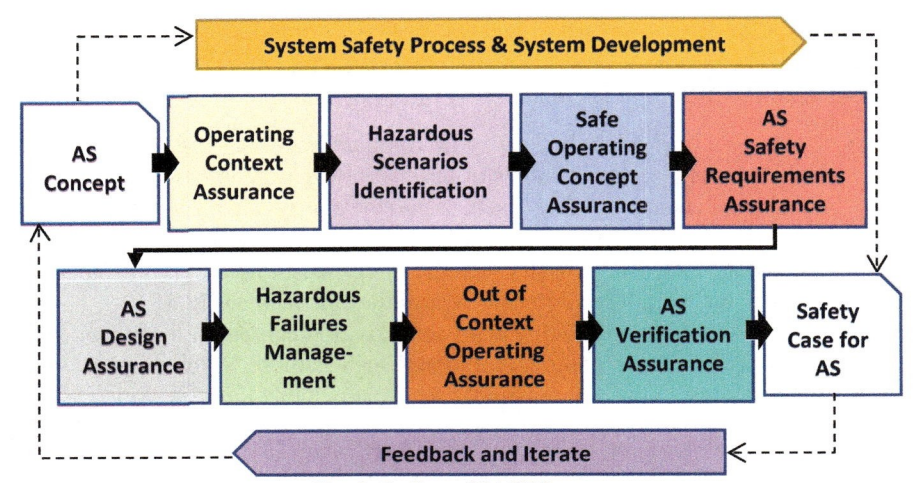

Fig. 3. Outline of SACE Process

The guidance suggests that these early stages be undertaken at the functional level. Upon application within the nuclear context, however, a different reality is revealed. Our use case has suggested that, as autonomy is used to simplify operation, reduce complexity, or expand capability, very few (if any) autonomous systems would be designed from a truly blank slate, particularly in nuclear applications. In the context of this project, for example, there were constraints around hardware from the outset. Enabling the incorporation of this information in the early stages of safety case development may limit the number of Operating Scenarios and subsequent Hazardous Scenarios, thus enabling efficient utilisation of resource in authoring the Safety Case and a greater focus on the elements which could truly present hazards.

5.1 Phase One – Operating Context Assurance

Guidance from the ISA suggested there were strong and heavily iterative connections between these early phases of the SACE and our experience in implementing it confirmed this.

This became particularly apparent when developing the Context of Safe Operation (CSO) during Phase 1. The CSO consists of the Operational Domain Model (ODM), the Autonomous Capabilities and the Operating Scenarios for the autonomous system. The development of any one of these areas directly influences the other two and the effect of this can be a process of developing one area to maturity only to find that a small change in another area forces redevelopment of the initial document. Whilst challenging, it is these connections which represent the true nature of autonomous decision making and the contextual importance of elements like the operating domain on the AS capability. No revised work was considered lost work in this process. With all changes logged and rationales captured, these were then used to inform the validation reports for each of the activities. In terms of providing a safety case that is complete, compelling, and accurate, reflecting on all these changes is essential.

As well as highlighting the relationships within the CSO, identifying Operating Scenarios also involved the consideration of existing approaches to nuclear safety cases and subsequent SACE activities. For example, equipment failures should not be considered as Operating Scenarios as these would, instead, be captured within a Failure Modes and Effects Analysis (FMEA). Additionally, outcomes of decisions made by the autonomous system (e.g. Robot collides with Object) were not considered Operating Scenarios as they are elicited as outcomes of the AS Decision Analysis.

5.2 Phase Two – Hazardous Scenarios Identification

This phase marked the first point at which safety issues began to be elicited and provided a concrete idea about the effectivity of our prior analyses and specification for use in future phases.

The Operating Scenarios identified within Stage 1 present the decision points of the autonomous system. Options are then elicited for each of these decision points to outline the potential actions of the autonomous system in response to the scenario. These decisions are analysed in the context of real-world state and system belief state; disparities between the two belief states present a space in which hazards can arise and enable the identified of hazardous scenarios associated with operation of the autonomous system.

It is noted that this decision analysis is similar to a Hazard and Operability (HAZOP) study in that it aims to identify the points at which a hazard may arise within a process/set of actions. It is, therefore, advisable that this analysis is undertaken with a multi-discipline team to capture knowledge gaps.

When applied as written in SACE, the decisions analysis identified a large number of potential outcomes. It was, therefore, beneficial to apply a severity rating to the outcomes (as recommended within SACE) to enable straightforward distinction between seriously hazardous scenarios and those which are simply inconvenient This allowed more effective analysis to take place by identifying scenarios that led to harm to people.

Hazardous scenarios in SACE are elicited by applying environmental conditions that may influence the outcome of an autonomous decision. The Robotic Glovebox offers a self-contained micro-environment of pressure, humidity, lighting etc. meaning it is far more controllable than may otherwise be the case. This limited the number of applicable environmental conditions that could be introduced to the system that actively posed a hazard to a person. The constrained environment of the Robotic Glovebox is something that also became apparent when creating the severity scale for the hazardous scenarios; the extent to which hazards can impact a person was limited to potential wounding/laceration, indirect radiation exposure from glovebox operations, and to direct exposure to radiation by a complete system failure.

It is noted that SACE does not provide guidance around the means of validating that all appropriate environmental conditions have been considered in the identification of hazardous scenarios and, as such, there is uncertainty around the completion of the AS decision analysis. Completeness of the AS decision analysis for the robotic glovebox was demonstrated through peer review rather than taking a systematic approach.

The identification of these hazardous scenarios is essential because traditional safety analysis does not fully analyse the consequence or hazardous output of decisions that an AS can make. Decision analysis does this in a comprehensive way that accounts for misunderstandings within the AS.

By identifying the high severity hazardous scenarios, proper requirements can then be written that mitigate these scenarios, through either AS limitations or hardware choices.

5.3 Phase Three – Safe Operating Concept

The Safe Operating Concept (SOC) encompasses system-level safety requirements that dictate how an autonomous system should behave to mitigate hazardous events. Progressing through Phases One and Two, we observed the emergence of requirements when discussing the interactions between system elements. While there was a temptation to move directly to the requirements and hardware allocation, completing the preceding phases established a robust foundation for decision-making.

The link between hazardous scenarios, requirements and design choices signifies comprehensive hazard identification and assessment. This method instils greater confidence in the final safety case.

Implementing hardware decisions prior to the identification of hazardous scenarios and SOC may unnecessarily constrain the autonomous capability of the AS. These constraints limit the number of available options at the design stage and could, therefore, stifle innovation.

As previously discussed, SACE Phases One and Two favour functional-level analyses to influence safety-driven design. Making hardware decisions without a clear grasp of hazardous scenarios and associated requirements can lead to sub-optimal design choices. Detailed knowledge of hazards and requirements is essential for effective optioneering studies.

Example 1:
During the AS decision analysis, the following hazardous scenario was identified:

<The Robot Arm is travelling with an Object> <with the Robot Arm Mounting Frame in the path of the Robot Arm> AND <The Robot Arm continues along its current path>.

This could challenge the integrity of the Mounting Frame and result in a breach of glovebox containment. From this, the following requirement was produced as part of the SOC:

> "While travelling, the Robot Arm shall maintain safe separation from the Robot Arm Mounting Frame".

Example 2:
During the AS decision analysis, the following hazardous scenario was identified:

> <The Robot Arm is Grasping a radioactive Object> <with the incorrect End Effector attached> AND <The Robot Arm continues with Grasp>.

This could result in the spread of contamination within the glovebox through contamination of the End Effector and/or damage to the radio-active Object. From this, the following requirement was produced as part of the SOC:

> "When Grasping an Object, the Robot Arm shall ensure that the correct end effector is attached".

While many of the requirements derived from the hazardous scenarios can be decomposed and addressed through hardware decisions, some may pertain to machine learning function in SACE Phase Four. For instance, Example 1 (above) could lead to safety requirements related to the Machine Vision System. The safety assurance of such elements may be undertaken in accordance with the guidance for Assurance of Machine Learning for use in Autonomous Systems (AMLAS). An understanding of AMLAS is, therefore, recommended when undertaking implementation of SACE.

Requirements within the SOC prioritise prevention of the hazardous scenario over protection or mitigation. This aligns with the ONR Safety Assessment Principles with respect to the five levels of defence in depth (*Office for Nuclear Regulation, July 2019*); safety functions associated with normal operations typically relate to Levels 1 and 2 of the Defence in Depth hierarchy. The SOC also includes the identification of Reduced Operating Domains (RODs) in response to system or component failure modes, making it advisable to conduct a functional failure analysis at the beginning of SACE Phase Three.

6 Conclusions

6.1 Nature of the Strawman Safety Case and the Need to Narrow the Project Scope

Creating a comprehensive safety argument through the SACE framework is a resource-intensive endeavour that exceeds the scope of this project. Consequently, we've prioritised certain framework elements and documented our progress and lessons learned as we gain proficiency in each step.

Rather than duplicating well-established analyses for the entire operational scope of the AS, we focussed on four specific use cases of interest. This approach allowed us to gain a broader understanding of the SACE process while efficiently testing various components of the Safety Case framework.

The decision to narrow the scope occurred when identifying AS Operating Scenarios. The complexity of the Robotic Glovebox resulted in a vast number of activity diagrams and potential use cases. Identifying Operating Scenarios for the full scope was deemed too time-consuming and labour-intensive within the context of this project. The decision to reduce scope has meant that hazard analysis has not been performed for some tasks of the Robotic Glovebox. This however has had limited impact as some of the Use Cases carried forward (e.g. Travel to Destination and Grasp Object) were representative of many other activities within the Safety Case.

The "Prepare to Cut sample" operation was retained in the down-selection process as it was a clear candidate for presenting hazards across the AS and traditional safety elements. Both the project team and the regulators recognised the value of assessing its associated risks. Additionally, the "Object Classification" use case was retained due to the recognised hazard of object misclassification and its potential impact on other use cases.

Lastly, autonomously posting items out of the glovebox was known to involve hazardous operations, but it was not considered feasible given the current state of technology. It is considered a future candidate for more detailed assessment.

6.2 Lessons Learned in Applying SACE

A critical outcome of this project is its ability to inform the industry of potential strengths and weaknesses with both the SACE framework and the process of delivering an autonomous system at large. These strengths and weaknesses are expressed below in a list of lessons learned:

- The relationship between SACE and conventional system safety activities should be considered prior to any of the implementation activities. There are natural synergies between the two lifecycle approaches, and without explicit consideration of these projects may find themselves either delayed as they wait for information required from the conventional design, or overly constraining the system because of requirements over the AS.
- The SACE process cannot be implemented after hardware is allocated or a system has been built. The iterative process of defining an ODM, the operating scenarios and the autonomous capabilities directly drives design. There can be no mistaking the extensive influence that the safety assurance process has over system design. Dependent on the aspirations of the system

or the complexity of the environment, the safety elements may either shape the design or preclude it entirely. It is in the design organisations best interests to be aware of this at project initiation.
- The application of AI to a given system may be at best detrimental to the process itself or at worst objectively add unsafety to an otherwise robust system. In summary, the desire to make a process autonomous should not override the drawbacks of doing so and, as previously stated, a robust justification should be provided for the implementation of an autonomous system. In a significant number of cases, it became apparent that autonomous decisions and functionality could easily be replaced with automated (i.e. pre-defined closed loop) behaviours.
- The securing of an effective governance framework in which to operate the autonomous system is as challenging and important as developing the technology and the safety case itself. Acceptance, to a large extent, is driven by trust factors such as transparency, intentionality, and education. Acceptance arriving from these factors should be considered with equal weighting to the safety case itself.
- An AI safety case is an additional stream of work, and whilst complimentary to the existing safety case, requires at least the same level of effort. Like all processes, generating talent and corporate memory for the AS design process will inevitably lead to time saving in the long term. Its short-term application can be expected to approximately double the time invested into safety assurance.
- Irrespective of intention to develop autonomous capabilities, there is benefit to all organisations undertaking safety evaluation in complex environments in considering the creation of a domain specific ODD. The ability to interrogate an ODD against specific conditions and design considerations is among the most powerful elements of the SACE process and yielded consideration of failures and conditions outside the AS that were not present in previous dialogue.
- The use of specific language has been demonstrably vital within our application of SACE. Clearly defining the scope of autonomous operations and the associated decision points enables accurate identification of potential outcomes/hazardous scenarios. It is, therefore, recommended that terms are clearly defined and consistently applied throughout documentation. Failure to define semantically correct definitions may directly lead to incorrect safety requirements.
- The Goal Structuring Notation (GSN) that underpins the SACE approach calls for the validation of the output of each phase. There is, however, no specific guidance for performing this validation at any phase. As previously noted, this lack of clarity has the potential to introduce uncertainty around the accuracy and completeness of work undertaken within a given task/phase. The validation activities did offer an opportunity to review the contents of the phases' outputs in detail of which the importance cannot be

understated. It also allowed for an opportunity to justify the decisions and progression of the Robotic Glovebox Safety Case as it was being developed.

7 The Future of the AI Glovebox Project

The project is approximately 40% complete and we have recognised a significant amount of effort required to complete the process is front-loaded into phases 1-3, with these steps forming the foundation of future activity. The project will continue to move forward with its reduced scope to assess overall fitness for purpose of the SACE framework within the nuclear sector. Should there be a desire to continue, this project scope can be returned and omitted use cases can be analysed for remaining hazardous scenarios. By this point, the process for analysing, mitigating, and implementing the remaining scope of the Robotic Glovebox Safety Case will be understood by the completion of the reduced scope. Updating the remainder of the Safety Case should be a comparatively low effort endeavour given no unexpected or unmanageable risks.

When complete it is hoped this project will have produced the following outputs:

- A template for implementing SACE in future robotic systems in a nuclear environment.
- A gap analysis of current regulatory requirements against those produced during the SACE and traditional system safety case process.
- A body of knowledge to be used by other safety engineers undertaking this work to provide detail over the intention and rationale of various steps within the SACE process.
- An accord with the ONR as to the viability of autonomous systems in the nuclear regulatory regime

8 Opportunities for Improving our Approach

Progressing through the SACE process has highlighted some interesting technical and process-related work that could be pursued to either improve the process or generate a higher level of confidence in its outputs. A list of these elements can be found below.

8.1 Implementation Opportunities

- Considering responsible innovation as a key element of the complete safety argument for the system alongside conventional and AS safety processes.
- Detailing the process of interacting with the regulator. Creating a short document listing concerns from the regulator and potential answers from within SACE could be used to guide early-stage conversations in new or similar domains.
- Forming a panel of independent assessors comprised of customer and regulator representatives to conduct the assurance steps of each part of the SACE process.
- Automating the AS analyses that support the SACE process such that expected links between these elements are automatically formed ready for population with data.

8.2 Project/Hardware Opportunities

- Add additional complexity to the system by considering the fully autonomous interaction of two robot arms within the glovebox, ensuring their safe operation as independent parts of an autonomous whole.
- Instantiating this safety case in contexts where the operator doesn't have full control of its ODM. This would mean we have to accommodate a wider range of parameters within the safety analyses.
- Incorporation of new techniques/technologies such as chemical sampling replacing the need for swabbing.

8.3 Regulatory Opportunities

The project continues to work with the regulator to identify opportunities to better ease the coming of AS in the context of nuclear safety. We plan to better define these opportunities in future papers but highlight three key learnings below:

- Existing guidance for nuclear safety cases focusses on sites and facilities rather than smaller systems. If this approach is accepted and implemented more widely, guidance around the development of system safety cases would facilitate innovation across the industry.
- As a result of point one, this autonomous system and the approach used to define its safety characteristics has some incompatibilities with the current license conditions. We have identified there may be some opportunities to draw parallels between the two, but ultimately this would require a separate more focused study.

- If this approach is accepted and implemented more widely, it would be beneficial for Nuclear Safety Committees to have representatives with a detailed understanding of AI and the implementation of Nuclear Safety Cases for Autonomous Systems. Further guidance may enhance this.

Acknowledgements The authors are grateful for the pivotal support and funding provided by the Robotics and AI Collaboration whose funding and encouragement have been instrumental in advancing our research in this whitepaper.

References

Hawkins, et al., July 2022. Guidance on the Safety Assurance of Autonomous Systems in Complex Environments. *Assuring Autonomy International Programme (AAIP) The University of York, York, 2022* https://www.york.ac.uk/assuring-autonomy/guidance/sace/sace-download/

Office for Nuclear Regulation, July 2019. Nuclear Safety Technical Assessment Guide – NS-TAST-GD-094 Revision 2.2. Office for Nuclear Regulation, 2019

UL Standards and Engagement. (2023). Presenting the Standard for Safety for the Evaluation of Autonomous Vehicles and Other Products. https://ulse.org/ul-standards-engagement/presenting-standard-safety-evaluation-autonomous-vehicles-and-other-1

SCSC Safety Assurance Objectives SC135b for general AI safety guidance. Version 3.0. Safety of Autonomous Systems Working Group.

Poster: Using Rust for Safety-Critical Systems

Jonathan Pallant

Ferrous Systems UK Limited

Abstract *Ferrocene is a downstream project of the main Rust Programming Language compiler ("rustc") that is qualified for use in safety-critical systems in accordance with ISO 26262 ASIL D and IEC 61508 SIL 4. It is the first of its kind in that is completely open source (https://github.com/ferrocene) and it does not diverge from the upstream codebase. But what does that mean exactly? This poster walks through the documentation and tooling behind Ferrocene - and with that, the ways in which the project produces continuous daily releases that each meet the same high bar for quality as a production release.*

© Jonathan Pallant 2024.
Published by the Safety-Critical Systems Club. All Rights Reserved

How to Assure a Cloud

Mike Parsons

Ebeni Ltd and SCSC

Abstract *There is increasing pressure to adopt Cloud-based IT as it so much cheaper and simpler for an organisation to contract for the IT services needed rather than actually owning and maintaining their own IT infrastructure. The same pressures exist for safety functions and some safety-related IT is now provided by Cloud services in areas such as healthcare, policing and government. In the near future safety-critical functions such as those used in air traffic management (ATM) may be provided in this way. Other sectors are moving in the same direction. This is a fundamental shift as, using paradigms such as Software as a Service (SaaS), Infrastructure as a Service (IaaS) and Platform as a Service (PaaS), the IT implementation is to some extent hidden from view and operated and maintained using commercial imperatives. This means that traditional methods of assurance involving detailed knowledge of the components, the engineering design, the organisation and methodologies employed do not work any longer: new methods are needed. The presentation explains work done by the SCSC Service Assurance working group to address these problems, and shows how the Service Assurance Guidance can be mapped to an air traffic management context. Examples are given of recent work with a major European ATM provider to develop a framework involving principles, objectives and workflow to assure critical IT functions provided by a Cloud.*

© Mike Parsons 2024.
Published by the Safety-Critical Systems Club. All Rights Reserved

Assurance 2.0: experience and automation

Ben Philips

Adelard part of NCC Group

Abstract *This talk will introduce Assurance 2.0, discuss those features that are being taken up by industry and outline the automation support that we have been developing as part of the DARPA ARCOS programme on the automation of certification.*

Poster: Adaptive Safety Measures: A Concept to Optimize Safety in Automated Driving Systems

Anil Ranjitbhai Patel, Peter Liggesmeyer

Chair of Software Engineering: Dependability, RPTU Kaiserslautern, Germany

Abstract *This poster introduces an approach in the field of Autonomous Driving Systems (ADS), focusing on enhancing safety in complex and rapidly changing driving conditions. Central to this research is the development of a dynamic risk rating system. Leveraging runtime data from On-board sensors (OBS), this system continuously evaluates and responds to risk levels based on key parameters, such as relative velocity, distance to the lead vehicle, and driving environment conditions. By incorporating Machine Learning techniques, it adapts its risk management algorithms to be more proactive and less reactive.*

The research then integrates this risk level prediction with a system service monitor to translate risk assessments into actionable safety measures. This integration identifies safety rules that could prevent hazardous situations during operation, marking a key step in operational safety. Subsequently, a reconfiguration strategy is employed, involving a configuration manager that includes a system service monitor, a set of safety rules, and various configurations. It works with the risk assessment module to select and activate configurations that mitigate identified risks while maintaining functionality. Each safety rule correlates specific vehicle risk levels with restorative measures, ensuring operational safety.

The poster details a comprehensive simulation study in a highway lane-following scenario with an adaptive cruise control system. This environment replicates various failure conditions, such as sensor malfunctions, unexpected behaviours of the lead vehicle, and adverse weather conditions. The results demonstrate the model's ability to dynamically adapt to unsafe situations, offering a granular understanding of evolving risks and enabling the ADS to make safer, more risk-informed decisions.

The advanced transportation field of ADS necessitates a shift from traditional static risk assessment methods to dynamic, adaptable models. This research contributes to this field by providing a conceptual framework for dynamic risk management. The adaptive risk rating system not only improves the ability of ADS to navigate complex environments but also sets a new way forward for runtime risk perception and management. It is a step toward more intelligent, adaptive, and safe autonomous driving technologies, capable of handling the unpredictability and diversity of real-world driving scenarios.

Acknowledgements This poster discusses research conducted within the framework of a broader project sponsored by the Performance Center Simulation and Software-based Innovation (Leistungszentrum Simulations- und Software-basierte Innovation) based in Kaiserslautern, Germany.

© Anil Ranjitbhai Patel, Peter Liggesmeyer 2024.
Published by the Safety-Critical Systems Club. All Rights Reserved

Lithium-ion Batteries: Safety in Second-Life Applications

Anne Seldon

>Product Safety and Compliance
>
>WAE Technologies Ltd

Abstract *As the world begins to finally acknowledge the devastating impact of climate change and the need to move towards more sustainable alternatives, industries are increasingly moving towards lithium-ion battery technology to power the future. A recent report from McKinsey indicates that Li-ion battery demand is expected to grow by about 27 percent annually, increasing the demand on battery manufacturers and consumption of finite resources leading to further negative environmental impacts. Experts in the field have proposed that a solution to limit consumption of resources is to remove batteries from their primary applications and utilise them in a second-life application such as stationary storage. Whilst this proposal helps to reduce the potential environmental impact on the planet, it potentially introduces safety risks which must be effectively managed to ensure that the use of aged lithium-ion batteries does not result in catastrophic failure. This presentation explores the risks associated with aged lithium-ion batteries and proposes a model for managing the safety of lithium-ion batteries when installing in second-life applications.*

© Anne Seldon, 2024.
Published by the Safety-Critical Systems Club. All Rights Reserved

How do we make the case for "Safe" software and AI systems? - the Horizon Example

David Slater

Cardiff University

Abstract *This short paper outlines the steps for creating an initial FRAM model of a typical software solution to the counter operations Post Office Horizon assisted by ChatGPT 4.0.*

1 The Background

"Programming is a human task and programmers make mistakes; an error rate in writing software code of 10 errors per thousand lines of code is considered good, 1 error per thousand lines is rarely if ever achieved."

Harold Thimbleby et al

The current public inquiry into the causes and implications of the failures of the Post Office's Horizon software, has served to bring to the fore an issue which has been a problem for software and safety engineers for a long time. The issue has been outlined[1] in a think piece which asks the question as to why we have not manged to do this more effectively to date. One of the main problems seems to be the lack of a universally acceptable and accepted method of demonstrating this to designers and users alike. This has resulted in a reliance on a catalogue of qualitative assurances from the number of precautions and tests involved that the system must be safe.

But in reality, we are all aware that this is more hope than confidence. Software is getting more capable, but also more complex all the time. We have a real problem with assuring ourselves that the coding does exactly what it says 'on the tin', no more and no less. With more conventional engineering systems, risk assessments and safety cases would be made by analysing and predicting the reliability and security of the system from detailed engineering process flow or wiring diagrams. Unfortunately, software systems are not built that way and the necessary detailed documentation is almost impossible to construct, or to find. This is because they are

---

[1] https://www.linkedin.com/pulse/what-took-you-so-long-david-slater-ty14e%3FtrackingId=1B%252F7CL%252FXTrqpVhE1IvD64A%253D%253D/?trackingId=1B%2F7CL%2FXTrqpVhE1IvD64A%3D%3D

© David Slater 2024.
Published by the Safety-Critical Systems Club. All Rights Reserved

predominantly built in an "agile" way, involving groups and teams progressing through sprints and scrums, to add layer after layer of developing code, one on top of another (like papier mâché?) to form "the package", (essentially a black box?). So, the only way to demonstrate reliability, security and safety, in its intended application is to test, test, test in development and monitor continuously in use. And in use we know that errors and bugs are inevitable, common, frequent and (Perrow) "normal"! – thus we accept this reality and hope it is acceptable?

So how can we develop a way of producing the realistic system "models" that we need to systematically probe for performance in operation. Many attempts have been made using conventional approaches to detail the hard wiring diagrams of what is happening (e.g. Model Based System Engineering, MBSE) so that established quantitative methodologies such as "Fault and Event Trees", Probabilistic Risk (or Reliability?) Analysis, and HAZOP's can be carried out. The problem is the resource intensity and detailed databases need and the abovementioned lack of definitive "wiring diagrams" for the integrated software packages.

Thus, in an increasingly complex world there is a real, urgent need for methodologies to enable engineers to model complex socio-technical systems, as these now seem to encompass the majority of systems in use today. This is of course exacerbated by the increasing involvement and augmentation with "black box" AI contributions. We need methodologies which will allow the analyst insights into these complex systems'.

A group of safety system professionals in the Safety Critical Systems Club are actively concerned and involved in finding better, more responsible and transparent way of assuring the safety of the black boxes and they do indeed 'do what it says on the tin', no more, no less!

We are looking at an approach developed to model systems as sets of interactive, interdependent "functions", (abstracted from agent or component details, FRAM, (Hollnagel, 2020)) and this has now been developed to the point where it can take the basic data and structures from the current component focussed system engineering "models", and can pull it all together into dynamic models, (as opposed to static, fixed System Theoretic Process Accimaps), from which analysts can discern how they really work in practice, and predict the emergent behaviours characteristic of complex systems. It can now provide the numbers and a quantitative approach that the model-based system engineering applications demand.

Furthermore, as the methodology merely builds the system "visualisation ", or FRAM model, it still needs the safety professional to analyse the model to discern behaviours expected and emergent.

Since the building of a system model is often seen as the most laborious, resource intensive and critical (Garbage in Garbage out?), part of the process, mastering yet another model building methodology seems too onerous. The big difference is that the FRAM model building is an iterative process with the initial attempts inevitably being improved with further examination, so the first model just needs to be a first approximation. With that caveat, a number of studies are now underway using Large Language Models to build these initial FRAMs to work on. As well as being extremely rapid, the results have been encouragingly accurate in the analyses enabled.

(Syringe filling, CPR, Microprocessor operations and Runway incursions are recent applications).

The runway incursion FRAM was produced by ChatGPT 3.5, and the model was built with the visualisation software, in less than an hour. This was judged to have produced a valid analysis of the issues involved and identified a critical reliance on a single communication link to prevent inadvertent runway incursion – a single point of failure. So, it seemed appropriate to test it on the Post Office Horizon software issues, a quintessentially software reliability case.

As a first step we asked ChatGPT 4.0 to build us an initial FRAM model of a typical software solution to the counter operations Horizon deals with. The result of a couple of hours' work is shown below.

2 The Horizon Analysis FRAM Model

To construct a detailed FRAM model for the process of a postmaster entering payments and receipts into a central database, we will follow a systematic approach. This includes identifying the functions from the Hierarchical Task Analysis (HTA) and mapping their interdependencies, variabilities, and aspects (INPUT, OUTPUT, PRECONDITION, RESOURCE, CONTROL, TIME).

Let's break down the steps:

Step 1: Identify the key Functions from HTA

Based on the HTA we've conducted, we identify the primary functions involved in the process. Each function is an activity or task that is crucial for the system's operation. These functions are:

1. Authenticate Postmaster's Access
2. Select Transaction Type
3. Enter Transaction Details
4. Review and Confirm Transaction
5. Update Central Database
6. Manage Personal Records

Step 2: Map the Aspects for Each Function

For each identified function, we map the six types of aspects. This includes identifying the inputs that trigger the function, the outputs produced, preconditions required, resources needed, control mechanisms in place, and time constraints if any. This step is crucial for understanding how each function operates within the system.

Example: Function - Authenticate Postmaster's Access
- **Input:** Postmaster's credentials
- **Output:** Access granted or denied
- **Precondition:** Credentials must be valid

- **Resource:** Authentication system, secure database
- **Control:** Password policies
- **Time:** Immediate response required

Step 3: Identify Interdependencies Between Functions
Here, we examine how the output of one function becomes the input for another, how resources are shared, and how control aspects influence multiple functions. This step is critical for understanding the system's dynamics.

Example:
- The output of "Authenticate Postmaster's Access" (access granted) becomes the input for "Select Transaction Type."
- The control aspect of "Data validation rules" in "Enter Transaction Details" influences the "Review and Confirm Transaction" function.

Using the FRAM Model Visualiser, (FMV) we create a visual representation of the model as shown in the attached figure. Each function is represented as a hexagon, and the aspects are represented on the hexagon's corners. Arrows and lines are drawn to show the flow and interdependencies between functions.

Step 5: Identify Variabilities and Potential Issues
After constructing the model, we analyze each function for variabilities – the differences in how they perform under varying conditions. This step is vital for identifying potential issues and hazards in the system.

Example:
- Variability in "Authenticate Postmaster's Access" might be the response time fluctuating under different server loads.
- Variability in "Enter Transaction Details" could be data entry errors due to user fatigue.

3 Now attempt the FRAM analysis

To perform a comprehensive FRAM analysis for the process of a postmaster entering payments and receipts into a central database with unique access for managing personal records, we'll first conduct a Hierarchical Task Analysis (HTA) to identify and sequence the tasks. This will be followed by the FRAM analysis.

3.1 Hierarchical Task Analysis (HTA) for the Postmaster's Task

1. **Function: To Authenticate Postmaster's Access**
   - **Inputs:** Postmaster's credentials (username, password)
   - **Outputs:** Access granted or denied message
   - **Preconditions:** Postmaster must have valid credentials
   - **Resources:** Authentication system, secure database
   - **Control:** Password policies, access control mechanisms
   - **Time:** Immediate response required

2. **Function: To Select Transaction Type**
   - **Inputs:** User input (payments or receipts)
   - **Outputs:** Appropriate transaction interface
   - **Preconditions:** Successful authentication
   - **Resources:** User interface
   - **Control:** User input validation
   - **Time:** User-dependent

3. **Function: To Enter Transaction Details**
   - **Inputs:** Transaction data (amount, date, payee/payer details)
   - **Outputs:** Transaction recorded
   - **Preconditions:** Correct transaction type selected
   - **Resources:** Data entry interface, keyboard
   - **Control:** Data validation rules
   - **Time:** User-dependent

4. **Function: To Review and Confirm Transaction**
   - **Inputs:** Entered transaction details
   - **Outputs:** Confirmation or correction prompt
   - **Preconditions:** All transaction details entered
   - **Resources:** Review interface
   - **Control:** Review and edit options
   - **Time:** User-dependent

5. **Function: To Update Central Database**
   - **Inputs:** Confirmed transaction details
   - **Outputs:** Database updated, success message
   - **Preconditions:** Transaction confirmation
   - **Resources:** Database management system
   - **Control:** Transaction processing logic
   - **Time:** Immediate processing required

6. **Function: To Manage Personal Records**
   - **Inputs:** Request to access/update personal records

- **Outputs:** Updated personal records
- **Preconditions:** Valid access to personal records section
- **Resources:** Personal records management interface
- **Control:** Privacy and access control policies
- **Time:** User-dependent

3.2 Identification of Issues, Hazards, and Variabilities

1. **Authentication Failures:** Variability in input (incorrect credentials) can lead to access denial.
2. **Data Entry Errors:** Variabilities in the 'Enter Transaction Details' function can lead to incorrect database updates.
3. **Transaction Confirmation Errors:** Incorrect confirmations can lead to false records.
4. **Database Synchronization Issues:** Any delay or error in updating the central database can lead to discrepancies.
5. **Personal Records Management:** Unauthorized access or errors in managing personal records pose privacy and accuracy issues.

To address these issues, additional functions like "To Validate Data Entry", "To Audit Transactions", and "To Backup Database" may be necessary.

3.3 Reflecting on Software's Impact

The details of computer software, particularly in a transactional system like the one used in a Post Office, significantly impact various operational aspects, including data transfer, time-outs, and error detection. These software characteristics directly influence certain functions in the FRAM model. Let's explore how:

1. Data Transfer
- **Function: Update Central Database**
    - **Resource:** The software's data handling capabilities, including its algorithms for database updates.
    - **Time:** How quickly the software processes and transfers data to the central database. Slow processing can lead to delays.
    - **Control:** Error handling mechanisms in the software to manage data transfer failures.
- **Function: Ensure Data Integrity and Security**
    - **Control:** The software's encryption protocols during data transmission to protect against data breaches.

o   **Resource:** Secure data transfer technologies integrated into the software.

2. Time-Outs
- **Function: Authenticate Postmaster's Access**
    o   **Time:** Software's session management could enforce time-outs for security, logging out users after periods of inactivity.
    o   **Control:** Settings within the software to determine the duration before a time-out occurs.
- **Function: Monitor and Audit System Access**
    o   **Control:** The software's ability to log time-out events, which is crucial for security audits.

3. Error Detection
- **Function: Enter Transaction Details**
    o   **Control:** Software's built-in validation rules to detect errors in transaction entries.
    o   **Resource:** Error detection algorithms to identify anomalies or incorrect data formats.
- **Function: Monitor Transaction Integrity**
    o   **Resource:** Software features that continuously check for transactional discrepancies or data corruption.
    o   **Control:** Automated alerts or flags raised by the software in response to detected errors.

The software's capabilities and design choices have a direct impact on the system's efficiency, security, and reliability. For instance, if the software has sophisticated error detection mechanisms, the likelihood of transactional errors decreases, enhancing the overall integrity of the system. Similarly, efficient data transfer and well-managed time-out protocols contribute to both operational efficiency and security.

In the FRAM model, these software-related aspects would be considered under 'Resource' and 'Control' for the relevant functions. The model helps to visualize how software intricacies affect various parts of the transactional process, revealing areas where software improvements could enhance system performance.

Understanding these interactions is crucial for system optimization, risk management, and ensuring that the software aligns with the operational goals and security requirements of the Post Office's transaction system.

3.4 And discovered Errors like the Callendar bug?

Incorporating potential errors like the Callendar Square bug and the Receipts and Payments Mismatch (RPM) bug into the FRAM model involves explicitly representing the functions where such errors could manifest and the interdependencies that might be affected. Let's consider how to integrate these issues into the existing model:

1. Callendar Square Bug
This bug, related to database lock timeouts and message replication failures, primarily affects the following functions:

- **Function: Update Central Database**
    - **Control Variability:** Add a control aspect to represent potential issues in database lock mechanisms, which could lead to transaction duplication.
- **Function: To Manage Data Transfer and Processing**
    - **Control and Time Variability:** Include variabilities to account for potential delays or failures in data replication due to software issues.

2. Receipts and Payments Mismatch (RPM) Bug
This bug affected the accuracy of transactions in the Horizon Online system, creating discrepancies that are contrary to double-entry bookkeeping principles. It impacts these functions:

- **Function: Enter Transaction Details**
    - **Control Variability:** Introduce a control aspect for the potential of software-induced discrepancies in transaction entries.
- **Function: To Reconcile Accounts**
    - **Output Variability:** Highlight that the reconciliation process may not always catch discrepancies due to software bugs, affecting the integrity of financial records.
- **Function: Ensure Double-Entry Bookkeeping Compliance**
    - **Control Variability:** Acknowledge the potential for software errors to cause non-compliance with double-entry bookkeeping standards.

3. Reflecting on Error Detection and Correction

- **Function: To Perform Error Detection and Correction**
    - **Resource Enhancement:** Strengthen this function to include resources for detecting specific types of software errors, like those experienced in the Callendar Square and RPM bugs.
    - **Control Enhancement:** Implement more robust error detection and correction mechanisms that can identify and resolve such discrepancies.

How do we make the case for "Safe" software and AI systems? - the Horizon Example   237

3.5 Updating the FRAM Model

These modifications to the FRAM model help in visualizing not just the standard operational flow, but also the potential points of failure and their systemic impacts. By mapping these bugs within the model, we can better understand how software issues propagate through various functions, affecting overall system integrity and reliability.

4 Now complete the list of all these Functions that need to be included in building the initial (Work as Imagined) FRAM model

The updated and comprehensive list of functions for the FRAM model, specifically tailored for the Post Office transaction system with a focus on security, double-entry bookkeeping, and operational integrity:

The complete list with 30 functions for the FRAM model of the Post Office transaction system:

1. **To Initiate a Transaction**
    - Starting the entire transaction process.
2. **Authenticate Postmaster's Access**
    - Ensuring secure system access for authorized personnel.
3. **Select Transaction Type**
    - Choosing the appropriate type of transaction.
4. **Enter Transaction Details**
    - Recording specifics of transactions, adhering to double-entry bookkeeping.
5. **Review and Confirm Transaction**
    - Verifying and finalizing transaction details before submission.
6. **Update Central Database**
    - Reflecting transaction details accurately in the central database.
7. **Manage Personal Records**
    - Enabling postmasters to manage their personal transaction records.
8. **To Reconcile Accounts**
    - Balancing and verifying transaction records for accuracy.
9. **Validate User Privileges**
    - Confirming appropriate access levels for system users.
10. **Ensure Data Integrity and Security**
    - Protecting the integrity and confidentiality of transaction data.
11. **Logging and Tracking Access and Changes**
    - Maintaining logs for system access and modifications.

12. **To Pay in Money**
    - Facilitating cash deposits and related transactions.
13. **To Provide a Receipt**
    - Generating receipts for each transaction.
14. **To Identify Purpose or Type of Transaction**
    - Categorizing transactions based on their purpose.
15. **To Make a Balance at the End of a Trading Period**
    - Calculating and reconciling transactions at the end of a business period.
16. **Monitor and Audit System Access**
    - Overseeing system access to prevent unauthorized access.
17. **Conduct Regular System Audits**
    - Performing comprehensive system checks for compliance and accuracy.
18. **Monitor Transaction Integrity**
    - Continuously verifying the accuracy of transactions.
19. **Audit Financial Records**
    - Inspecting financial records for accuracy and compliance.
20. **Report and Analyze Audit Findings**
    - Compiling and analyzing audit results for improvements.
21. **Ensure Double-Entry Bookkeeping Compliance**
    - Enforcing and verifying adherence to double-entry accounting principles.
22. **Monitor and Enforce Role-Based Access**
    - Ensuring system access is consistent with user roles.
23. **Review and Update Security Protocols**
    - Regularly enhancing system security measures.
24. **Conduct Financial Discrepancy Investigations**
    - Investigating and resolving any financial discrepancies.
25. **Provide User Training and Support**
    - Offering training and support to system users.
26. **Regularly Update Software and Hardware**
    - Keeping system technology up to date.
27. **To Complete a Transaction**
    - Finalizing the transaction process.
28. **To Manage Data Transfer and Processing**
    - Handling the efficient transfer and processing of transaction data.
29. **To Handle System Time-Outs**
    - Managing system time-outs for security purposes.
30. **To Perform Error Detection and Correction**
    - Detecting and correcting errors in transaction entries and system operations.

This list now accurately reflects the functions required for a comprehensive FRAM analysis of the Post Office transaction system. Each function plays a specific role in the system, contributing to its overall efficiency, security, and reliability.

These functions encompass the entire range of activities involved in the Post Office transaction process, from initiating a transaction to completing it, including all the critical steps for security, accounting, and operational management in between. They provide a comprehensive framework for the FRAM model, allowing for a detailed analysis of the system's functionalities and interdependencies.

Using the FRAM Model Visualiser[2], the following FRAM model was built (Figure 1, below).

---

[2] https://functionalresonance.github.io/FMV_Community_Edition/

240 David Slater

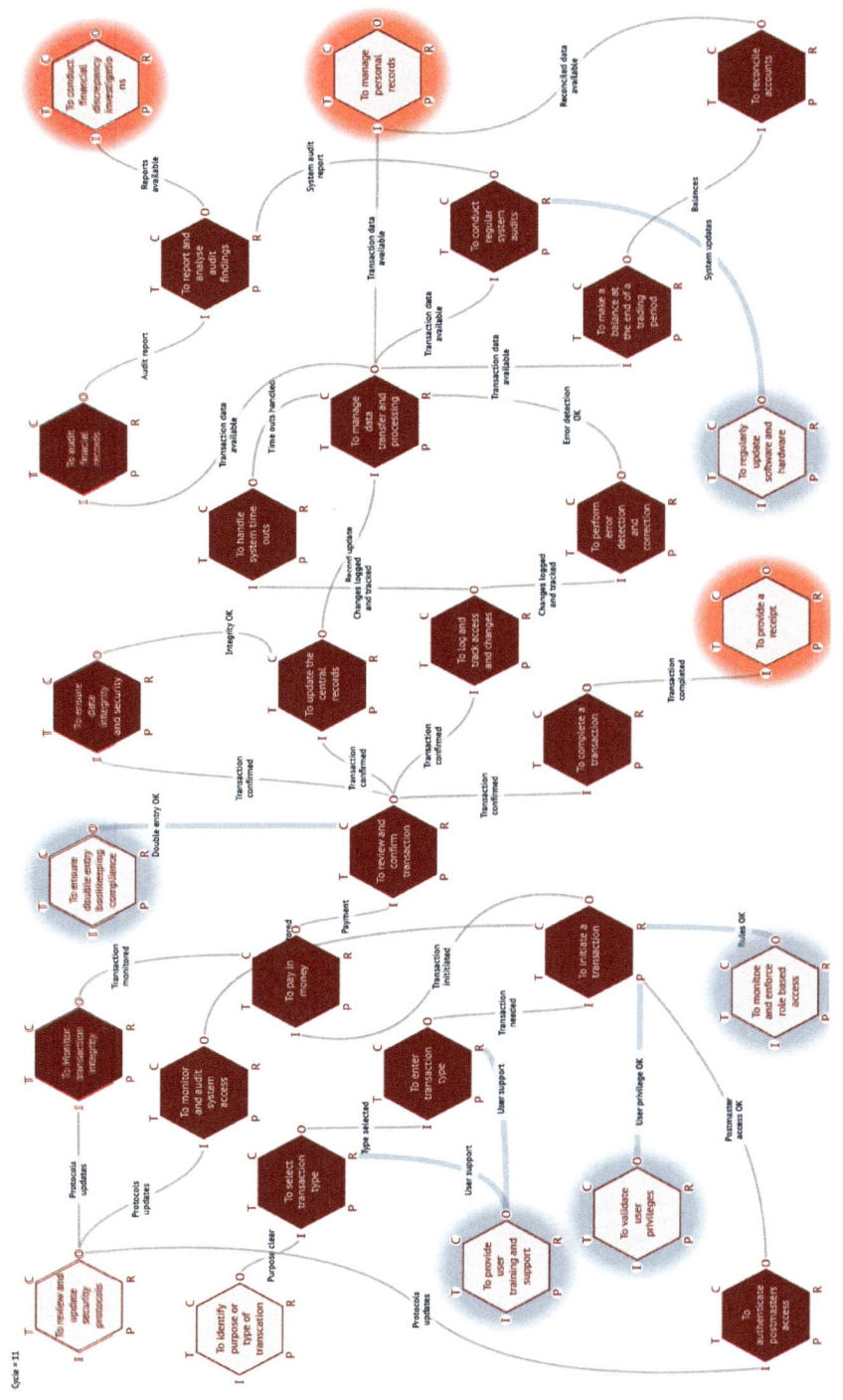

Fig. 1. Initial FRAM Model Built Using the FMV

5 Conclusions

This note reports on the initial attempts to develop and validate a better way to model and assure the performance of modern software packages. It sets out to address systematically the issues which are proving difficult to obtain consensus solutions to analysing and assuring the performance of safety-critical software systems.

It thus looks at the potential for applying more advanced methods of modelling and analysing these systems.

- The first approach to be investigated is the use of the Functional Resonance Analysis Method to build the system visualisations – models.
- Secondly the feasibility of using Large Language Models (LLM's) to produce initial outline systems models which can then be used to examine in detail the behaviours possible in these complex systems.

It is suggested that the above is an encouraging start.

References

Hollnagel, Erik, 2020, A brief introduction to the FRAM, https://functionalresonance.com/brief-introduction-to-fram/, Accessed January 2024

Seeing beyond the Post Office Horizon

Harold Thimbleby

Swansea University

Abstract *The Post Office Horizon case is the largest miscarriage of justice in the UK. While voiding convictions and providing adequate compensation is an immediate priority, the technical complexity of the case and the on-going Post Office Horizon Inquiry have paralysed decision making, and distracted from the strategic urgency of addressing the poor IT culture that led to and fed the problems. Horizon is a symptom of deeply-entrenched cultural problems with IT, including poor programming causing errors, and undermining the reliability of computer evidence for use in court. Failure to understand IT led to the misleading common law presumption that computer evidence is reliable, which undermines disclosure requirements in courts and further reduces scrutiny of computer evidence. Legal reasoning on the reliability of computers in court is flawed. Throughout the Horizon scandal, the inability to distinguish naïve and dishonest IT optimism from rigorous scientific thinking and evidence ensured that incompetence knew no limits. In short, what started (put charitably) as incompetence transformed into a scandalous "delay and deny" cover-up.*

IT problems have a wide impact in many areas far beyond the Post Office Horizon scandal. As AI gains wider use it will create worse problems, particularly for legal evidence. Raising, debating and taking steps to manage these generic and besetting IT problems are of fundamental importance in the digital age to achieve a safe and just society.

1 Introduction

Lee Castleton opened his Bridlington Post Office in 2003, but soon found discrepancies in his financial accounts run by the Post Office system called Horizon. Castleton made 91 calls to the Horizon helpline. By March 2004, his unexplained losses had grown to £25,000. He was suspended by the Post Office, and taken to court. Summing his case up, the judge said *"The losses must have been caused by his own error or that of his assistants,"* and *"it is inescapable that the Horizon system was working properly in all material respects."* Castleton was left with costs of £321,000. He went bankrupt.

© Harold Thimbleby 2024.
Published by the Safety-Critical Systems Club. All Rights Reserved

2 Background

Over a 16-year period starting around 1999, the Post Office prosecuted over 900 postmasters for shortfalls the Post Office claimed were theft, false accounting, and fraud.

We now know these shortfalls were due to errors in the Post Office's Horizon and other software as well as unauthorised remote access to accounts. Although some postmasters have had their convictions overturned by the Court of Appeal, as of January 2024, most of those wrongly convicted are still waiting to have their convictions overturned. None have had adequate compensation. The Court of Appeal Judge, Peter Fraser said the Post Office's malicious prosecutions and failures were so egregious as to make their prosecutions an affront to the conscience of the court.

A public inquiry[1] is ongoing, and is revealing more problems and mendacious behaviour daily. The police are now investigating both the Post Office and Fujitsu for perjury, fraud, and other offences. (Horizon was originally implemented by ICL, a British company that was later taken over by Fujitsu.) Ironically, the Inquiry itself has become a standard excuse not to say or do anything: Fujitsu, for example, has repeatedly said they cannot comment while the Inquiry is ongoing.

At root, the horrendous Post Office failures can be traced back to poor software and poor IT culture and poor management, plus a culture of denial that spread across the Post Office.

Initially this might be explained as a toxic mix of naïve optimism of people with little technical knowledge, perhaps being motivated by first needing to present Horizon as a wise investment, then needing to keep Horizon looking like a successful political initiative, and, finally, deliberately avoiding upsetting wider UK-Japan relations (Fujitsu is Japanese).

3 Prosecutions

When cases were prosecuted, one might have assumed that the courts would be critical and objective, but there is a common law presumption that assumes computers are correct, so court scrutiny was minimised (Marshall *et al*, 2021). Post Office prosecutors never needed to face serious cross-examination on the Post Office claims about the reliability of Horizon. Under the presumption, defendants have no way of finding out what documents or computer records might show relevant computer errors to support their case. Defendants trying to find such evidence would be accused of fishing.

Problems were covered up by management apparently more interested in Horizon maintaining a public image as a successful project and maintaining the public

---

[1] https://www.postofficehorizoninquiry.org.uk

image of the Post Office as a successful company. Some of the cover up and inertia against doing anything may have been sustained by believing the successful court prosecutions exonerated Horizon — to this way of thinking, one successful prosecution after another reinforces the apparent reliability of Horizon. To another way of thinking, the extraordinary numbers of prosecutions and the consistent complaints by postmasters on the unreliability of Horizon suggests a systemic failing, and certainly a profound lack of curiosity.

One argument presented in court was that if a system like Horizon correctly processes thousands of transactions every day, as no doubt it did, then it must be reliable, and therefore any postmaster's claims that Horizon is unreliable cannot be taken seriously. This reasoning is false, and is an example of the Prosecutor's Fallacy[2].

The common law presumption might perhaps be justified because a typical court cannot be expected to understand technical arguments about computer programming or bugs one way or the other. If computer evidence wasn't assumed to be reliable, perhaps we would all be trying to argue against speeding fines, unpaid parking tickets, bank fees, and much more. It is plausible that the Law Commission who created the presumption were as technically incompetent and desperate to cover their ignorance as the Post Office. Indeed, the Post Office itself gave evidence to the Law Commission to encourage creating the presumption. The presumption significantly reduces the cost of prosecutions relying on digital evidence regardless of whether that evidence is valid.

The common law presumption papers over large cracks. In reality, we have no idea whether any computer evidence is reliable, because the people who built the computer systems that produce the evidence do not even have to be competent. Their programs could easily make a mess of any evidence. A court simply cannot tell if the software they are relying on for evidence is wonderful or terrible. The common law presumption side-steps this worry by saying the questions don't even need to be raised.

Inside and outside of courts, then, we are unable to distinguish between safe and unsafe computer systems. We cannot tell whether the systems providing evidence

---

[2] Consider a simple analogy between accounting faults with mechanical faults in cars. From publicly available UK figures, the chance a random car is under repair on any given day is about 1 in 10,000, but this low figure does not mean that you would most likely be lying if you claimed your car was faulty. Your car (if faulty) is not a random car: your car has not been selected at random from all cars in the UK, most of which are not faulty, as it is one of the few that have problems. Whether your car is faulty should be established by examining *your* car and by identifying one or more faults, not by abstractly comparing it to the thousands of *other* cars that do not have faults. Unfortunately the common law presumption removes pressure on the courts to examine relevant evidence, and then it becomes easy for prosecutors to fallaciously claim the average evidence is relevant — why should they disclose faults when the law presumes there are none? Indeed, the presumption means the defendant has to prove their car is faulty when the prosecution does not even need to reveal the specific fault it may have. The defendant may know their car does not work, but the prosecution need not disclose the specific reason it is faulty — so the prosecution can argue, if the defence is unable to identify a specific fault, the claim that there is a fault must be a lie.

are reliable (and managed reliably), and we certainly cannot tell whether the expert witnesses are competent to provide reliable professional advice to the court.

4 Delusions

However the seeds were sown, soon claiming the correctness of Horizon became an article of faith, which was reinforced by silencing critics, like Second Sight. There was a self-fulfilling cycle of not disclosing evidence of problems, and believing there was no evidence of Horizon problems because nobody had disclosed any. And, of course, successful convictions were taken to confirm that Horizon was blameless, which would in turn drive even more prosecutions. The Post Office was soon prosecuting one postmaster a week.

Then there was the delaying and denying compensation to postmasters, and lying to Parliament.

All of it can only be understood as a shared delusional world, paralysing action, paralysing all critical thinking. To do anything, like compensating a few postmasters fairly, would expose decades of staggering incompetence and open flood gates of conscience for all the many people who have done nothing.

Nobody wants that cognitive dissonance (Tavris & Aronson, 2015), as it is *far* easier and more comfortable to stay in denial, especially if no colleagues understand computers. Indeed, the Post Office is a textbook case of the Dunning-Kruger Effect (1999): inaccurate self-assessment leads people to make bad decisions, and inhibits them from noticing or addressing their shortcomings. They are then unable and unwilling to improve themselves. *Unconscious incompetence.*

News reports, like many in the persistent *Computer Weekly* and *Private Eye*, were trying to cover complex cases against the powerful public persona of the Post Office. They never gained traction. Nick Wallis's powerful book, *The Great Post Office Scandal* (Wallis, 2015), was detailed and thick, but perhaps overwhelming in the wrong way. Even the Post Office Inquiry was as turgid as it was damning.

And then the postmaster, Alan Bates, was portrayed as the protagonist in an extraordinarily powerful 2024 ITV drama *Mr. Bates vs The Post Office*, playing in our own homes very human stories of injustices and suffering. The drama turned the rumbling scandal into front page news, and quickly into a political priority. Suddenly, one-time Post Office CEO, Paula Vennells handed back her CBE. Suddenly, Prime Minister Rishi Sunak promised legislation to quash convictions wholesale – dramatically challenging British traditions about separation of powers.

Bad software is nothing new, but the constricting cultural spiral of:

digital incompetence → ignorance → denial → corruption → institutionalised incompetence

drove the Post Office Horizon scandal. The Post Office has the power, has the law on its side, has the legal and financial resources, has managers and politicians needing it to stay on brand; and the Post Office incentivised its prosecutors. The Post Office only has one shareholder, the Government's Department for Business, Energy & Industrial Strategy, and presumably avoided all the scrutiny that is routine in normal diverse shareholder meetings.

The Post Office never needed to reflect why it was not just claiming to be victim, but was the prosecutor as well. We can only speculate on its lack of diversity and lack of technical skills, but the Horizon scandal is the culmination of four centuries of, literally, just paper-pushing and failing to prepare itself to understand digital technology, getting out of its depth, maybe at first unwittingly but soon ending up in a whirlpool of intentional cover-up and denial.

5 Beyond the Horizon

Apart from sheer scale, there is nothing unique in the Post Office's drift into failure. There are other serious failures and miscarriages of justice over faulty software, as terrible to the individual victims concerned but harder to acknowledge because there isn't a popular drama to highlight the human tragedy in a way the public cannot ignore.

The new booklet, *Patient Safety — Stories for a digital world* (Thimbleby & Thimbleby, 2024) gives many examples paralleling Horizon taken from across the NHS and international healthcare — situations caused by misunderstanding digital systems, leading to unnecessary patient harms and staff convictions. In some ways the NHS mirrors the Post Office — centuries of routine, very human, work suddenly computerized and made incomprehensible to everyone in the organisations.

One example concerns over 70 nurses who were disciplined. Some of the 70 nurses were prosecuted for alleged criminal negligence, on the basis of missing patient data that should have been recorded by the nurses. The court found that the data been deleted by an engineer. How could the hospital have been so blind to their own IT failings?

Or consider that when an anaesthetist presses a button to put a patient to sleep, by law they have to be competent and must have up to date qualifications backed by substantial training. Yet what happens when they press that button is anyone's guess, because a computer will do it, and we have no idea whether the computer is reliable: there are no regulations governing the qualifications, supervision, oversight, or insurance of people programming systems, whether that is for accounting (as in Horizon) or delivering anaesthetics (as in hospitals). It is ironic and dangerous that programmers need have no insight or supervision into what they are doing. Nobody has to take responsibility or sign off that their code is safe.

Many developers don't even realise they are incompetent. They know so little about good programming, they don't realise they are not good programmers. It is called, as hinted above, *unconscious incompetence*. While our laws are written and voted on by people with negligible computer knowledge or expert advice, our laws will hold back and undermine both safety and justice.

There are ways to fix this sorry mess.

Centuries ago, quack doctors were a danger to society, and so the government responded by passing the Medical Act of 1858 because, in the Act's opening words, *"it is expedient that Persons requiring Medical Aid should be enabled to distinguish qualified from unqualified Practitioners."* We now think the idea of registering educated and qualified doctors is self-evidently sensible. Indeed, one of the solutions Dunning and Kruger proposed in their original 1999 paper was education, as it is only with education that we are reliably calibrated to see (and for our employers and clients to see) our skills and limitations.

Not all education is equal. In the UK, there is a long traditional of professionalising computer education, leading to professional recognition such as becoming an incorporated or chartered engineer, but these qualifications do not in and of themselves assure an engineer is a competent developer (or auditor, or tester, etc) able to develop systems that generate electronic evidence of probative value.

In comparison, to be a qualified electrical engineer who could, for instance, legally install electrical wiring, very specific technical qualifications are required (e.g., AM2E) followed with regular continuous professional development (CPD) to ensure continued competence. So, instead of certifying existing, generic computer science education qualifications, we need to develop new educational standards that are designed to ensure more reliable code and more reliable forensic evidence generated by that code. Again, we take regulation of electrical engineers for granted — yet we do not worry that high voltage electrical installations may be controlled by unregulated computer systems, implemented by unregulated programmers. (The unsafe, poor programming of a regulated electrical safety test tool is provided in Thimbleby, 2022.)

Just as there was resistance to the Medical Act (and the Pharmacy Act, regulating pharmacists, that soon followed it), there will be strong resistance to analogous legislation for computers. But resistance does not mean the idea is wrong; arguably, resistance is confirmation that there is an unsafe culture that needs addressing by such an Act.

It is time, then, that the Government legislated so that everyone can avoid being unwitting victims of quack computer systems. A computer Act based on the uncontroversial Medical Act would require programmers to be registered, have a decent education (to be defined), and have respectable, relevant qualifications, and, as in healthcare, the professionals around them would also need to be suitably qualified.

Of course, this wouldn't apply to hobbyists and children programming. But if you wanted to build a serious system then you would have to be registered as competent.

Working out how to crack the chicken-or-egg problem will not be trivial: nobody will want qualifications until they are required, and it is unreasonable to require qualifications until there are enough people with them and enough appropriate qualifications available. Some incremental process, perhaps implemented over a decade, will be required. Perfection is the enemy of the good, and here perfection may be set up as a strawman; on the contrary, there is a lot that can be done now that is worth doing, even though less than immediate perfection. It is a big job — but very worthwhile.

The point of this article is to provoke and stimulate debate, showing that there is models in other critical areas, and a plausible start to a solution. Regulations requiring competence, even as taken for granted in other industries, may not be sufficient to solve all the types of problems covered in the story of Horizon and outlined in this article. There may be other possible solutions that are better (more are discussed in Marshall *et al*, 2021), or that can be leveraged on better qualifications or clearer definitions of competence. If there are better ideas, or ways to improve the ideas suggested here, we urgently need to find them — and meanwhile we should start moving in the right direction.

Peter Fraser, a judge who heard appeals arising out of the Horizon cases, said that the Post Office's stubborn pursuit of convictions over Horizon was equivalent to maintaining that the earth is flat. It is time, then, that we started looking beyond the Post Office Horizon to find broader more general solutions, not just to avoid another Horizon, not just for postmasters, but to build a more rounded, safer, world for everybody using and affected by computers.

APPENDIX: Example poor code from the Horizon Inquiry

The code examples in this appendix are taken from section 7.3, *Report on the EPOSS PinICL Task Force, Post Office Inquiry document FUJ00080690*.

The examples of poor code below do not in themselves prove that the programs do not work, or even that the programs this code has been sampled from are buggy. What the examples do show is that the code is unprofessional and unreliable. The code is so bad that it would be pointless to debug it. Its confused and confusing style suggests there were no adequate requirements. Without clear requirements there is no standard to even define correctness.

Compare this situation with other industries, where poor quality can be illegal without having to prove a product is actually dangerous. Electrical installations, for example, are required to be wired to the relevant safety standards, and checked as compliant to those standards. Sloppy wiring is (in the appropriate circumstances) a criminal offence, even if the specific details of the sloppy wiring may have no direct causal link to any particular problems.

Just as electricians are expected to use appropriate standards and test equipment, there are plenty of standards and test tools available for programmers. The code examples below, taken verbatim from Inquiry evidence, imply that basic standards and software tools were not used (or, if used, their results were misunderstood or ignored).

This evidence shows extraordinary incompetence and lack of awareness of basic IT skills. Failing to notice or fix the problems shows extraordinary managerial incompetence.

Example 1

```
Public Function ReverseSign(d)
    If d < o Then
        d = Abs(d)
    Else
        d = d -(d*2)
    End If
    ReverseSign = d
End Function
```

This pointlessly obscure and inefficient function `ReverseSign` returns the negative value of its parameter.

Note that the variable o [sic] was copied from the report to the Inquiry. It is probably supposed to be zero, not the letter o. It is possible that o is a global variable so this code would compile and run, but it is unlikely to do what was intended (however it will work correctly provided the value of o ≤ 1).

On a typical computer, `Abs(d)` will require a function call and a further test. Since the if statement guard ensures `d < 0`, it would be faster to write `d = -d` instead of `Abs(d)`, as this is what `Abs` will do after its own internal repeat test.

Since compilers will typically optimise `d = d-(d*2)` to `d = -d` this expression has no advantage over the clearer `d = -d`. In fact, the subexpression `d*2` can overflow and cause incorrect results that `-d` does not generate. Many optimisers do not implement checks for overflow, so in this case optimisation may make the code more robust. (It would seem bizarre for a programmer to *want* undetected incorrect results under overflow conditions, and unprofessional not to comment the code to warn of its peculiar properties.)

A function like `ReverseSign` could be used for tracing or assertions, such as checking there is no overflow (e.g., on a twos complement machine, `-MinInt = MinInt`). There are no signs of tracing or assertions in any code exhibited to the Inquiry.

Example 2

```
If lstockrootnode = 3013 Or lstockrootnode = 3016 Then
    bremedprods = False
    intbalancerootlevel = 5
    lbalancerootenode = 3017
    If lstockrootnode = 2493 Then
        bremedprods = False
        intbalancerootlevel = 3
        lbalancerootenode = 3006
    End If
Else
    bremedprods = True
    intbalancerootlevel = 5
    lbalancerootenode = 3017
End If
```

Node numbers here are hard-coded and not documented. Typos in the ID values (3013, 3017, 2493, etc.) would be very hard to detect. The purpose of the conditions are not commented.

The shaded code above is unreachable, as after testing `lstockrootnode` is 3013 or is 3016 it cannot possibly become 2493 with the code shown. If the inner test `lstockrootnode = 2493` is not incorrect, the code is pointless. Indeed, the line of code `bremedprods = False` repeats an assignment a few lines earlier and is pointless — or perhaps the programmer meant to assign to a different variable or assign a different value to the variable?

Furthermore, the variables `intbalancerootlevel` is set to 5 and `lbalancerootnode` set to 3017 *regardless* of the main test conditions — the assignments are duplicated.

Overall, the code implies the programmer did not understand (and/or did not check) what was being written. Standard static analysis tools would have detected the unreachable code and the duplicated code; and standard testing practice would have been to ensure coverage (i.e., that all code was tested), and that cannot have happened with this code.

Example 3

```
If s<>"" Then
    Do
        If s<>"" Then
            // Significant code removed to save space
            Exit Do
        End If
    Loop
    End If
    Next
End If
```

At face value (i.e., the report comments out any details to the contrary), the loop is only executed at most once and is equivalent to the following clearer code:

```
If s<>"" Then
        // Significant code removed to save space
End If
```

It is possible the commented-out large body of code (the comment is in the Inquiry evidence) contains repeat loop commands, but if so the report writer who commented out the code missed them, and it should have been simplified (for instance) with function calls.

We also note the code in the report has incorrect indentation, a dangling `End If`, and the loop control `Next` appears to be outside any loop (at least any loop in the code as presented).

Example 4

```
Select Case Val(ObjAtributeValue(SCAMapping, "Data.Leaf.N")
    Case
```

```
            99995026,  99995027,  99995028,  99995029,
            99995030,  99995031,  99995032,  99995033,
            99995046,  99995056,  99995057,  99995058,
            99995059,  99995060,  99995061,  99995062,
            99995063,  99995064,  99995065,  99995066
               stxn = stxn &
            ObjMake("SuspenseContainer","S")
               Exit Do
      Case Else
   End Select
```

The object value IDs here are hard-coded and have no documentation. Typos would be very hard to detect.

The fact that the cases cover all consecutive IDs `99995026-33` and `99995056-66` inclusive, plus an isolated value `99995046`, is not clear. Anyone reviewing this code needs to know what the ID values mean, and needs to know how they are related: how else can a reviewer check whether, say, `99995035` has been missed out or not?

The line `stxn = stxn &` ... appears to be bit fiddling, with no documentation on the meanings of the bits affected; this sort of code is very obscure (e.g., what it does is not commented); it should have been written with explicitly-named methods (that would also hide the low-level bit implementation).

Acknowledgments Many thanks to Martyn Thomas who made many very perceptive and helpful comments.

Disclaimers The author was not funded for this article, and declares no conflicts of interest.

References

P Marshall, J Christie, PB Ladkin, B Littlewood, S Mason, M Newby, J Rogers, H Thimbleby & M Thomas, "Recommendations for the probity of computer evidence," *Digital Evidence and Electronic Signature Law Review,* 2021. DOI 10.14296/deeslr.v18i0.5240

H Thimbleby, "Cowboy digital undermines safety-critical systems," in *Safer Systems: The Next 30 Years, Proceedings of the 30th Safety-Critical Systems Symposium*, M Parsons & M Nicholson eds., SCSC-161:203–226, Safety-Critical Systems Club, 2022.

H Thimbleby & P Thimbleby, *Patient Safety — Stories for a digital world*, https://www.harold.thimbleby.net/booklet, 2024.

N Wallis, *The Great Post Office Scandal*, Bath Publishing, 2021.

C Tavris & E Aronson, *Mistakes Were Made, but Not by Me: Why We Justify Foolish Beliefs, Bad Decisions, and Hurtful Acts*, Pinter Martin Ltd, 3rd ed, 2015.

J Kruger & D Dunning, "Unskilled and Unaware of It: How Difficulties in Recognizing One's Own Incompetence Lead to Inflated Self-Assessments," *Journal of Personality and Social Psychology,* **77**(6):1121–1134, 1999. DOI: 10.1037/0022-3514.77.6.1121

Safety Monitoring for Large Language Models: A Case Study of Offshore Wind Maintenance

Connor Walker, Callum Rothon, Koorosh Aslansefat, Yiannis Papadopoulos, Nina Dethlefs

AURA CDT, University of Hull

Abstract *It has been forecasted that a quarter of the world's energy usage will be supplied from Offshore Wind (OSW) by 2050 (Smith 2023). Given that up to one third of Levelised Cost of Energy (LCOE) arises from Operations and Maintenance (O&M), the motive for cost reduction is enormous. In typical OSW farms hundreds of alarms occur within a single day, making manual O&M planning without automated systems costly and difficult. Increased pressure to ensure safety and high reliability in progressively harsher environments motivates the exploration of Artificial Intelligence (AI) and Machine Learning (ML) systems as aids to the task. We recently introduced a specialised conversational agent trained to interpret alarm sequences from Supervisory Control and Data Acquisition (SCADA) and recommend comprehensible repair actions (Walker et al. 2023). Building on recent advancements on Large Language Models (LLMs), we expand on this earlier work, fine tuning LLAMA (Touvron 2018), using available maintenance records from EDF Energy. An issue presented by LLMs is the risk of responses containing unsafe actions, or irrelevant hallucinated procedures. This paper proposes a novel framework for safety monitoring of OSW, combining previous work with additional safety layers. Generated responses of this agent are being filtered to prevent raw responses endangering personnel and the environment. The algorithm represents such responses in embedding space to quantify dissimilarity to pre-defined unsafe concepts using the Empirical Cumulative Distribution Function (ECDF). A second layer identifies hallucination in responses by exploiting probability distributions to analyse against stochastically generated sentences. Combining these layers, the approach finetunes individual safety thresholds based on categorised concepts, providing a unique safety filter. The proposed framework has potential to utilise the O&M planning for OSW farms using state-of-the-art LLMs as well as equipping them with safety monitoring that can increase technology acceptance within the industry.*

Keywords: Large Language Model, Safety Assurance, AI Safety, Statistical Distance Measure, SafeML, Safe Machine Learning, SafeLLM

© AURA CDT, University of Hull 2024.
Published by the Safety-Critical Systems Club. All Rights Reserved

1 Introduction

As the Offshore Wind (OSW) sector grows to meet demand for renewable energy in line with net-zero targets, it is estimated that OSW will supply 1150 GW, or 25% of global electricity usage by 2050 (Smith, 2023). In the OSW sector, approximately one third of the Levelised Cost of Electricity (LCOE) arises from Operations and Maintenance (O&M), which includes inspections, routine maintenance, and repairs.

As wind turbines have grown larger and more complex, and wind farms have moved further from shore, increasing emphasis has been placed on Condition-Based Maintenance (CBM). Current wind turbines include a wide range of embedded sensors in their Supervisory Control and Data Acquisition (SCADA) systems and increasing amounts of research have focused on the diagnosis of faults from this live data.

When in operation, wind farms generate large volumes of data, so nuisance alarms are an increasingly pressing issue. Nuisance alarms may include false alarms and chattering alarms that repeat in quick succession (Wei et al. 2023). Reports exist of up to 500 alarms in a 24-hour period at the Teesside wind farm, corresponding to an alarm roughly every 3 minutes on average (Walker et al. 2022). This complicates the accurate diagnosis of faults and the recommendation of required repair actions, increasing lead times on maintenance operations.

Whilst Large Language Models (LLMs) continue to become accepted as tools in the workplace, it is crucial that they are reliable and trustworthy, especially in safety-critical applications. Issues have been identified with hallucinations (Huang et al. 2023) and unsafe recommendations (Inan et al. 2023), which must be mitigated before LLM-based tools can be relied upon fully. While safety measures against high-risk inputs and outputs are recommended by developers (Meta 2023), it has been found that they can be bypassed with relative ease (Rando et al. 2022).

The key contributions of this paper are:

1. We propose SafeLLM, a method for the recommendation of repair actions based around LLAMA, with a safety layer implemented to detect unsafe recommendations, using Wasserstein distance.
2. We fine-tune the safety layer to an OSW task, using thresholds based on safety standards from industry, demonstrating our approach in a specialised task.

We present up to date literature on alarm and repair prediction and safety in LLMs in the Literature Review, define key concepts for this work in the Project Definitions, present our approach in the Proposed Methodology, then test on an OSW task in the Results section, and present our findings in the Discussion section.

2 Literature Review

Recent work in the OSW sector has focused on diagnosis of faults from alarm data, the prediction of subsequent alarms based on previous alarms, and the reduction of chattering alarms leading to alarm overload. Gonzalez et al. (2016) present an approach for categorisation of alarms, to reduce confusion arising from large amounts of data, highlighting the relationship between faults in a range of components and environmental conditions. Zhang and Yang (2023) present a Long Short-term Memory (LSTM) based Variational Autoencoder Wasserstein Generational Adversarial Network (VAE-WGAN) for anomaly detection on wind turbines, using Wasserstein distance to compare the model fit and true distributions.

Work has also been proposed which aims to predict the required maintenance actions from alarm sequences, supporting human decision making in O&M planning. Chatterjee and Dethlefs (2020) present a transformer-based system for data-to text generation, predicting faults and required maintenance for wind turbines based on SCADA data, showing good performance for both alarms and repair actions.

Walker et al. (2022) proposes a system based around LSTMs and Bi-directional LSTMs (BiLSTMs) for prediction of repair actions from sequences of alarms in the OSW domain, differing from previous works which aim to predict subsequent faults as opposed to the required action. This work also proposes adding a HITL layer to an LSTM based system, harnessing the knowledge base of experienced O&M staff for RL.

Wei et al. (2023a) apply word embeddings and Siamese convolutional neural networks to diagnosis of faults based on alarm sequences and validate their approach on alarm data from an operating wind farm. Similarly, Wei et al (2023b) proposes the use of domain knowledge-fused Word2Vec to transform alarms into numeric representations and uses an improved K-means clustering to group alarm sequences. Word2Vec (Mikolov et al. 2013) and word embeddings are techniques borrowed from Natural Language Processing (NLP), treating alarms in a sequence as analogous to words in a sentence.

Wasserstein distance has been shown useful as a metric for comparison of probability distributions in a range of tasks (Panaretos et al. 2018), including in Machine Learning (ML) and fault detection. Li and Martinez (2021) present a methodology for attack detection in cyber-physical systems, using Wasserstein distance to detect faults which lie outside of the distribution of expected noise in the system, and seek to determine the impact of "stealthy" attacks which lie within this distribution.

In recent years, progress on LLMs has been rapid, leading to wide interest in their adoption for a range of tasks. Zhao et al. (2023) survey recent progress on LLMs, considering pre-training, adaptation tuning, utilisation, and capacity evaluation. Open AI's Chat GPT (Open AI, 2022) is the most famous such example, based on GPT-3 (Brown et al., 2020). GPT 4 (OpenAI, 2023) is the most recent development in this family and has been reported to shown human-level capabilities in a range of tasks, although the definition of "human-level" is highly subjective and situational.

Touvron et al. (2023) present LLAMA, a set of LLMs with a range of parameter sizes trained on publicly available data, which was released to the research community. Models included in LLAMA have been shown to be competitive with the state of the art, so are considered a valuable resource. Carta et al. (2023) use an LLM as a policy which is updated via Reinforcement Learning, to remedy the current lack of grounding between LLMs and the environments in which they are applied.

As greater reliance is placed on ML-based systems with limited human oversight, it is vital that measures are put in place to reduce safety risks. Hawkins et al. (2021) present Assurance of ML in Autonomous Systems (AMLAS) and follow this with Safety Assurance of Autonomous Systems in Complex Environments (SACE) (Hawkins et al., 2022). AMLAS contains safety case patterns and processes for integrating safety into the development of ML components and justifying the acceptable safety of said components. SACE extends this work to full autonomous systems. Rando et al. (2022) finds that safety filters on stable diffusion image-generation models can be relatively easily bypassed and argues for a community-based approach to safety measures in generative AI.

A significant issue encountered with LLMs is that they can make non-factual statements, known as hallucinations. Huang et al. (2023) present a survey of hallucination in LLMs, including a taxonomy of hallucinations and identification of causes. Detection of hallucinations has been a field of rapid development, in tandem with the rise of LLMs. Manakul et al. (2023) present SelfCheckGPT, a hallucination detection algorithm, which is capable of fact-checking outputs from LLMs without external resources by comparing stochastically sampled responses. The offline approach proposed is effective in many applications but can fail if hallucinations are present in all sampled sentences. Rateike et al. (2023) proposes a method for detection of hallucinations in LLM activations from pre-trained models.

Inan et al. (2023) present Llama guard, a safeguarding model built around models in LLAMA using a safety risk taxonomy to classify prompts and responses. This work presents a taxonomy of safety risks that may arise when interacting with an Artificial Intelligent (AI) agent, including violence and hate speech, sexual content, and criminal planning. Llama guard takes this taxonomy as input and classifies user inputs (prompts) and agent outputs as encouraged (safe) and discouraged (unsafe) using a single model. By using a different taxonomy, the model can be fine-tuned using zero-shot and few-shot methods.

3 Problem Definitions

Developing a system focused on safety specific to the OSW domain requires a clear proposal of what the term refers to. Section 3.1 therefore refines the generic safety definition to clearly determine the meaning of safety within SafeLLM. Section 3.2 then identifies the problem definition in which we propose to address.

3.1 LLM Safety Definition for OSW O&M Applications

Safety is defined: "the freedom from unacceptable risk of physical injury or of damage to the health of people, either directly or indirectly as a result of damage to property or to the environment" (International Electrotechnical Commission 2018).

Safety of a system is then subject to, "Interactions with its environment and other systems also have an effect on the Safety of the system." (UK MOD 2018).

Hawkins et al. (2021) states that it is not possible to make any claim regarding safety of an ML component for all possible systems and environmental contexts. It is therefore essential that the term safety is defined within the scope of the work proposed in this paper. Furthermore, Hawkins et al. (2022) adopts the commonly used definition of a safety case; "structured argument, supported by a body of evidence that provides a compelling, comprehensible and valid case that a system is safe for a given application in a given operating environment." (UK MOD 2018).

In the context of OSW maintenance, safety has a wide scope of meaning, both in the physical environment and safety of personnel. Working in harsh offshore environments harbours its own safety risks. For the application of SafeLLM, we refine the above definitions of safety to the protection of maintenance personnel's exposure to risk, danger, or injury resulting directly from responses generated by the conversational agent. Further, protecting the environment from unnecessary harm caused by unsafe practices. Our aim is therefore to eliminate any additional risks that exceed acceptable levels currently in the OSW industry.

3.2 Maintenance Planning for OSW Farms

As identified in our previous work, operators face more than 500 simultaneous alarms in a single day (Walker et al. 2022). This will potentially overwhelm staff – alongside pressures applied by windfarm operators and energy companies – resulting in irrational decisions being made in the interest of reducing downtime.

Alleviating this pressure, in turn would improve overall safety throughout the maintenance process.

Currently, it is expected that maintenance crews have the knowledge and experience to understand and diagnose faults. The alarm notes, such as "WTG1A HV MAINTENANCE", also being ambiguous in definition presents further difficulties in implementation of suggested actions.

OSW, in its nature, is progressively exploring into deeper waters with the introduction of floating turbine structures. These introduce further maintenance complexities as the distance from shore increases from a current average of 44 km to consented farms more than 200 km (Interreg Europe, 2018). As the distance from shore increases, harsher conditions are present, shortening weather windows for safe transfer and maintenance. Where onsite alarm fault diagnosis is apparent, this results in a reduction in time to complete repairs, leading to either multiple days of maintenance scheduling, or, more critically, reduction in safety awareness of crews to complete tasks.

As such, we look to address the issue of reduced safety critical awareness, stemming from pressures applied by the drive to reduce turbine downtime. Through filtering our trained conversational agents' responses, we can eliminate unsafe practices, whilst maintaining concise yet intelligible actions. Section 4 introduces the methodology proposed to achieve SafeLLM within OSW maintenance scheduling.

4 Proposed Methodology

We address the defined problems by developing and integrating safety layers, aimed to capture unsafe concepts generated by the conversational agent. Existing models utilise Cosine Similarity of both word and sentence embeddings. Exploiting the text embeddings creates inputs for various Empirical Cumulative Distribution Function (ECDF) statistical distance measures.

Embedding this into our wider work, the sentence input becomes the response generated by the LLM. To benchmark our results against existing methodologies, each sentence is tested on both measures: Cosine Similarity and Wasserstein Distance. These are defined and discussed in detail in sections 4.4 and 4.5 respectively.

Figure 1 shows a block diagram of a process flow using a SafeLLM: Fine-tuned LLM within a safety-critical system, in the domain of OSW turbine O&M. The process can be addressed in the following steps:

1 - Input Prompt: The process begins with the input prompt, which contains alarm sequences from a SCADA system. These alarms may include various error messages or status reports such as "Grd. Inv. Communication error," "Converter tripped, waiting," "GenInv: 38 D1 volt high," etc.

2 - Obtain LLM's Embeddings: The input prompt is fed into a fine-tuned LLM in which LLAMA 2 has been used. The LLM processes the input and produces embeddings, which are high-dimensional vector representations capturing the semantic and syntactic features of the input data.

3 - Pre-defined Embeddings for Unsafe Concepts: The diagram shows a radar chart representing the embedding space. This space is pre-defined with embeddings for unsafe concepts associated with turbine operation, e.g. "No Power Isolation". The LLM's embeddings are compared against these to calculate a distance metric (WD_Dist), using the Wasserstein distance or a similar metric.

4 - Context: A sidebar lists unsafe contexts or practices in the turbine operation, such as "Ignoring Weather Conditions" and "Skipping Regular Inspections." These contexts may be used to inform or adjust the model's understanding and evaluation of safety.

5 - SafeML Score and Threshold Decision: The system uses SafeML (Aslansefat 2020, Aslansefat 2021), a framework for measuring statistical similarity between the LLM's embeddings and unsafe concepts, to produce a SafeML score. If the score is below a certain threshold, it indicates potential safety issues, and the system proceeds to "Verify the Outcome." If the score is above the threshold, the process moves to "Filtering the Results and regenerating a new one."

4 - Repair Action: On the right side of the diagram, there is a potential outcome where a repair action is suggested. For example, if the SafeML score is above the threshold, it may be recommended to filter the outcome and generate a new one.

5 - Turbine Knowledge Graph: In the background, there's an OSW Turbine domain-specific knowledge graph that is used to consider interconnected concepts and entities relevant to turbine O&M and improve the accuracy of the LLM results.

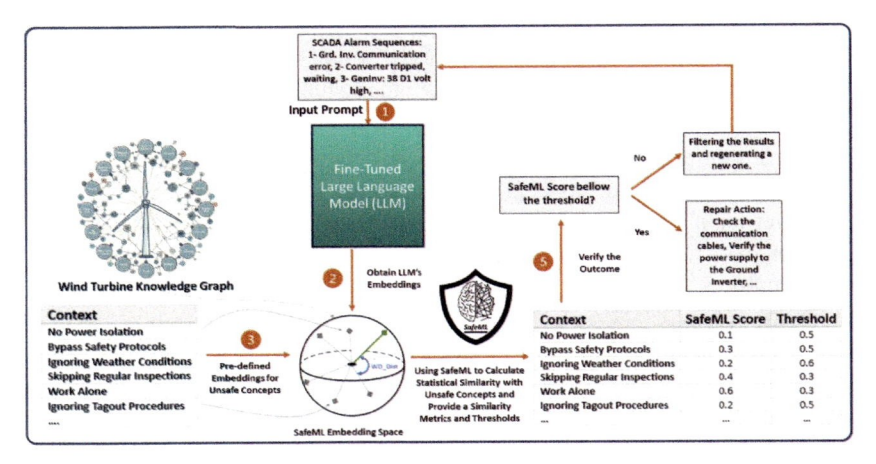

Fig. 1. Diagram showing the overall procedure of SafeLLM.

In the following subsections, we discuss the procedures involved in the implementation of SafeLLM in detail.

4.1 Data Gathering and Pre-processing

Due to restricted availability of domain specific maintenance data, we were able to generate datasets from ChatGPT 4.0 to use for testing prior to validation. As a foundation for what should be deemed as an unsafe practice, we asked ChatGPT to provide multiple datasets.

The first dataset generated consists of 2400 sentences generalised to maintenance tasks and considerations within OSW. The sentences have not been validated for accuracy of application to the industry. Each sentence also has a Boolean of safe/unsafe determined by ChatGPT's safety filter. The unsafe sentence data was then split 20:80; 20 % creating an 'unsafe dictionary' to compare against, and 80% for testing. All safe sentences were used for testing.

A second dataset has also been generated to analyse on category specific thresholds. This dataset consists of the sentence, safe/unsafe Boolean, and an assigned maintenance category.

Categories 1-10 are defined as:

- Procedural Compliance
- Emergency Procedures
- Personal Protective Equipment (PPE)
- Risk Assessment

- Communication Protocols
- Environmental Awareness
- Equipment Handling
- Training and Certification
- Regulatory Compliance
- Incident Reporting

Once sentence embeddings had been extracted from each sentence, these were stored dynamically in a data-frame, each instance containing the sentence, embeddings, safety category (undefined for the large dataset), list of Wasserstein distances and cosine similarities; each initialised as 0 prior to calculating. Finally, a list of data-frames is created for each category of sentences: Unsafe Dictionary, Unsafe Test Sentences, and Safe Test Sentences.

4.2 Latent Space of LLMs

LLMs, such as LLAMA2, utilise deep learning architectures to encode linguistic information into a high-dimensional latent space. This latent space, or embedding space, is critical for representing the complex semantic and syntactic structures of language.

Consider language model with L layers, where each layer transforms its input to a higher level of abstraction. Latent space at layer l for a given input sequence $f(x) = (x_1, x_2 ... x_n)$ can be represented as:

$$h^l = Transform^l(h^{l-1}), \text{ where } h^0 = Embed(x)$$

In this equation, $Embed(...)$ is the initial embedding function mapping the input sequence to the first latent representation h^0. Each $Transform^l(...)$ signifies the transformation at layer l, which may involve self-attention and feed-forward neural networks in transformer-based models. The final latent representation h^L encapsulates the contextualised embeddings, utilised for various downstream tasks, including text generation, classification, or summarisation.

The latent space dimensionality, typically ranging in the hundreds to thousands, allows the model to capture a wide range of linguistic nuances. Methodology for representing the datasets is further discussed in the following section.

4.3 Sentence Embeddings

Sentence embedding is defined as the numerical representation of a sentence, capturing both semantic meaning and context (Helwan 2023). Using the Universal Sentence Encoder (USE) model from Google Research (Cer et al. 2018), we can easily extract these for analysis.

Vaswani et al. (2017) present framework to compute context aware word representations; considering both the ordering and identity of all other words within a sentence. Figure 2 shows the transformer model architecture.

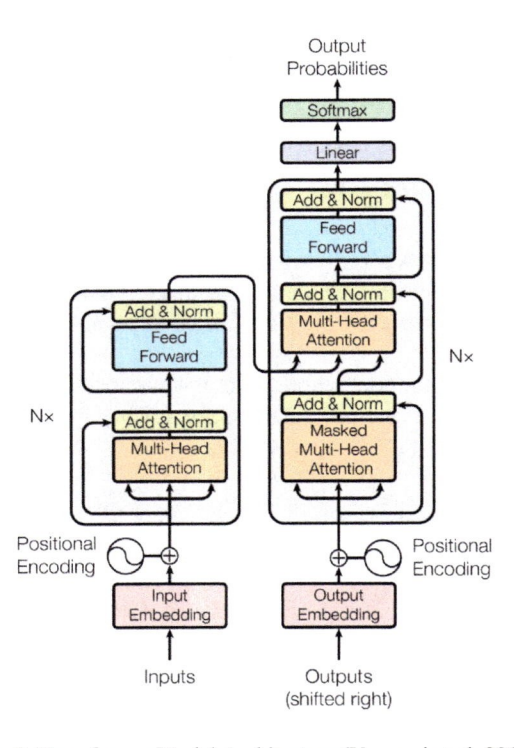

Fig. 2. Transformer Model Architecture (Vaswani et al. 2017)

Cer et al. (2018) then processes the outputs by computing the element-wise sum at each work position, before dividing by the square root of the sentence length. The final output is given as a 512-dimensional sentence embedding.

4.4 Cosine Similarity

As mentioned, Cosine Similarity is utilised as a benchmark for accuracy of the proposed Wasserstein Distance methodology. This is defined as:

$$\cos(\theta) = \frac{A \cdot B}{\|A\|\|B\|}$$

Where A and B are the input vectors, or sentence embeddings, of the two sentences being compared; θ is the angle between the input vectors. A·B is the dot product of A and B. ‖A‖ and ‖B‖ are the magnitude of vector A and B respectively.

Comparing the sentence embeddings for Cosine Similarity of three example sentences, and visually representing them gives the result shown in Figure 3 below.

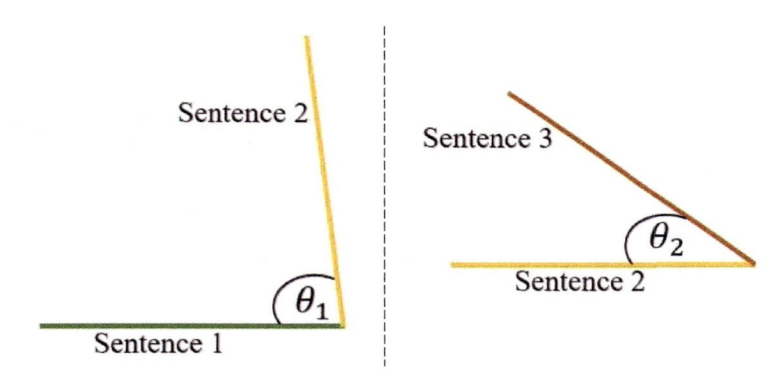

Fig. 3. Visualised Cosine Similarity

As can be seen in Figure 3, Sentence 1 has low similarity to Sentence 2 with Cos θ = 0.11579657. Changing one word between Sentence 2 and Sentence 3, keeping word order the same has a much higher similarity: Cos θ = 0.80871284.

- Sentence 1: "Complete maintenance on the wind turbine."
- Sentence 2: "Follow safe practices."
- Sentence 3: "Ignore safe practices."

4.5 Wasserstein Distance

Optimal Transport Theory (OTT) provides a baseline foundation for Wasserstein Distance. Therefore, we define this first. OTT provides a framework for moving a mass distribution into another in the most efficient way possible (Kim et al. 2021). Given C as the cost – cost defined as the mass and distance moved – it is required to associate each data point 'x' in X with exactly one 'y' in Y, where X and Y are the sentence embeddings. C is therefore defined simply as $C(x,y) = |x - y|$, with N! possibilities, where N is the number of data points within an embedding (Kim et al. 2021).

OT can be formulated both using the Monge (practical) and Kantorovich (theoretical) formulations (Thorpe 2018); we discuss only Monge formulation. Thorpe defines transporting one measure to another as:

$$T : X \to Y \text{ transports } \mu \in P(X) \text{ to } \nu \in P(Y)$$

Cost is therefore again determined as transporting one unit from $x \in X$ to $y \in Y$. With this, the aim being to transport from μ to ν whilst reducing C. Monge Formulation is further defined as:

$$\inf_T \int \|x - T(x)\|^p dP(x)$$

Limitations to the above are presented where no optimal transport map (OTM) exists. This is reliant on both P and Q having densities, where the above $\frac{\inf}{T}$ is $T_\# P = Q$ measuring the distance moved from P to Q. Without a density in both, no OTM exists.

To resolve this, Wasserstein Distance allows the mass at x to be moved to multiple locations, defined as:

$$W_p(P,Q) = \left(\inf_{J \in j(P,Q)} \int \|x - y\|^p dJ(x,y) \right)^{1/p}$$

$j(P,Q)$ denotes all joint distributions J for (X,Y) with marginals P and Q. In scenarios where $p = 1$, this can also be referred to as Earth Mover Distance (EMD). J is then called the Optimal Transport Plan (OTP). Where Wasserstein Distance is used and an OTM exists, J is a singular measure.

Calculating P and Q as the Cumulative Distribution Function (CDF) of p and q respectively as:

$$F_P(p) = Probability(P \leq p)$$

$$F_Q(q) = Probability(Q \leq q)$$

Wasserstein Distance is then commonly simplified to:

$$W_p(p,q) = \int_{-\infty}^{+\infty} |P - Q|$$

4.6 Defining Safety Threshold Ranges

Cosine Similarity is limited to the range of 0 – 1, meaning increments between the two can be tested for accuracy of safe and unsafe sentences. For the large dataset, increments were reduced to be in range of 0.6 – 1 determined by the results gained. Where no change of accuracy happened on either safe or unsafe sentences, the increments were then reduced further. This allowed us to identify the highest accuracy of both combined, with increments reducing as far as 0.0005. Within the small, categorised dataset, a uniform increment of 0.05 across the full range 0 – 1 was used to find the limits of accuracy on all categories.

Wasserstein distance can produce a range of 0 – N, having no discrete upper bound. Incrementing the threshold started as 1×10^{-5}, reducing as far as 1×10^{-8} at points of static accuracies. As with cosine similarity, on the smaller categorised data, we set a uniform increment of 0.0005 in range of 0.001 – 0.005.

5 Results

A summary of main results is presented in this section, with a full discussion of results provided in section 6. Section 5.1 summarises the results using a single safety threshold on the large dataset; 5.2 summarises the results using 10 category-based thresholds on the smaller labelled dataset.

5.1 Single Safety Threshold

Table 1 and Table 2 provide summaries of accuracies achieved at varying thresholds for Cosine Similarity and Wasserstein Distance respectively.

Table 1. Accuracies achieved at varying thresholds for Cosine Similarity.

Thresholds (Cosine Similarity)	Safe	Unsafe	Overall
0.6	77.25	86.125	84.35
0.625	78.5	78	78.1
0.6255	78.5	77.813	77.95
0.626	78.5	77.75	77.9
0.627	78.5	77.5	77.7
0.6275	78.5	77.188	77.45
0.63	78.75	75.938	76.5
0.65	79.75	70.125	72.05
0.7	91	51.688	59.55
0.75	98.75	31	44.55

Table 2. Accuracies achieved at varying thresholds for Wasserstein Distance

Thresholds (Wasserstein Distance)	Safe	Unsafe	Overall
0.001275	69.5	54.937	57.85
0.00129	65.5	58.813	60.15
0.001295	63.5	60.188	60.85
0.0012975	63	60.425	61.1
0.0012985	62.7499	60.75	61.15
0.0012995	62.7499	60.938	61.3
0.0012999	62.7499	61.063	61.4
0.0013	62.7499	61.125	61.45
0.001325	54.499	67.313	65.15
0.00135	51.5	72.25	68.1

When considering the overall accuracies provided for both results, it is important to acknowledge that the dataset was not balanced. Safe test sentences totalled 400, unsafe totalled 1600. The accuracy is defined by the number of sentences correctly categorised as safe and unsafe when compared to the Boolean provided by ChatGPT.

5.2 Category Based Safety Thresholds

Figure 4 below displays example confusion matrix heatmaps generated for 4 of the 10 categories, demonstrating the relationship between correctly and incorrectly categorised sentences at each Wasserstein safety threshold for both unsafe and safe sentences. Each category contains 20 unsafe and safe sentences.

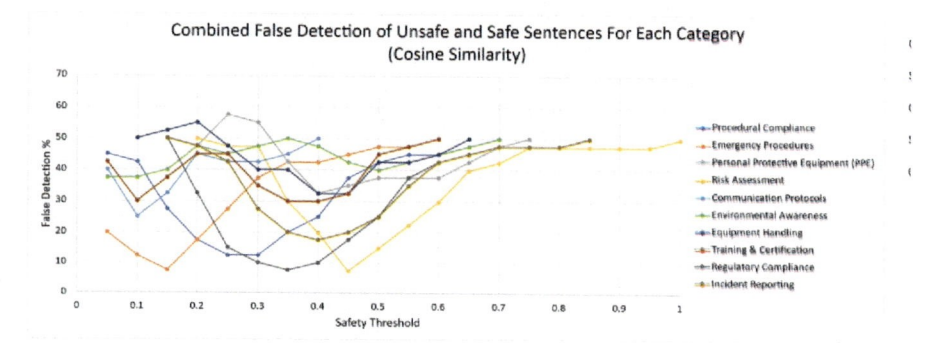

Fig. 5. Categorised False Detection Rate for Cosine Similarity

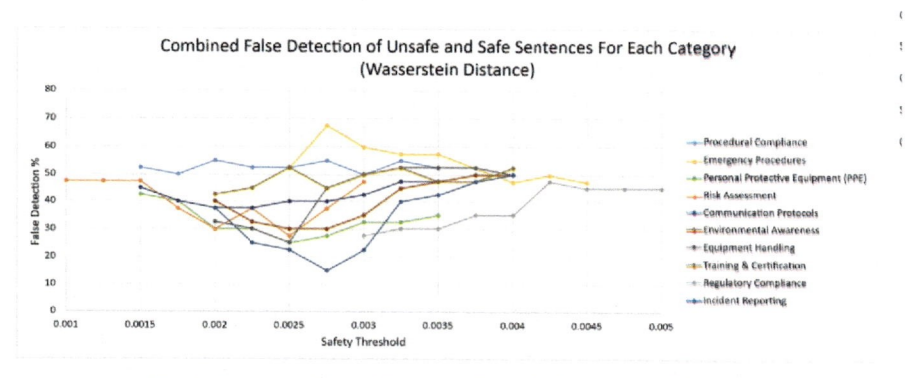

Fig. 6. Categorised False Detection Rate for Wasserstein Distance

Figure 5 shows the false detection rate of cosine similarity for both unsafe and safe sentences combined at each safety threshold for all 10 categories. Figure 6 then shows a comparative plot for the combined failure rate of Wasserstein Distance. Where plot ranges differ for each category, it can be assumed that the accuracy remains the same when changing the safety threshold outside of these bounds. These points have been removed from the plots for clarity.

Figures 7 and 8 below present the false detection rate of safe sentences for both Cosine Similarity and Wasserstein distance. False detection is determined by the number of safe sentences incorrectly categorised as unsafe during testing. When comparing these it is important to note that the scales for the two measures are mirrored; sentence similarity increases as the Wasserstein Distance shifts towards 0, whereas similarity decreases as the Cosine Similarity shifts toward 0. Therefore, it can be assumed that both plots follow the same trend and are comparable.

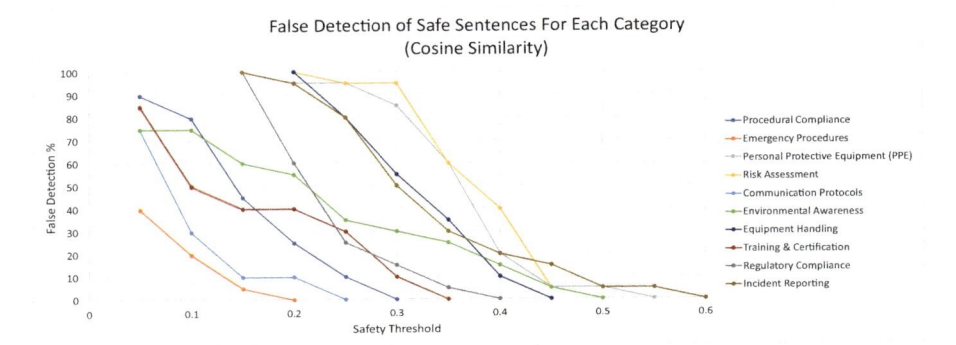

Fig. 7. Categorised False Detection Rate of Safe Sentences (Cosine Similarity)

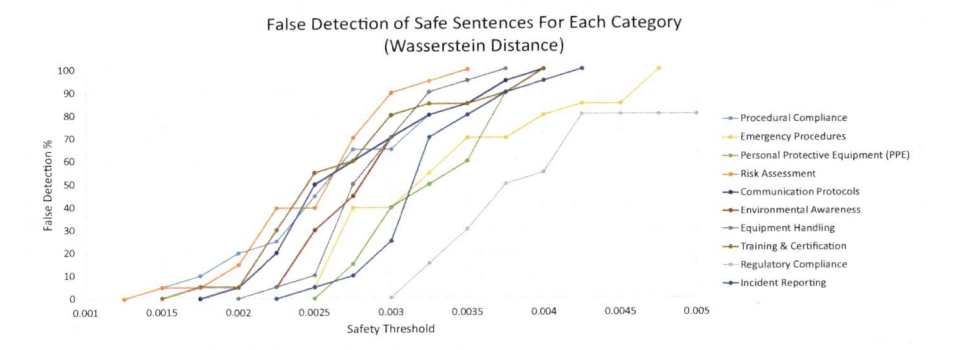

Fig. 8. Categorised False Detection Rate of Safe Sentences (Wasserstein Distance)

Figure 9 and Figure 10 present the false detection rate of unsafe sentences, for Cosine Similarity and Wasserstein Distance respectively. False detection is determined by the percentage of unsafe sentences incorrectly categorised as safe during testing. As with the false detection of safe sentences, these plots are comparable and follow similar trends as the similarity shifts.

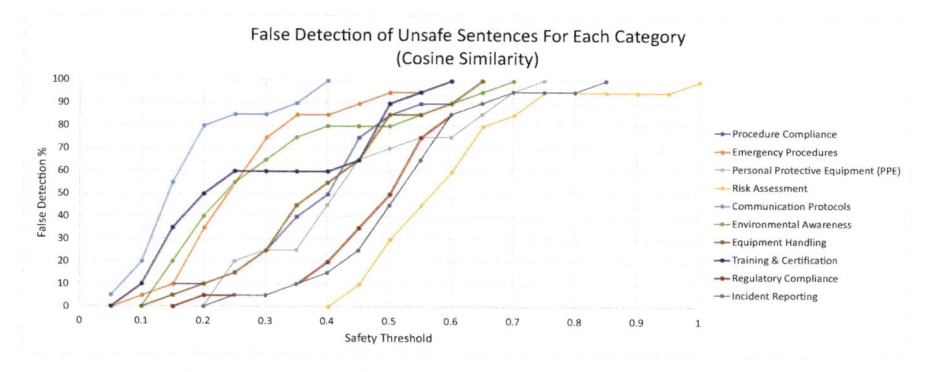

Fig. 9. False detection of unsafe sentences (Cosine Similarity)

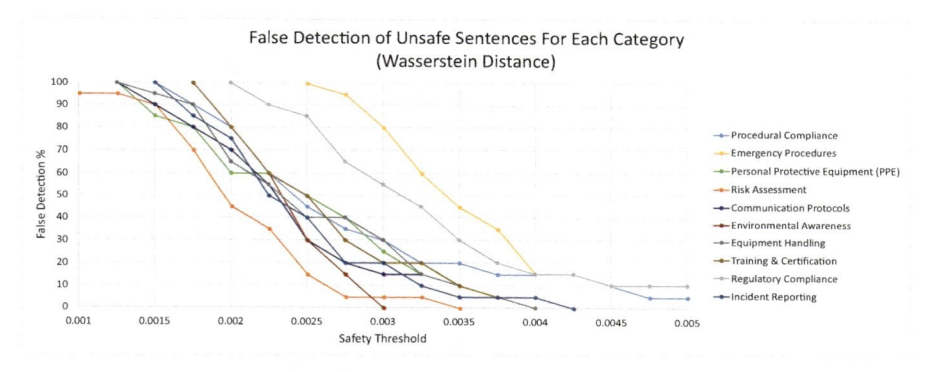

Fig. 10. False detection of unsafe sentences (Wasserstein Distance)

Finally, Figure 11 presents the maximum overall accuracy of safe and unsafe sentences for both Cosine Similarity and Wasserstein Distance.

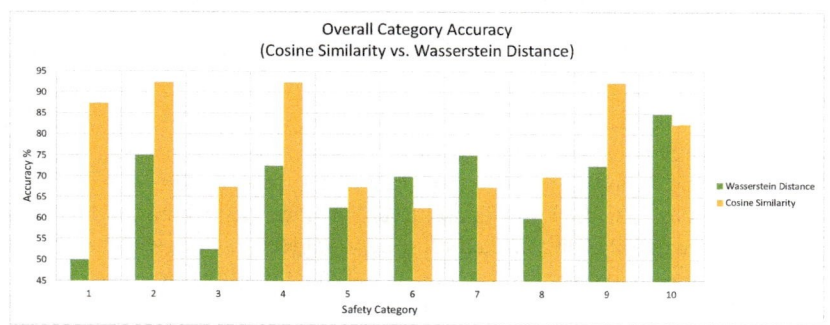

Fig. 11. Overall category accuracy of Cosine Similarity and Wasserstein Distance.

From this, categories 6, 7 and 10 provide higher accuracies from Wasserstein Distance. All other categories, excluding category 1 can be deemed within comparable ranges. Accuracies of Wasserstein Distance have a range of 50 % - 85 %; Cosine Similarity being 62.5 % - 92.5 %.

6 Conclusion

In this paper, we defined the Wasserstein Distance statistical distance measure as a framework to identify and eliminate unsafe concepts being suggested to maintenance personnel through our previously proposed Conversational Maintenance Agent. The aim of this work is to improve the safety – as defined in section 3.1 – of maintenance scheduling and compliance through decreasing reliance pressure on maintenance personnel. These pressures include, but are not limited to, reducing downtime of turbines, and reducing task completion time in already limited weather windows; determined by safe weather conditions.

In most cases, it has been observed that Cosine Similarity outperforms Wasserstein Distance and provides better accuracy overall at this stage. However, Wasserstein Distance performs comparably, and in three categories outperforms Cosine Similarity, so cannot be ruled out as a valuable method as proposed in this paper. Where Cosine Similarity has proved more accurate, Wasserstein Distance follows the same trends across all results.

The results presented are preliminary, with scope for further optimisation in future. A foundation for using this framework has been developed with the results being comparable to current published work. Wasserstein Distance as a method is therefore believed to hold significant benefit in its application into the development of SafeLLM.

Limited testing of the generated datasets has been conducted, with a limited range of threshold intervals tested. Parameterising these thresholds moving forward will therefore be implemented to further optimise and improve on accuracies.

Results have been seen to be somewhat volatile, highly dependent on the dataset produced by ChatGPT, specifically when generating a dictionary of unsafe concepts to test against. This was presented as a limitation whilst asking ChatGPT to categorise the large dataset to test on the category-based thresholds. As such, this dataset was only used for testing a single safety threshold. However, in future, it is hoped that we can use this to validate the categories by testing and manually analysing the results to determine accuracy.

As highlighted, a significant limitation to achieving validation of results is caused by lack of OSW specific data. It is hoped that through discussions and further development, we can validate the safety categories, as well as the unsafe concepts within each. This will allow for the creation of a dictionary containing concepts which align with current industry standards and processes. The data generated by ChatGPT can also then be validated by domain experts, with the availability of data increasing over time, leading to continuous improvement of the complete system.

Code and Data Availability Regarding the research reproducibility, codes, generated data and functions supporting this paper are published online at GitHub: Safe-LLM: A new approach for making LLM results Safe (github.com)

Acknowledgements This project is partially supported by the Secure and Safe Multi-Robot Systems (SESAME) H2020 Project under Grant Agreement 101017258. The authors would like to thank the AURA Innovation Centre for its support.

References

Aslansefat K, Sorokos I, Whiting D, Tavakoli Kolagari, R, Papadopoulos Y (2020, September). SafeML: safety monitoring of machine learning classifiers through statistical difference measures. In *International Symposium on Model-Based Safety and Assessment* (pp. 197-211). Cham: Springer International Publishing.

Aslansefat K, Kabir S, Abdullatif A, Vasudevan V, Papadopoulos Y (2021). Toward improving confidence in autonomous vehicle software: A study on traffic sign recognition systems. Computer, 54(8), 66-76.

Brown T.B, Mann B, Ryder N et al (2020) Language models are few-shot learners.

Carta T, Romac C, Wolf T et al (2023) Grounding large language models in interactive environments with online reinforcement learning.

Cer D, Yang Y, Kong S et al (2018) Universal sentence encoder.

Chatterjee J, Dethlefs N (2020). A Dual Transformer Model for Intelligent Decision Support for Maintenance of Wind Turbines. International Joint Conference on Neural Networks (IJCNN), Glasgow, UK, 2020, pp. 1-10, doi: 10.1109/IJCNN48605.2020.9206839.

IEC Safety and functional safety. http://iec.ch/functional-safety. Accessed 15 December 2023

David R (2020) An introduction to system safety management in the mod part 1. https://assets.publishing.service.gov.uk/government/uploads/system/uploads/attachment_data/file/904238/SSM_Whitebook_PART_1_2020_update_2.pdf. Accessed 15 December 2023

Europe I (2018) Future energy industry trends. https://northsearegion.eu/northsee/e-energy/future-energy-industry-trends/. Accessed 15 December 2023

Gonzalez E, Reder M, Melero J.J (2016) Scada alarms processing for wind turbine component failure detection. Journal of Physics: Conference 757(7)

Hawkins R, Osborne M, Parsons M et al (2022) Guidance on the safety assurance of autonomous systems in complex environments (sace).

Hawkins R, Osborne M, Parsons M et al (2021) Guidance on the assurance of machine learning in autonomous systems (amlas)

Helwan A (2023) Introduction to word and sentence embedding. https://abdulkaderhelwan.medium.com/introduction-to-word-and-sentence-embedding-991c735a2b0b. Accessed 15 December 2023

Huang L, Yu W, Ma W et al (2023) A survey on hallucination in large language models: Principles, taxonomy, challenges, and open questions

Inan H, Upasani K, Chi J et al (2023) Llama guard: Llm-based input-output safeguard for human-ai conversations

Kim Y, Pal S, Pass B (2021) What is optimal transport? https://kantorovich.org/post/ot_intro/. Accessed 15 December 2023

Lees A, Tran V.Q, Tay Y et al (2022) A new generation of perspective api: Efficient multilingual character-level transformers

Li D, Martinez S (2021) High-confidence attack detection via Wasserstein-metric computations. IEEE Control Systems Letters 5(2). 379-384

Manakul P, Liusie A, Gales M.J.F (2023) Self-checkgpt: Zero-resource black-box hallucination detection for generative large language models

Markov T, Zhang C, Agarwal S et al (2023) A holistic approach to undesired content detection in the real world

Mikolov T, Chen K, Corrado G et al (2013) Efficient estimation of word representations in vector space

OpenAI (2022) OpenAI: Introducing chatgpt. https://openai.com/blog/chatgpt#OpenAI. Accessed 15 December 2023

OpenAI (2023) OpenAI: Gpt-4 technical report

Panaretos V.M, Zemel Y (2019) Statistical aspects of Wasserstein distances. Annual Review of Statistics and Its Application 6(1). 405-431

Rando J, Paleka D, Lindner D et al (2022) Red-teaming the stable diffusion safety filter

Rateike M, Cintas C, Wamburu J (2023) Weakly supervised detection of hallucinations in llm activations

Thorpe M (2018) Introduction to optimal transport. https://www.damtp.cam.ac.uk/research/cia/files/teaching/Optimal_Transport_Notes.pdf. Accessed 15 December 2023

Touvron H, Lavril T, Izacard G et al (2023) Llama: Open and efficient foundation language models

Vaswani A, Shazeer N, Parmar N et al (2027) Attention is all you need. Advances in neural information processing systems, 30.

Walker C, Rothon C, Aslansefat K et al (2022) A deep learning framework for wind turbine repair action prediction using alarm sequences and long short term memory algorithms. In: Seguin C, Zeller M, Prosvirnova T (eds) Model Based Safety and Assessment. Pp 189-203. Springer International Publishing

Wei L, Qu J, Wang L et al (2023a) Fault diagnosis of wind turbine with alarms based on word embedding and Siamese convolutional neural network. Applied Sciences 13(13)

Wei L, Wang L, Liu F, Qian Z. Clustering Analysis of Wind Turbine Alarm Sequences Based on Domain Knowledge-Fused Word2vec (2023b). Applied Sciences. 13(18):10114. https://doi.org/10.3390/app131810114

Zhang C, Yang T (2023) Anomaly detection for wind turbines using long short-term memory-based variational autoencoder Wasserstein generation adversarial network under semi-supervised training. Energies 16(19)

Zhao W.X, Zhou K, Li J et al (2023) A survey of large language models. arXiv preprint arXiv:2303.18223

Poster: SafeLLM: A Novel Framework for Safety Evaluation of Large Language Models: A Case Study of Offshore Wind Maintenance Planning

Connor Walker, Callum Rothon, Koorosh Aslansefat, Yiannis Papadopoulos, Nina Dethlefs

AURA CDT

University of Hull

Abstract *Offshore Wind's (OSW) contribution to the renewable energy sector is paramount as the demand for global net-zero heightens. Estimations currently suggest that up to 1150 GW; 25 % of the world's usage being supplied from OSW by 2050 (Smith 2023). Up to one third of levelised cost of energy (LCOE) is belonging to Operations and Maintenance (O&M), driving competition to lower costs. There are previous reported cases whereby more than 500 alarms occurring within a single day at Teesside Wind Farm. Thus, making optimal O&M planning without automated systems unfeasible and somewhat impossible. Increased pressure on maintenance strategies to ensure safety and dependability in progressively harsher environments demonstrates the need to integrate dependable Artificial Intelligence (AI) and Machine Learning (ML) systems. To eliminate these issues, we recently introduced a specialised conversational agent trained to interpret alarm sequences from Supervisory Control and Data Acquisition (SCADA) and recommend comprehensible repair actions (Walker et al. 2023). Acknowledging the recent advancements of Generative AI and Large Language Models (LLMs), we expand on this earlier work, fine tuning LLAMA (Touvron 2018), using available maintenance records from EDF Energy. An issue presented by LLMs is the risk of responses containing unsafe actions, or irrelevant hallucinated procedures. In response to these issues, this paper proposes SafeLLM as a novel framework for safety monitoring of OSW, combining previous work with additional safety layers. Generated responses being filtered ensures that raw responses of this agent do not endanger personnel and the environment. The algorithm represents such responses in embedding space to quantify dissimilarity to pre-defined unsafe concepts using the Empirical Cumulative Distribution Function (ECDF)-based statistical distance measure including Wasserstein and Anderson-Darling. In addition, a secondary layer to identify hallucination in responses has been added; exploiting probability distributions* *to analyse against stochastically generated sentences. Combining these layers, the paper aims to fine tune individual safety thresholds based on categorised concepts, providing a unique safety filter. Finally, a human-in-the-loop feature layer is discussed, using expert-approved predictions for online reinforcement learning, improving safety over time. The proposed framework has potential to utilise the O&M planning for OSW farms using state-of-the-art LLMs as well as equipping them with safety monitoring that can increase technology acceptance within the industry*

A Position Paper on Safety Culture Assessment and Improvement

Michael Wright

Safety Culture Working Group

Safety-Critical Systems Club

Abstract *The Safety Culture Working Group has produced "A position paper for assessing and managing safety culture". It provides high-level guidance on the assessment and improvement of safety culture for organisations that design, build, assure and operate complex safety-critical systems. It synthesises recognised good practice and can act as a benchmark and guidance. It (a) exemplifies how safety culture manifests itself, (b) provides guidance on good practice that organisations should aim to achieve and (c) draws out methods that are of particular importance to organisations involved in development and operation of safety-critical systems. The position paper summarises lessons learned on how to improve safety culture, such as engaging with staff, and clearly communicating behavioural expectations. These lessons draw on evidence of what has and "has not" worked. There are well known examples of organisations that had been regarded to be industry leaders, subsequently suffering major accidents due to the erosion of their safety culture, changes in organisational imperatives and a loss of corporate memory of past incidents. The position paper offers some tactics for guarding against the erosion of safety culture. It concludes by reinforcing the position that safety culture influences all aspects of safety performance and all stages of the system lifecycle, including design, safety assessment and assurance, manufacture, operations and maintenance. The position paper will help organisations understand how they can effectively assess, improve, and maintain their safety culture.*

© Safety Critical Systems Club CIC, 2024.
Published by the Safety-Critical Systems Club. All Rights Reserved

1 Introduction

1.1 Poor safety culture and system safety

"Poor" safety culture within the design, safety assurance and operation of safety-critical systems has been a key factor in catastrophic accidents. The 2006 fire and crash of the United Kingdom's NIMROD maritime reconnaissance/strike aircraft exemplifies the role of safety culture in the assurance of system safety. A fuel leak contacted hot pipework and ignited. The Assistant Deputy Coroner stated (UK Ministry of Defence, 2007):

> *"This cavalier approach to safety must come to an end. There were failures... [in monitoring the aircraft's safety]...that should, if the information had been correctly recorded and acted upon, have led to the discovery of this design flaw within the Nimrod fleet."*

The inquiry said that there had been a failure or leadership in producing the safety case, with inadequate priority given to the safety case. There was a general "malaise" and assumption that the aircraft was safe, having entered service in 1969. The inquiry thought that fuel probably overflowed during air-to-air refuelling, using a refuelling modification fitted in 1989. The fuel was probably ignited by the Cross Feed/Supplementary (air) Conditioning Packs (SCP) duct. The SCP duct was fitted in 1979 and increased ignition risk. These were considered to be "latent" design flaws. There had been a number of previous incidents and warning signs that should have been a "wake up call", including the rupture of the SCP duct in 2004.

The safety case was considered a 'tick box' exercise. The safety case was reported to be rushed and to contain significant errors and omissions. 40% of hazards were left 'open' and 30% were 'unclassified', including the Cross Feed/SCP duct hazard. Outstanding risks were sentenced in an unrealistic basis. The Cross Feed/SCP duct hazard was classified as "Tolerable".

If the safety case had been drawn up properly, the latent design flaws introduced by the modifications to the plane could have been identified and the accident could have been avoided.

This incident brought a focus of interest onto the role of safety culture in the design, build, safety assessment and in service management of complex safety-critical systems.

The recent Titan submersible implosion in June 2023 highlights the ongoing need to understand and manage the safety culture in the design, manufacture and operation stages of safety-critical systems. The inquiry by the US Coastguard, Canadian Transport Safety Board into the Titan incident is ongoing at the time of authoring this paper. Public news reports have suggested that the vessel was knowingly operated despite: i) not being subject to any safety regulations, ii) having adopted a non-standard design using novel (inappropriate?) materials, and iii) that safety concerns had been raised about the vessel. For example, it is reported (Porter and Guenot, 2023) that a 2018 letter to OceanGate highlighted safety concerns around the Titan. They report that Bart Kemper (a forensic engineer) told the New York Times that OceanGate's vessel evaded regulations by being deployed in international waters, where Coast Guard rules do not apply

Fig. 1. Titan submersible. Courtesy of OceanGate, Fair use

Two more recent events are summarised below.

1.2 Accident case study: VSS Enterprise crash, 2014

The Virgin Space Ship (VSS) Enterprise crash occurred on October 31, 2014, when the VSS Enterprise, a SpaceShipTwo (SS2) experimental spaceflight test vehicle operated by Virgin Galactic, suffered a catastrophic in-flight breakup during a test flight.

The SS2 was meant to unlock a feather mechanism at 1.4 Mach to ensure it was in position during re-entry. The feather flap assembly with twin tail booms upwards to stabilise attitude and increase drag on re-entry. The feather mechanism was deployed too early while still under rocket propulsion at 0.8 Mach. The feathering mechanism then began moving due to aerodynamic forces on the tail and inertial loads and the craft disintegrated.

Cockpit image recording showed that the pilots' voices were strained, with high levels of vibration and loads from acceleration. It is thought that the pilot deployed the mechanism early due to high workload and stress in the short time span available, just ~30 seconds for three tasks recalled from memory. The conditions of high acceleration and vibration had not been replicated in simulator training and the pilot had no recent experience of this effect.

The hazard analysis had recognised this to be a single point catastrophic failure but had not considered the possibility of error of premature unlocking of feather mechanism. It assumed pilots would always operate correctly due to training/simulation runs. The craft operated under an experimental licence from Federal Aviation Authority (FAA) who found that the hazard analysis did not meet requirements but issued a waiver and did not determine if there was mitigation against single point (human) failure. The US National Transport Safety Board (NTSB) found that:

Fig. 2. VSS Enterprise Space Ship Two and NTSB crash scene

> *"An FAA/AST[1] evaluator added that there was "a lot of pressure, political pressure" to issue experimental permits, even when FAA/AST evaluators were uncomfortable with an application, which diminished AST's safety culture."*
>
> *"FAA/AST management appeared to be more concerned about ensuring that the FAA's authority in this emerging industry was not being exceeded beyond defined limits and maintaining the timeframe in which to approve experimental permit applications."*

---

[1] AST is the Office of Commercial Space Transportation

"Many of the safety issues that we will hear about today arose not from the novelty of a space launch test flight, but from human factors that were already known elsewhere in transportation."

NTSB chairman Christopher Hart

SS2 has since been modified with an automatic mechanical inhibit device to prevent locking or unlocking of the feather during safety-critical phases.

1.3 Accident case study: Mid Staffordshire NHS Foundation Trust, 2005-2008

In 2007 concerns were raised about the mortality rate of patients at Mid Staffordshire NHS Foundation Trust, with potentially hundreds of more deaths occurring in a three-year period (2005-2008) than expected for this type of hospital.

A subsequent public inquiry (Francis, 2013) reported that in this period:

> *"...conditions of appalling care were able to flourish" and persist, including a lack of basic care of patients. The inquiry concluded that the failings were:*
> *... primarily caused by a serious failure on the part of a provider Trust Board. It did not listen sufficiently to its patients and staff or ensure the correction of deficiencies brought to the Trust's attention. Above all, it failed to tackle an insidious negative culture involving a tolerance of poor standards and a disengagement from managerial and leadership responsibilities.*
> *This failure was in part the consequence of allowing a focus on reaching national access targets, achieving financial balance and seeking foundation trust status to be at the cost of delivering acceptable standards of care."*

The organisational culture resulted in a focus on business performance rather than patients and their safety, with a tolerance of poor standards, and lack of managerial accountability. Many recommendations were made, such as to foster a common culture that put the patient first, openness, candour and transparency about matters of concern.

2.0 Position paper aims

The Safety Culture Working Group (SCWG[2]) of the SCSC has produced a position paper ((SCWG, 2023). The SCWG is a volunteer interest group within the Safety Critical Systems Club. The SCWG seeks to 'Improve safety culture in safety-critical organisations focussed on product and functional safety, by sharing examples and latest approaches collated from real life case studies'.

The SCWG's position paper aims to:

- Exemplify how safety culture effects the process of specifying, designing, manufacturing, operating and assuring complex safety-critical systems;
- Provide guidance on good practice that member organisations should aim to achieve;
- Draw out key methods that are of particular importance to the activities of organisations involved in safety critical activities.

The SCWG recognised that there is already extensive guidance on how to assess and improve safety culture. The position paper does not aim to provide detailed guidance nor worked examples. Instead, the position paper aims to provide a view on good practice that can be used to review and improve organisation's approaches. To this end, further reading and references are offered in the SCWG's position paper.

3 Key positions

3.1 The concept of safety culture

The SCWG position is that the concept of safety culture is a valid concept. Numerous regulators and agencies have published guidance on safety culture, its importance and the need to systematically assess and manage safety culture.

The position paper uses the term "safety culture" to refer to the safety-related norms, values, beliefs, attitudes and behaviours of the person's organisation. Safety culture is part of a wider organisational culture, but will have distinct values, beliefs and behaviours. Moreover, it is necessary to understand these safety-related values, beliefs and behaviours, and how they influence safety performance, to be able to manage and maintain an effective safety culture.

---

[2] https://scsc.uk/gu

Numerous assessments of organisations find that safety culture is not the same everywhere in large organisations and may differ across departments, roles, and through levels of an organisation (see Mannion and Davies, 2018, for example).

There is also evidence that safety culture does vary between different safety domains, such as between occupational safety and process safety. This evidence includes the major accidents at Texas City refinery, Longford gas processing site, Deepwater Horizon, and British railway incidents. In each case, the organisations had a strong focus on, and good performance in occupational safety. However, this did not reflect equal focus onto, and good performance in other safety areas, such as design, maintenance or operations of safety-critical systems.

The implications of the potential for divergent safety cultures include:

- A need to understand if and how culture can vary between different parts of an organisation or between different safety domains; and
- A need to consider how to best implement a safety culture improvement programme for it to be effective.

3.2 The assessment of safety culture

The assessment of safety culture is relevant good practice and is common practice amongst many safety-critical organisations. Assessment can serve a number of purposes including:

- Insights to support improvements, such as:
  - Strengths and weaknesses
  - Which departments or roles have stronger-weaker cultures?
  - What are the factors contributing to poorer culture?
- An understanding of the current culture and hence an indication of the need to improve;
- Tracking over time whether culture is steady, improving or declining;
- Demonstrating to stakeholders that the organisation is a responsible and safe operator.

The absence of incidents does not necessarily mean that safety is being achieved, especially with low frequency major accident risks, or where the effect of behaviour (such as during design) is not revealed until a later point in time such as when the system is first operated. An assessment of safety culture can provide insights into safety performance especially where incident rates are not a reliable nor practical measure of safety performance.

Safety culture is a critical aspect of the entire system lifecycle through typical phases of design, build, operation and disposal/termination. Organisations should assess safety culture at each phase as the culture can influence all aspects of safety performance, including but not limited to:

- The specification and design of systems;
- The procurement, manufacture and testing of components and their integration into systems;
- Assurance, such as safety assessment and safety cases;
- Operation and maintenance of systems;
- Learning lessons from operational experience.

Some examples of behaviours and attitudes that are specific to a stage in the system lifecycle and safety domain include:

- Design: The extent to which inherent safety is prioritised in the specification and design of a new system.
- Safety assessment and assurance, such as:
    - The tolerance of single point failures within safety assessment and approval of systems.
    - The 'openness' of hazard identification workshops.

Various tools, techniques, and methods have been developed, for example:

- The Hearts and Minds safety culture assessment toolkit (Energy Institute, undated) for use across oil and gas, petrochemical and other energy sectors.
- Just Culture assessment method (Civil Aviation Authority, undated).
- 'Safety Culture Discussion Cards' (Eurocontrol, undated) which are a practical resource to aid real discussion about safety culture. They cover the same scope as the Eurocontrol safety culture survey. They ask, for example that a workshop group "Reflect openly on an experience, situation, event or idea".

These and other methods have been tried and tested over a number of decades and they are advocated for use along with other guidance to help develop improvement plans, to benchmark and track progress over time.

Assessment usually combines methods, usually staff surveys, workshops, root cause analysis and key performance indicators such as frequency of near miss reporting. For example, surveys can capture the perceptions of large numbers of people, while workshops can provide in-depth understanding of attitudes and perceptions. Thus, a common approach is to combine quantitative methods such as the aforementioned surveys, with qualitative methods such as outputs from workshops.

The SCWG's position paper offers some examples of safety culture assessment.

3.3 What does a "good" safety culture look like?

There are models of safety culture which are intended to represent what "good" looks like. Some examples include:

- Hearts and Minds (Energy Institute, undated)
- Just culture (NHS England, undated)
- Institute for Nuclear Power Operators (INPO) attributes of an effective nuclear safety culture (Morrow, S. 2012).

The common elements of "good" safety culture cited in these models are summarised in Figure 3. The assessment methods noted in section 3.2 are used to determine the extent to which an organisation fulfils these criteria, as a form of "goodness" measure.

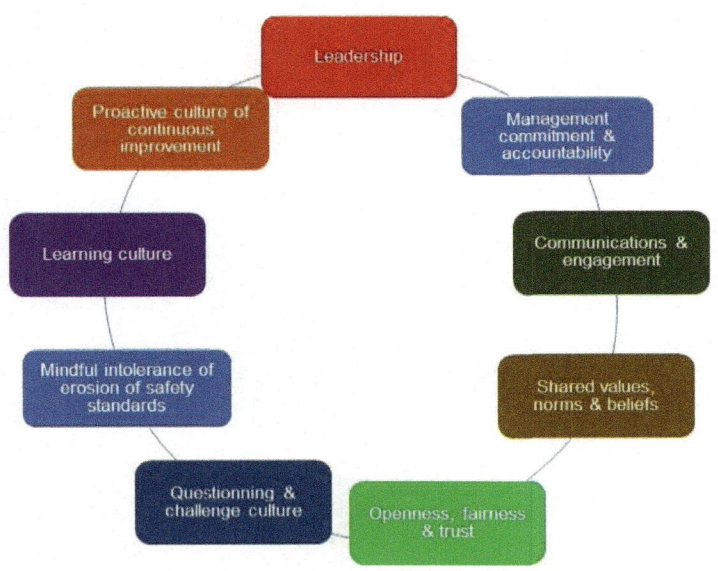

Fig. 3. Common elements of a "good" safety culture

Recent work (Dekker et al, 2022) has explored the idea of "restorative just culture", especially in areas such as healthcare, and where people have been harmed by an event. This approach identifies who has been impacted by an incident and aims to "repair" harm to them. This includes listening to harmed persons, appreciating their perspectives and developing their trust in the implementation of changes. This concept builds on the element of openness, fairness and trust in Figure 3 above.

Some models of safety culture describe a "maturity scale", rather than a singular set of attributes to be achieved. These "maturity models" help to characterise the organisation's current culture and put it on a progressive "scale".

One such "maturity model" is the aforementioned Hearts and Minds toolkit, as shown in Figure 4. This leads to the question of what standard of safety culture is required for organisations responsible for safety-critical systems. While the toolkit was first developed for use in the oil and gas sector, versions of it have been developed and applied in other sectors, including rail (Gliddon et al, 2017), healthcare (NPSA, 2006) and defence (Lockwood et al, 2015).

A "pathological" culture is typified by prioritising objectives such as reputation, finance, legal liability and schedule over safety to an extent that safety is adversely affected. A "reactive" culture entails only acting on safety in response to an adverse event, such as an accident or enforcement action from a regulatory organisation. A "Calculative" culture aims to understand and comply with the law and minimum standards, without aiming to understand and minimise risk.

None of these three cultures are likely to support the required level of safety performance for a safety-critical system with the potential for major accidents. Organisations with the potential to contribute to catastrophic accidents tend to be expected to have a "Proactive" culture of continuous improvement, as a minimum.

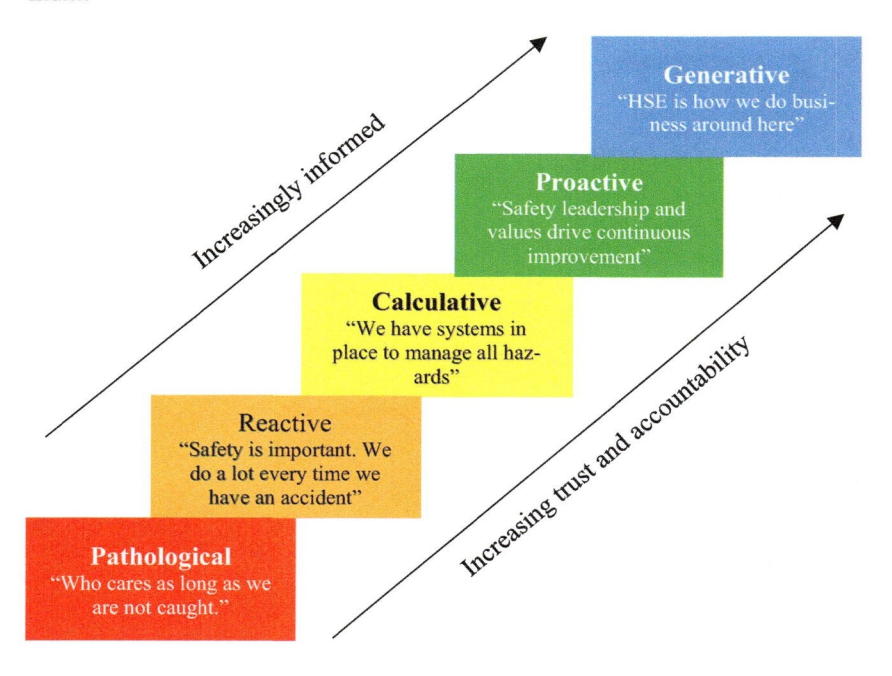

Fig. 4. Hearts and Minds safety culture maturity model
(reproduced from Energy Institute, undated)

3.4 Improving safety culture

There is extensive experience in the improvement of safety culture which offers many lessons learned. These lessons learned should be understood and used to inform improvement programmes. Some lessons learned on tactics for improving culture include:

- Defining and communicating clear behavioural expectations and values, such as not tolerating 'Open' hazards in safety cases;
- Communicating a clear "case" for why safety culture needs to change or adopt a particular model;
- Engaging all sections of staff and other affected persons in the definition of objectives, and change plans – thereby securing their understanding and "buy in";
- Consistently exemplifying the behaviours through day-to-day decision making and actions, such as not accepting 'concessions' that permit operating equipment that has known design flaws.

In mature organisations people may have behaved in a certain manner for many years, with implicit or explicit endorsement of these behaviours and values. Sentient staff are more likely to engage with change where they can understand the "case" for change and agree with the validity and importance of these changes.

Culture can take a long time to change. People need to believe that there is a "real" intent to change and that the organisation truly wants people to adopt the new behaviours. This requires the communication and exemplification of new behaviours to be sustained and to be consistent amongst senior managers. It also requires realistic timescales for change programmes, with effective management and resourcing.

The SCWG's position paper offers some examples of successful culture change.

3.5 Why might a good safety culture be eroded?

There are well known examples of organisations that had been regarded to be industry leaders, subsequently suffering major accidents due to the erosion of their safety culture (Dekker, 2012). The Haddon-Cave inquiry (Charles Haddon-Cave QC, 2009) concluded that safety had been sacrificed for cost, quoting an officer stating that:

> *"There was no doubt that the culture of the time had switched. In the days of the RAF chief engineer in the 1990s, you had to be on top of airworthiness. By 2004 you had to be on top of your budget if you wanted to get ahead."*

Boeing was portrayed (New York Times, 2020), with respect to internal communications released to the inquiry about the 737 Max, as:

> *"For generations, Boeing represented the pinnacle of American engineering...But the newly released messages portray a company that appears to have lost its way. ...Once relentlessly focused on safety and engineering, Boeing employees are shown obsessing over the bottom line. Though Boeing is one of the American government's biggest contractors, the FAA[3] was viewed as a roadblock to commercial goals that would "impede progress" when it tried to "get in the way."*

Some observed reasons for the erosion of safety culture are:

- Changes in organisational imperatives leading to a greater focus on objectives such as delivering new products, increased throughput, reduced costs – sometimes coinciding with a change in leadership;
- A loss of corporate memory of past incidents and the rationale for safety requirements, sometimes involving a change in leadership and subject matter experts leaving the organisation. This was highlighted in healthcare - the quick turnover of senior execs led to loss of corporate memory and lack of appropriate safety oversight structures (Kirkup, 2022).
- A reduction in the weight given to opinion of subject matter experts, such as engineers or safety specialists, especially where there are new business imperatives and new leadership lack (for example) appreciation of systems engineering.

The achievement of safety often includes the introduction of safeguards (engineered, managerial and administrative) to protect against past safety issues such as near misses, incidents and defects. With the passage of time and loss of experienced personnel, the reasons for these safeguards and the risks exemplified by past events can be forgotten or judged to no longer be relevant. Where new leadership lack an appreciation of the lessons learned from past events, and instead focus on new business imperatives, safety concerns can be overridden and dismissed and the opinions of safety and other specialists devalued below these new imperatives.

---

[3] Federal Aviation Authority

A "poor" safety culture can also be one that relies too much and too statically on engineered, managerial and administrative safeguards and expects that everything will be 'fine' as long as people follow the rules. "Good" safety culture 'embraces' the complexity of systems and appreciates that the changing nature of risk and the complexity and uncertainty inherent in the system can undermine safeguards or render them out dated.

3.6 What are the signs and symptoms of an eroding safety culture?

A challenge with the erosion of safety culture is that it can be slow and may not be easy to recognise. Some indicators include what are termed "weak signals", such as behavioural signals. These include where people normalise lower standards, accept decisions and practices that were previously rejected, accept work arounds as normal practice or are silent about poor safety decisions.

The challenge in detecting "weak signals" can be exacerbated if leaders demand "hard" evidence of safety concerns, for example, to change business decisions, or view the expression of safety concerns to be disruptive, a threat to the organisation or as opposition to organisation's goals. Organisation may also not have the mechanisms to detect "weak signals". This leads to the idea of safety intelligence and safety wisdom (Future Sky Safety Consortium, undated), whereby safety information is effectively drawn upon in safety decision making. The Future Sky Safety Consortium defines these as follows.

> *"Safety Intelligence is generally being used to refer to the various sources of quantitative information an organisation may use to identify and assess various threats. This has traditionally been incident data and other safety information on precursor events which, when put together, can give reasonable predictions about likely accidents and measures to avoid them.*
>
> *Safety Wisdom refers to the judgement and decision-making of those in senior positions who must decide what to do to remain safe and how they also use quantitative and qualitative information to support those decisions. This could be proactively in relation to a future or emerging threat, or reactively to an accident that has happened to another similar organisation."*

Safety Wisdom includes using intelligence to maintain safety under pressure and to anticipate the next threat, thereby mitigating the erosion of safety standards.

Safety culture can be eroded slowly and imperceptibly. Where safety culture is being eroded, at least in part, due to change in leadership and/or new organisational imperatives, this creates challenges with respect to a potential loss of corporate memory and new imperatives that may change the approach to safety. The erosion of safety culture may be masked by other organisational changes, distracting attention. It can also be that some people are aware of the erosion of safety, but are not heard.

3.7 How can the erosion of a good safety culture be prevented?

Some common tactics elaborated in the position paper for preventing the erosion of safety culture include:

- Formal checks and balances that can help recognise, challenge and control the erosion of safety culture. These are noted below.
    - Independent safety function and independent assurance who scrutinise engineering and managerial decisions that may impact safety
    - Management of Organisational Change
    - Key Process Indicators
- Retention of organisational memory and a mature and resilient safety leadership that can counter pressures to reduce safety standards. Some common mitigations of loss of corporate memory include:
    - Succession planning with a period of briefing and knowledge transfer;
    - Onboarding and mentoring processes for new staff;
    - Maintaining a culture where experts and experienced people are respected and listened to;
    - Retention of expert functions within the organisation, at least to act as "intelligent customers".

Equally important is a culture that values "lessons learned" from past experiences and does not dismiss these as being no longer relevant ("that was then") or "distances by differencing" (a view that the lessons do not apply to us because we are different).

- Organisational mindfulness (Liu et al 2023), chronic unease (Fruhen, 2014) and combating "normalisation of deviance" (Furst, 2021):
    - Organisations need to adopt a set of attitudes and behaviours to mitigate the tendency to downplay the "weak signals" of poorer safety. They need to recognise that long periods of success can cause complacency.
    - Organisational mindfulness entails being alert to the types of behaviours noted above and includes maintaining a sense of chronic unease, scepticism, and challenging the normalisation of deviance

Finally, the maintenance of effective safety leadership, that maintains a high priority for safety and commitment to honestly assess safety performance, risks and to make objective safety decisions is key.

4 Concluding points

Safety culture is equally relevant to the design, safety assessment and manufacture of systems as to operations and maintenance. Organisations responsible for safety-critical systems and operations can help achieve high standards of safety performance by proactively assessing and improving their safety culture. This is good practice and a common expectation. There is an extensive body of experience, guidance and tried and tested methods that can be drawn on. A proactive and sustained approach to safety culture helps to maintain trust and confidence in the capability of an organisation, its values and behaviour.

The SCWG's position paper will help organisations understand how they can effectively assess and improve their safety culture.

As with all areas of safety science, further studies could help provide rigorous evidence about the impact of safety culture on performance and the impact of interventions intended to have an impact on safety culture.

Disclaimers All statements in this paper are those of the Safety Culture Working Group and do not necessarily represent the opinions of their member organisations.

Acknowledgments The SCWG's position paper was developed by the membership of the Safety Culture Working Group, with special thanks to Paul Leach, Mark Sujan, Darren Mcminn, Dr James Laughton, Sarah Lay, Fraser Mellstrom, Kathryn Mearns, Mark Westwood, Jane Fenn, Matthew Twiselton, Jeremy Hubbard and Kirk Mayes. This symposium paper was reviewed and edited by Jeremy Hubbard, James Laughton, Paul Leach, Kirk Mayes, Darren Mcminn, Kathryn Mearns and Mark Sujan.

References

Charles Haddon-Cave QC. The NIMROD Review. An independent review into the broader issues surrounding the loss of the RAF Nimrod MR2 Aircraft XV230 in Afghanistan in 2006. October 2009. https://assets.publishing.service.gov.uk/government/uploads/system/uploads/attachment_data/file/229037/1025.pdf Accessed January 2023

Civil Aviation authority: Safety culture. https://www.caa.co.uk/safety-initiatives-and-resources/how-we-regulate/state-safety-programme/safety-promotion/safety-culture/ Accessed October 2023

Dekker, S, Rafferty J and Oates A. Restorative Just Culture in Practice: Implementation and evaluation. Routledge, 2022.

Dekker, S. Drift into failure: from hunting broken components to understanding complex systems: Ashgate Publishing, Ltd.; 2012.

Energy Institute. https://heartsandminds.energyinst.org/home Accessed January 2023

Eurocontrol. Safety Culture Discussion Cards - Complete Collection. https://skybrary.aero/articles/safety-culture-discussion-cards-complete-collection Accessed October 2023.

Francis, R. The Mid Staffordshire NHS Foundation Trust Public Inquiry. February 2013. https://assets.publishing.service.gov.uk/media/5a7ba0faed915d13110607c8/0947.pdf Accessed October 2023.

Furst, P. Normalization of Deviations in Performance. OHS Online. 2021. https://ohsonline.com/Articles/2021/10/01/Normalization-of-Deviations-in-Performance.aspx Accessed October 2023

Future Sky Safety Consortium. Keeping the aviation industry safe. Safety Intelligence and Safety Wisdom. https://www.futuresky-safety.eu/wp-content/uploads/2016/04/FSS_white_paper_keeping_aviation_industry_safe-1.pdf Accessed October 2023

Fruhen L.S, Flin R.H. and McLeod R. (2014) Chronic unease for safety in managers: a conceptualisation, Journal of Risk Research, 17:8, 969-979, DOI: 10.1080/13669877.2013.822924

Gliddon V, Canham R, Wright M, Pirapakaran B, Nichols D, Barron M, Selman D. Showing success in assessment and improving safety culture on the DLR: Industrial application. The Sixth International Human Factors Rail Conference. 2017, 6th - 9th November https://rhf2017.exordo.com/files/papers/104/final_draft/GSBKAD_RHF_2017_Full_paper_AssessingSafetyCulture_PPR1_V2_B_W_AF.pdf Accessed October 2023

Kirkup, B. Reading the signals. Maternity and neonatal services in East Kent – the Report of the Independent Investigation. October 2022. https://www.gov.uk/government/publications/maternity-and-neonatal-services-in-east-kent-reading-the-signals-report Accessed October 2023.

Liu Z, Hoff K, Baranski E, Snyder G, Flin R, Lindner P, and Spitzmueller C. Mindfulness and workplace safety: An integrative review. Journal of Organizational Behaviour, Vol 44, Issue 8. April 2023.

Lockwood, F., Canham, R. & Wright, M. (2015) Developing a framework for assessing Workplace and Product Safety culture in BAE Systems. In Proceedings volume of the 2015 Safety-critical System Symposium (SSS'15). http://scsc.org.uk/paper_129/Lockwood - Developing a Framework for Assessing Workplace and Product Safety Culture in BAE Systems.pdf?pap=980 Accessed October 2023

Mannion R, and Davies H. Understanding organisational culture for healthcare quality improvement. BMJ (Clinical research ed). 2018; 363:k4907.

Morrow, S. Independent Evaluation of INPO's Nuclear Safety Culture Survey and Construct Validation Study. June 2012. https://www.nrc.gov/docs/ML1217/ML12172A093.pdf Accessed October 2023.

NHS England: Safety culture: learning from best practice. https://www.england.nhs.uk/long-read/safety-culture-learning-from-best-practice/ Accessed January 2023

National Patients Safety Agency. Manchester Patient Safety Framework (MaPSaF). 2006. https://webarchive.nationalarchives.gov.uk/ukgwa/20171030124256/http://www.nrls.npsa.nhs.uk/resources/?EntryId45=59796 Accessed October 2023.

National Transport Safety Board. In-Flight Breakup During Test Flight Scaled Composites SpaceShipTwo, N339SS, Near Koehn Dry Lake, California, October 31, 2014. Aerospace Accident Report. NTSB/AAR-15/02. PB2015-105454 https://www.ntsb.gov/investigations/AccidentReports/Reports/AAR1502.pdf . Accessed January 2023

New York Times, Natalie Kitroeff. https://www.nytimes.com/2020/01/10/business/boeing-737-employees-messages.html Accessed October 2023

Porter, T and Guenot, M. The missing Titanic sub fell outside safety rules by operating in international waters beyond the law, experts say. Insider Today. https://www.insider.com/titanic-sub-avoided-safety-rules-by-diving-in-international-waters-experts-2023-6 Accessed October 2023.

Safety Culture Working Group. A position paper for assessing and managing safety culture. 2023. https://scsc.uk/gu Accessed October 2023.

Sky library. Assessing Safety Culture in ATM. https://www.skybrary.aero/articles/assessing-safety-culture-atm Accessed October 2023

UK Ministry of Defence. Board of Inquiry Into The Accident Involving Nimrod MR2 XV230. December 2007. https://web.archive.org/web/20090807195756/http://www.mod.uk/DefenceInternet/AboutDefence/CorporatePublications/BoardsOfInquiry/BoiNimrodMr2Xv230.htm Accessed January 2023.

Safety in unmanned aviation - how much have we got and how much do we need?

Steve Wright

Wright Airborne Computing

Abstract *The global aviation industry has decades-old (and very successful) methods for enforcing safety in conventional manned aerospace, evolved gradually around a set of mature technologies. However, regulators are now struggling to integrate the profoundly different implications of unmanned aviation. In this talk Steve discusses the fundamental differences in technology and operations between manned and unmanned aircraft and their implications for maintaining safety in both, and shares some of the thrills and spills of performing development at this new frontier*

© Steve Wright, 2024.
Published by the Safety-Critical Systems Club. All Rights Reserved

System Safety for Complex Projects – The Crossrail Approach

Hayat Zerkani

Crossrail Ltd

Abstract *This Technical Paper sets out the details of the System Safety approach used by the Crossrail Project and describes some of the solutions employed to resolve the key challenges faced during the lifecycle of the project. The paper is published in the Crossrail Learning Legacy website at:* https://learning-legacy.crossrail.co.uk/documents/system-safety-for-complex-projects-the-crossrail-approach/

© Hayat Zerkani, 2024.
Published by the Safety-Critical Systems Club. All Rights Reserved.

Author Index

Adiac Aguilar	23
Koorosh Aslansefat	253, 273
George De Ath	67
Edmond Awad	67
Tom Boden,	203
Stephen Bull	25
Guy Burroughes	203
Lavinia Burski	27
Laure Buysse	71
Richard Cannon	67
Carmen Carlan	35
Ben Carvell	67
Johan Catrysse	71
Greg Chance	193
Mikela Chatzimichailidou	37
Dewi Daniels	53
Paul Darnell	65
Nina Dethlefs	253, 273
Simon Diemert	157
Tim Dodwell	67
Sai Pavan Kumar Eswara	169
Richard Everson	67
Vincent Ganthy	69
Vikas Ghatge	71
Miriam Gonzalez-Atienza	95
Paul Hampton	115
Nikita Bhardwaj Haupt	141
Richard Hawkins	203
George Head	173
Chris Hobbs	143
Christopher Hobbs	157
Islem Jouini	169
Jeff Joyce	157
Rob Kleihorst	71, 95
Philip Koopman	171
Pavan Kumar	65
Benita Lawrence	173
Peter Liggesmeyer	141, 225
Alessio Lomuscio	191
Lacey-Jo Marsland	203
George Mason	193
Gavin McCall	197

Author Index

Ross McMurran 65
Niki Mok 199
Phillip Mulvana 203
Matt Osborne 203
Jonathan Pallant 219
Yiannis Papadopoulos 253, 273
Mike Parsons 221
Anil Ranjitbhai Patel 225
Ben Philips 223
Davy Pissoort 71, 95
Callum Rothon, ... 253, 273
Ravindra Sabbella 65
Anne Seldon 227
David Slater 229
Mikhail Tchernikov 169
Harold Thimbleby 243
Marc Thomas 67
Kath Uthay 25
Dries Vanoost, ... 71, 95
Connor Walker 253, 273
William H. Widen 171
Michael Wright 275
Steve Wright 293
Hayat Zerkani 295

Printed in Great Britain
by Amazon